A CULTURAL ARSENAL FOR DEMOCRACY

A VOLUME IN THE SERIES
Public History in Historical Perspective
EDITED BY
Marla R. Miller

A CULTURAL ARSENAL FOR DEMOCRACY

The World War II Work of US Museums

CLARISSA J. CEGLIO

University of Massachusetts Press
AMHERST AND BOSTON

Copyright © 2022 by University of Massachusetts Press
All rights reserved
Printed in the United States of America

ISBN 978-1-62534-625-4 (paper); 624-7 (hardcover)

Designed by Sally Nichols
Set in Filosofia
Printed and bound by Books International, Inc

Cover design by Frank Gutbrod
Cover art: *Know Your United Nations* at the Brooklyn Museum (September 16, 1947– November 23, 1947), UN Photo/Kari Berggrav. Courtesy of the United Nations Photo Library.

Library of Congress Cataloging-in-Publication Data
Names: Ceglio, Clarissa J., 1962–author.
Title: A cultural arsenal for democracy : the World War II work of U.S. museums / Clarissa J. Ceglio.
Description: Amherst : University of Massachusetts Press, [2022] | Series: Public history in historical perspective | Includes bibliographical references and index.
Identifiers: LCCN 2021017193 (print) | LCCN 2021017194 (ebook) | ISBN 9781625346247 (hardcover) | ISBN 9781625346254 (paperback) | ISBN 9781613769003 (ebook) | ISBN 9781613769010 (ebook)
Subjects: LCSH: World War, 1939–1945—Museums—United States. | Museums—Social aspects—United States—History—20th century. | Museums—Educational aspects—United States—History—20th century. | Public history—United States—History—20th century. | World War, 1939–1945—Propaganda. | Propaganda, American—History—20th century. | World War, 1939–1945—Social aspects—United States.
Classification: LCC D733.U6 C45 2022 (print) | LCC D733.U6 (ebook) | DDC 940.53/73—dc23
LC record available at https://lccn.loc.gov/2021017193
LC ebook record available at https://lccn.loc.gov/2021017194
British Library Cataloguing-in-Publication Data
A catalog record for this book is available from the British Library.

Portions of chapter 1 were previously published as "Imperfectly Progressive: The Social Mission of U.S. Museums in the 1930s," in *Radical Roots: Public History and a Tradition of Social Justice Activism*, edited by Denise Meringolo (Amherst: Amherst College Press, 2021), 363–93.

To John Cosimo, my truly one and only

AMDG

CONTENTS

Preface ix

INTRODUCTION
The American Museum as Social Instrument
1

CHAPTER ONE
Toward a Material Rhetoric of Social Instrumentality
16

CHAPTER TWO
Materializing the Good Neighborhood
The Exhibitionary Network and Hemispheric Citizenship
40

CHAPTER THREE
War Comes to the Museum
70

CHAPTER FOUR
Witnessing War Fare
The Construction of Home-Front Citizenship
93

CHAPTER FIVE
Gateways to Global Citizenship in a Postwar World
129

CONCLUSION
Museum Stories, Old and New
159

Notes 173
Index 211

PREFACE

This is a book about ideas forged in battle—and not only the battles a reader might expect from a history of US museums during World War II. The central struggle I examine emerged in the 1930s and met its field tests during the war years. It concerned newer ways of making and communicating meanings with and through material objects, ways that made plainly, even painfully, evident what had always been true but not fully acknowledged: exhibition craft is an interpretive act, not a neutral revelation of inherent object truths. This development occurred within the context of larger debates arising during the Great Depression that centered on whether museums should be, foremost, educational institutions and, if so, whether they should increase both their utility and popularity by directly engaging with contemporary issues of civic concern. Some in favor of these propositions envisioned museums as social instruments that not only educated citizens but also inspired them to useful action. Means to achieve such goals included lectures, classes, and publications, with many efforts being developed by some of the first professionals in the field to be specifically trained for museum-based education. They did so, too, in consultation with experts in the bourgeoning adult education movement. Alongside these activities came experimentations in exhibition craft intended for actively didactic education.

Museums in the 1930s continued to borrow display tactics and ideas for garnering public interest from department stores, expositions, and mass media, much as they had in the decades before. A closer look at the period's discussions about the civic purpose of museums and, relatedly, the function of exhibiting objects reveals this modernization to be more than a matter of window dressing. For some practitioners it marked a substantive re-envisioning of the exhibition as an explicitly narrative medium useful for conveying ideas not only as a means to educate the public but also to direct it toward civically useful ends. Objects, as tangible anchors rooted in material truths, endowed the museum narrative, its practitioners believed, with a credibility that other narratives in the public square lacked. Furthermore, if rightly arranged, material objects could uniquely appeal to the individual museumgoer's mental, emotional, and physical faculties.

The idea that objects and the various other elements of exhibit craft constituted in toto a type of material rhetoric for civic storytelling met with resistance and censure. In an age in which propaganda, still understood broadly as a form of persuasive mass communication, might as easily sell fascism as household goods, there was good reason for museums as democratic educational institutions to become vocal actors in the public square—savvy to propaganda's tactics while avoiding its abuses. Indeed, from the 1930s through to the immediate postwar period, this was a line that social instrumentalists in the museum field believed they could walk. It is this balancing act, amid a war and warring ideas about the museum's role in civic life, that this volume chronicles. I argue that attempts during the war years to fit exhibition craft to the aims of social instrumentality constitute an important but forgotten moment in the field's debates over whether museums should take active stances on public issues or, to use current parlance, remain neutral.

Issues of museum neutrality and civic engagement were very much on my mind when I began conducting research for this book. While in the archives I busily traced how museums talked and disagreed about what they should be doing in service to a public and nation at war; outside the stacks and reading rooms, I watched as museums contended with a different war as the 9/11 attacks became the bombing of Pearl Harbor for a new generation. Some museums responded with alacrity. In Chicago, the Field Museum offered free admission and held town hall–style meetings so that locals could meet to discuss the developing events.[1] As the damaged Pentagon smoldered, the Smithsonian Institution assured the public, "The doors of the Smithsonian remain open so we can explore our nation's past struggles, successes and the resilience of our people. The treasured icons of our past remind us of the values we hold dear and give us hope for the future."[2] In New York, the Metropolitan Museum of Art reopened on September 13, announcing, "Hospitals are open. They're around to fix the body. We're here to fix the soul."[3] Steeped as I was in museums' pronouncements across the course of World War II, such statements had an eerily familiar ring. Beyond these surface similarities, the War on Terror was not, of course, World War II redux either for museums or American society.

I was struck, for example, by how commentary in the field's literature in the weeks and months after the attacks remained oddly devoid of direct references to the nation's being newly at war. As civilian and combatant casualties in the various theaters of the war on terror increased, remembrance and healing from national and personal trauma became the neutral ground on which numerous museum exhibitions stood. In terms of stance taking, many such displays left it squarely and safely to each museumgoer to determine what the losses signified. Bolder takes on the complexities and fraught issues of the widening conflict would come much later—and largely through art exhibitions that allowed museums to act as equivocal frames for contemporary and historic positions taken by artists. There is, of course, much more to be said about the wartime work of US museums following 9/11, including the fact that we have not yet recognized it as such.

This project has had a slow germination and yet I feel it could not be better timed. Recent years have seen intensified calls for museums to own up to their political entanglements, past and present, *and* to become catalysts, if not outright activists, for civic change on pressing social issues. I see this book as suited to our present moment because it makes the argument that museums have a longer, more complex history of social instrumentality, of believing that they should be involved in civic matters, than the traditional bracketing of such activities to the Progressive Era and 1960s–70s allows. Past models can, to be sure, constitute a mixed bag of precedents by current standards, but they stand as proof that the impulse to bring museums' resources to bear on society's problems is an enduring one.

Research for this book drew from administrative records, correspondence, and reports held by the archives of the American Museum of Natural History, the Brooklyn Museum of Art, the Museum of Modern Art (New York), the National Art Gallery, the Newark Museum, the Rockefeller Archive Center, the Smithsonian Institution, and the Wadsworth Atheneum (Hartford). Consulted primary sources also included numerous books, periodicals, and conference papers produced by and for museum and allied professionals from the 1920s through the early 1950s; these include the American Association of Museums' biweekly members' bulletin, *The Museum News*, the annual reports and members' bulletins of numerous museums, and various studies of the field funded by the Carnegie Corporation and the Rockefeller Foundation. Several chapters include deep analysis of specific exhibitions for which adequately rich documentation made it possible for me to track their iterative development from initial conception on through to final implementation and reception. Here, I consulted multiple reworkings of floor plans and exhibition scripts, memos and other correspondence detailing decision making and logistics, installation sketches and photographs, and, in one case, audio recordings of a narration heard by museumgoers in 1942. I also gleaned insights from exhibition promotional materials (press releases, brochures, invitations, etc.), press coverage, exhibition reviews, and, where available, commentary from museumgoers.

Museums have not always been the best keepers of their own histories, particularly in terms of systematic documentation of their temporary exhibitions, such as those created during World War II. Furthermore, wartime cutbacks caused a number of institutions, such as the Newark Museum, to discontinue publication of members' bulletins and other materials that might normally carry news and opinions of goings on. Other deficiencies in the record produced and maintained by the period's museum mainstream are the result of the field's predominant whiteness. Museums, along with other institutional actors, cast normative forms of public being and belonging in the white likeness. In contrast to the distinctions that institutions made among potential museumgoers on the basis of age or educational attainment, race seldom earned explicit mention—either as whiteness recognizing itself or as a means to categorize segments of society as racially "other." Attentive to racial absence and presence in the sources consulted, I have incorporated both explicitly and implicitly expressed white racial attitudes that shaped the exhibitions and efforts detailed in this book. Likewise, I consulted newspapers and periodicals produced by Black and other communities to find and add where I could perspectives on museums and their work from a broader range of vantage points.

The debts I owe to those who made the research, writing, and production of this book possible are many. The generous support of a Rockefeller

Archive Center grant-in-aid not only made possible the research essential for the chapter on museums' hemispheric unity work but also augmented my perspectives on the Museum of Modern Art's operations during the war years. Critical funding for the book's final stages of production came from my home institution, the University of Connecticut (UConn), through the School of Fine Arts' Project Completion Grant and the UConn Humanities Institute's Humanities Book Support Award. I am grateful for the recognition of my work's value that such support betokens.

My research is also indebted to the aid of the knowledgeable and gracious professionals at the Rockefeller Archive Center, the Newark Museum Archives, the Museum of Modern Art Archives, the Wadsworth Atheneum Museum of Art Archives and Auerbach Art Library, the United Nations, and the Smithsonian Institution Archives. I am grateful, too, for those institutions, including the Brooklyn Museum, the Art Institute of Chicago, the American Museum of Natural History, and the Museum of Modern Art, that have made exhibition records, press releases, annual reports, and other archival materials available online through open-access databases.

For the gift of latitude, so essential to completing the manuscript, I thank my colleagues at Greenhouse Studios | Scholarly Communications Design and those in the Department of Digital Media and Design at the University of Connecticut. Among my many supporters are Tom Scheinfeldt, who constantly encouraged me make the book a priority, particularly when shiny new projects beckoned, and Alexis Boylan, who generously dispensed practical advice and perfectly timed boosts to flagging spirits. Credit for sharpening my thinking and writing through early drafts goes to Steven Lubar, Susan Smulyan, Bettina Carbonell, Eugene Leach, and Paul Lauter. None of you, I understand now, really had time to spare—but you did so anyway. I offer my thanks to all of you as a down payment on the promise to pay forward to others the investment you made in me.

I am also humbled by the professional generosity of the two anonymous readers who, in a time of pandemic and national reckoning with histories of racial oppression, devoted their time and expertise to the conscientious examination of my manuscript. The fact that my colleagues at the University of Massachusetts Press worked under these same conditions, which presented all of us with priorities far more urgent than any workaday concern, underscores the depth of their commitment to their authors. From Mary Dougherty's early encouragement and Marla Miller's incisive comments to Matt Becker's wise and supportive editorial guidance at every turn, I cannot imagine a better set of collaborators, including Sally Nichols for impeccable design and Rachael DeShano for steady management. For copy editing and indexing, my thanks go to Ivo Fravashi and Joan Shapiro, respectively.

Throughout this journey, family has been my unfailing bedrock. My parents, Jeune and Joseph Welsh, contributed a mother's prayers, a father's constancy, and countless acts of loving support across my lifetime. Andrew Welsh bolstered moments of doubt with a brother's pride. It is to them that I owe everything. Jack Ceglio, from beginning to seemingly never-ending end, gave his full support completely and without hesitation. He kept me caffeinated and listened with remarkably rapt attention to every clunky draft that I insisted on reading aloud to him so that my ears could hear the needed edits that my eyes had missed. Every word between these covers is his accomplishment, too. And it is to him, my remarkable husband, that I dedicate this book.

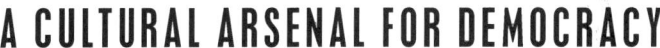

A CULTURAL ARSENAL FOR DEMOCRACY

Introduction

THE AMERICAN MUSEUM AS SOCIAL INSTRUMENT

> The conception of the museum as a social instrument is not a modern innovation in the history of museum philosophy.
>
> Theodore L. Low, 1942

In June 1941, a Central Press wire story declared, "The latest and strangest recruit in Uncle Sam's defense line-up is—the museum!" The release quoted John Hay Whitney, president of the "progressive-minded" Museum of Modern Art, as saying, "Does it seem strange to you to think of a museum as a weapon in national defense?"[1] To the field itself, the idea that museums constituted "another type of 'arsenal for democracy,'" as the article put it, was far from strange. In fact, this notion aligned with the paradigm of the museum as social instrument that had coalesced in the 1930s. This Progressive Era–inspired vision had called museums to engage with topics relevant to people's daily lives as a means to foster better-informed civic participation.[2] So, throughout World War II, museums across the United States of America responded to the national emergency in varied and creative ways. Their home-front activities included furnishing collections-based expertise, social services, and space. The Nevada Museum and Art Institute in Carson City, for example, installed an emergency hospital in its basement, and the Springfield Museum of Fine Arts in Massachusetts gave over a wing of its building for use as the city's United Services Organization center.[3] Other institutions created modest lounges, or canteens, where off-duty service personnel came for relaxation. Curators from the Metropolitan Museum of Art's Arms and Armor Department drew inspiration from their study collections to help design protective gear for bomber crews and infantry.[4] Researchers at the Smithsonian Institution undertook projects for the government and military. One such endeavor, "Survival on Land and Sea," provided troops with a portable guide to consult for such potentially lifesaving tasks as distinguishing edible plants from poisonous ones and estimating one's latitude from Polaris's location in the sky.[5]

Amid such activities, exhibitions served as the primary vehicle through which museums, large and small, engaged their publics with wartime topics. Fare ranged from displays on the tools of modern warfare, the cultures of Allied countries, and the basics of growing a victory garden to exhibits of soldiers' art, "living maps" charting actions overseas, and large-format photography shows created by US government agencies, corporations, and foreign information services that museums took on loan. This period in museum history, when not overlooked, is largely attributed to the national mobilization of people, industry, and culture to the purposes of waging war. At best, this frames museums' war activities as exceptions within the field's history and, at worst, as embarrassing lapses into propaganda work that can be explained away by pressures to conform to the prevailing culture. Scholarship that credits World War II with giving the nation's museums a forceful nudge toward active engagement with current events remains a rarity.[6]

To truly understand the wartime work of US museums, one must look beyond the tidy start and end dates that memorialize declarations and treaties but obscure the messy, longer edges, the windings up and drawings down, of armed conflict.[7] Hence, this wartime history of museums begins in the 1930s, an important period of deliberation and debate about whether museums should take more active roles in civic affairs—and, if so, what forms of involvement were and were not suited to their missions as collectors, preservers, and educational interpreters of natural and human-made materials. Such discussions also took up the matter of how the meanings held by objects could be made knowable to nonexperts not only through the adaptation of storytelling approaches employed by mass marketing and popular media but also through the unique connective capacities of material objects, capacities activated by the human-thing encounter if rightly arranged by the museum. These disputes, particularly as they concerned turning object display and exhibition craft toward the socially instrumental work of inspiring civic thought, feeling, and action on important issues of the day, are at the core of this book. They are covered, first, at the level of field-wide conversations as these took place through the profession's literature and convenings. These chapters provide grounding for those that are focused on how the discussions played out in practice by offering extended analyses of selected exhibitions attentive to the contexts, ambitions, and compromises that gave shape to the expression of social instrumentality at the institutional level. Examined exhibitions include those that sought to foster knowledgeable public participation in such national concerns as hemispheric unity (e.g., the Newark Museum's *Three Southern Neighbors: Ecuador, Peru, Bolivia,* 1941–42); home-front planning (e.g., the Museum of Modern Art's *Wartime Housing,* 1942); and the forging of a world reunited in peace (e.g., the Wadsworth Atheneum's *What the Boys Send Home,* 1945).

By tracing the experiments, collaborative entanglements, and fledgling ideal of the museum as social instrument from the 1930s through to the immediate postwar years, I argue that the storytelling approach to exhibition craft in service to social instrumentality posed a novel dilemma for the field—a dilemma greatly complicated by wartime concerns but ultimately about challenges to what would now be called museum neutrality. The matter of whether *and how* museum fare should pursue explicitly didactic aims intended to foster informed democratic decision making arose in the 1930s but met its test in the 1940s. In its pursuit of greater civic relevance, the museum field grappled actively in these decades with the issue of where the line between social instrumentality and indoctrination lay. To pass over wartime exhibitions as mere patriotic propaganda is to ignore how practitioners of the past sought to distinguish their efforts from jingoism. Likewise, to dismiss museums' wartime activities as unconnected to ongoing concerns of the field is to divest contemporary activist public history and museum work of its imperfect but instructive pasts.

To be clear, this book does not claim that the war produced a field-wide reordering or led to an evident embrace of social instrumentality by more museums. But histories of lasting transformation are not the only histories we need. Indeed, throughout the war, as ideals met the frictions of implementation, the field contended actively with such perennial questions as Who constitutes "the public"? What does it mean to put museums in service to civic issues? How are objects to be interpreted and made meaningful to others? And should museum exhibitions persuade? As will be explored in detail, the social instrument paradigm as it arose in this period looked to immersive storytelling exhibitions designed to engage museumgoers in their mental, emotional, and physical capacities so that thought, feeling, and action might be inspired and directed toward civic goals. Museum exhibitions today often employ similar means to educate publics, illuminate pathways to change, and galvanize social energies. Now, as then, the field debates the compatibility of such aims with traditional collections-focused mandates. This adaptation of material rhetoric to the aims of social instrumentality and what happened to museums' more progressive impulses once the nation went to war constitutes a chief through line of this book.

In the decades since Whitney's rhetorical query, scant attention has been given to museums' roles in wartime cultures.[8] The rare, sustained analyses of this topic are Gaynor Kavanagh's *Museums and the First World War: A Social History* and Catherine Pearson's *Museums in the Second World War: Curators, Culture and Change*, both of which focus on British institutions.[9] *Exhibiting War: The Great War, Museums, and Memory in Britain, Canada, and Australia* is unique for its comparative international focus and for its study of how vernacular and state-sponsored collecting, commissioning, and exhibition during the war set the foundations for war museums on three continents.[10]

Kavanagh and Pearson argue that the urgent, though different, circumstances of each war stirred British museums to sharpen their focus on meeting civic needs through educational programming and exhibits treating current events. Peacetime, the authors note, relegated such community-facing work to the back burner, well behind collection, preservation, and research activities. In 1919, for example, the Museums Association in Britain rejected the Ministry of Reconstruction's proposal that classing museums with libraries and schools presented the best administrative path for coordination of all-ages education. The stated grounds for the objection: museums "were not fundamentally educational institutions."[11]

Still, as Pearson notes, the interwar years across the United Kingdom saw increasing calls for museums to play a more deliberate part in preparing citizens for informed engagement in modern social democracy. As in the United States, Carnegie funds in the 1930s supported studies in Britain of the state of practice in both public education and exhibition craft.[12] The United Kingdom looked also to American museums for models of collaboration among groups focused on adult and child education.[13] Although World War II derailed the proposed reforms emerging from these British studies, its disruption of routine operations also created some leeway for champions of the socially engaged museum to implement their ideas. However, as happened after the Great War, UK institutions largely fell back into more traditional routines. Pearson argues that the lack of a single commanding social focus around which to marshal the field made it all the easier to resurrect the prewar status quo.

The US museum reports that provided inspiration to British museums in the 1930s emphasized museums' obligations to serve democracy by helping to foster an educated populace capable, as individuals, of clear-headed, informed decision making for the common benefit. These studies, undertaken by or in conversation with the adult education movement, underscored museums' place in cradle-to-grave education, with collection, preservation, and research being "merely preliminary" essentials to the ultimate "use of objects for the enrichment of the life of the people."[14] The writings also share an underlying concern for the future prospects of museums—and of the body politic—amid social currents stirred by the economic crisis at home and political trends abroad. For the authors, who still equated material objects with objective truths, museums represented a "powerful instrument for the transmission of ideas and emotions directly to the ordinary man" so that all might "form their own cultural, economic, or political opinions from a firsthand study of unvarnished facts."[15]

The expanding adult education movement and fear of fascist influences on the American mind also garnered consideration in the crowning study of the decade: *The Museum in America: A Critical Study*.[16] Written by Laurence Vail Coleman, director of the American Association of Museums (AAM), and published in 1939, the study's three volumes drew together observations from some two thousand site visits, with data from a census of the nation's institutions. Its pages also covered the implications for museums of increased reliance on government and private foundation funds (which carried expectations of clearer public benefit), recent signs of declining attendance, the influence of mass media and corporate publicity tactics on Americans, and entry into the field of a new class of professional, the purpose-trained museum educator.[17] Coleman, in addition to having served as the AAM's executive secretary from 1923 until his promotion to director in 1927, had earlier experience as lead for the department of preparation and exhibition at the American Museum of Natural History.[18] The study, produced by the AAM, then in its thirty-third year of operation and supported by the Carnegie Corporation (which also supported the AAM itself), describes a field reflecting on its accomplishments but, cognizant of pressures to change, envisioning itself as a "social movement" directly engaged with the concerns of people's daily lives.[19]

Social Progressivism in Tension with Social Control

By the 1930s, a mix of forces had reignited Progressive Era visions of the museum as an agent of civic transformation. Not all embraced this idea, of course, and even those who did pursued it in different forms and degrees. Its strongest boosters had been inspired by the work and writings of their Progressive Era predecessors; some had also trained in the professionalization programs those earlier advocates had helped found. And a few long-lived practitioners from that first wave remained active. It is not surprising that the field looked to the forty or so years preceding its current disruptions. Such leading lights as Louise Connolly (1862–1927), John Cotton Dana (1856–1929), and Robert W. DeForest (1848–1931) had recently passed, prompting assessments of their times and careers.

One of those assessors, Theodore Lewis Low, produced *The Museum as Social Instrument* on behalf of the AAM's committee on education.[20] Low, then in his late twenties, had taken Paul J. Sachs's now-famed museum course at Harvard just two years prior to the volume's publication and championed the minority view that art museums had a duty to provide education grounded in democratic principles and goals.[21] He reminded his readers, "The conception of the museum as a social instrument is not a modern innovation in the history of museum philosophy."[22] Rather, he argued, it was an idea whose growth since the 1870s had been "spasmodic" but could now reach fuller realization if social consciousness became as prized a job qualification as scholarship. Low credited the Great Depression as a blessing in so far as it had reawakened interest in Progressive Era principles and, by his reckoning, led many in the field to "recognize that the only real justification for the existence of a museum lies in its degree of usefulness to society as a whole and that museums today are failing miserably to attain the standards necessary for continued life."[23] It had been an earlier war, the Great War of 1917–18, that had fractured museum alignments with Progressive ideals. The postwar industrial arts movement, for example, largely turned from improving US workers' lot to outfitting corporate producers for competition overseas while equipping the American public for consumer citizenship.[24] Still, for some 1930s observers, such work by the Metropolitan Museum of Art and the Museum of Modern Art (MoMA), which the state of New York chartered in 1929 "to encourage and develop the study of the modern arts and the application of such arts to manufacture and practical life," stood as exemplars of civically engaged museum practice.[25]

In addition to the lingering impact of these war-altered models of museum engagement in national life, the New Deal with its populism, funding, and manpower not only helped to rekindle a reform-minded outlook but also established museum-government relationships that later smoothed the way to wartime cooperation. Support of the Works Progress Administration (WPA) allowed the Metropolitan, for example, to experiment for three seasons with neighborhood "extension" exhibitions drawn from its varied departments.[26] Publicized by radio, flyers, and notices in mainstream and foreign-language newspapers, the exhibits went out to high schools, settlement houses, public library branches, the Young Men's Hebrew Association, and other locations where museum staff teamed with that of host organizations to offer study groups, classes, and lectures. Government use of exhibitions as a medium for public outreach also expanded, with various relief agencies sending some 450 of them out to schools, city halls, and museums.[27] The WPA, the Works Division of the Department of Public Welfare, and similar units also supported projects in museums dedicated to history, science, and other fields. Efforts included restoration and expansion of facilities, cataloguing and care of collections, installation of exhibitions, expansion of research and education activities, and augmenting existing staff so that long-deferred projects as well as ambitious new undertakings could be tackled. The infusion of government funds gave some in the field reason to ponder the possible benefits of continued federal support along the lines of the European model.[28]

Woven through the more reform-minded writings of the 1930s and early '40s is an avid but nervous interest in the ability of mass media and advertising to capture public imaginations—and, in the wrong hands, become tools of antidemocratic indoctrination. For some advocates, the museum as social instrument would be a bulwark against fascism and a democratic means of social influence. As US concern over domestic implications of the political and military turmoil abroad grew, security-state rhetoric made more frequent appearance in texts. The adult education movement, for example, becomes characterized as "part of the defense reaction of the democratic process to the increasing threats of hostile forces within and without the state."[29] The Progressive Era now stood as a high-water mark in proving that museums, like other institutions for popular education, could be effective "weapons of social action" against "poverty and social inequality."[30] By decade's end, voices called anew for museums to be "modern weapons in the struggle for popular enlightenment," not only for the civic good but for the sake, too, of their continued relevance.[31] As one observer noted (and Low later quoted), "separated from its social content a museum is meaningless to anyone but its curators."[32]

The conceptualization of adult education in this period also held that it could serve not only as a means of individual uplift and informed civic participation but also as "a definite method of social control, an essential framework for political democracy."[33] Just as the social reform work of the Progressive Era as a whole, and within museums, contained tensions and contradictions, so too did the term "social control" during the 1930s. In its older sociological sense, it referred to a society's ability to regulate itself. Under this meaning, museums and other institutions would stand athwart cadres of in-the-know experts or media oligarchies with vested interests. They would do so by providing untainted, easy-to-parse information so that common folk could come to understand the technological, cultural, political, and scientific forces shaping their lives. Thus equipped, the public could then make clear-headed decisions in town hall meetings, at the polls, and with their dollars. This democratic version of social control sat in opposition to totalitarian and fascist states, where, from the US perspective, public ignorance had made it possible for small factions to manipulate opinions and thereby rise to power.

In the 1930s, however, social control took on added meaning as theorists increasingly focused on institutional structures and their capacities for informal, noncoercive indoctrination of individuals to value systems.[34] It is only with this twofold meaning of social control in mind that one can fully appreciate the dilemma facing the museum field as practitioners and institutions sought to demarcate the boundaries between education and propaganda, and between the objective ideal and the subjective reality of the museum as a social instrument. As noted, the exhibition analyses at the heart of this book foreground how specific institutions and groups of individuals attempted to define and mark this relatively new terrain.

Examining Wartime Imaginaries, Networks, and Storytelling in the Museum

In addition to exploring how each exhibition was understood, received, and critiqued in its day, the analyses also give critical consideration to the cultural work they performed. This aspect of the examination focuses on three core areas: museums' roles in materializing national and supranational imaginaries of the war period; their connections to corporate and government efforts that, together with museum work, constituted a wartime exhibitionary network; and how some storytelling formats designed to engage mind, emotion, and body constituted a material rhetoric of social instrumentality. Exhibition craft related to the war effort took on multiple forms, and while art shows of wartime subjects and of the cultural heritage of Allied nations abounded, they are not this work's focus. Rather, the exhibitions that the book considers in depth are exemplars of what I call the material rhetoric of social instrumentality. The paradigm of the museum as a social instrument helped place new importance on artifactual display as a form of storytelling believed by its practitioners to be capable of producing intellectual, emotional, and embodied forms of knowing. An aspect of the cultural work performed by such exhibitions is their function as performative acts of public witness to the civic belonging of museumgoer *and* museum alike. Civic belonging is treated here as form of cultural citizenship that, while it does not confer legal standing within the state, asserts a legitimacy predicated on shared sensibilities and social practices.[35]

One means that will be used to analyze the structuring of individual and institutional belonging to the national body is to approach the selected wartime exhibitions as materializations of culturally predominant imagined communities configured during the period. Indeed, as will be shown, numerous museum exhibitions materialized the national and supranational civic imaginaries that I define in the book as "the Good Neighborhood" of hemispheric unity; "the Home Front" as solidarity; and the hoped-for "One World" at peace. For public history as well as American and museum studies, the nation-state is a shared area of concern. Scholars in these fields have argued that nations and museums are conjoined products of modernity. Benedict Anderson, in his seminal work on nationalism, cited the museum (along with the census and the map) as a chief means of visualizing the imagined community of the state in order to cohere and extend its power. His assertion that "museums, and the museumizing imagination, are both profoundly political" resonates with theorizations of museums as spaces of civic ritual, colonial hegemony, contact, and activism, to name but a few examples.[36] In terms of analyzing museum materializations of civic imaginaries, the work of scholars who treat the national imaginary as an always-in-process narration is useful because it foregrounds the oppositions and instabilities present within the idea of statehood *and* in the cultural representations that seek to call it into being.[37] This literature also treats the role of emotional experiences, including those derived from mediated encounters, in heightening the desire for civic identification.[38]

The materializing of civic imaginaries through exhibitions also involved other actors. Hence, my analysis also situates museums, together with government agencies, corporations, and media firms, as participants in a wartime exhibitionary network of display and exchange. Treating museums not as standalone actors but as parts of larger social configurations has been key to understanding the nature of the cultural power that they wield. One widely used term to describe such configurations, particularly as they existed at the turn of the twentieth century, is the "exhibitionary complex."[39] It situates museums together with world expositions, department stores, and similar public spaces that through their displays of material goods structured citizens' sense of self-relationship to systems of knowledge and power. A revised formulation of this framework, renamed the "governmental assemblage" by its originating scholar, Tony Bennett, better connects museums to various forms of state power, such as colonialism; it also underscores that the relationships among any group of actors are a thing of ongoing reconfiguration.[40]

Informed by these ideas, I use the term "exhibitionary network" to emphasize the collaborative alliances, unintentional alignments, and borrowings among the involved government, institutional, corporate, and media actors that facilitated the circulation of materials and influence during World War II. Such institutional webs matter. Examining the social, ideological, and political uses of museums—and museums' own interests in these areas—provides historical context for study of these issues in our own time. Also, ideology is revealed not only in content but also in the form of the business arrangements and agreements that influence the production and distribution of that content.[41] Lastly, to consider museums as participants in this wartime exhibitionary network is to take into account the mutually constitutive relationships among state, capitalism, and cultural enterprise.

The matter of how, exactly, this exhibitionary network helped to materialize the wartime imaginaries considered in this book circles back to the material rhetoric of social instrumentality that some museums applied to storytelling with objects. While exhibitions cannot be reduced to texts, those in this study were consciously discursive in nature. Here, scholarship that brings rhetorical theory to bear on museum architecture, exhibitions, and human encounters in these spaces provides useful ways to center relational processes of becoming. This avoids the pitfalls of suggesting that gallery arrangements bypass museumgoer and displayed object agency to produce determinative outcomes.[42] With regard to object agency, this project draws from material culture studies by recognizing that while things are "a medium" through which humans "think the world," they are by no means passive participants in the communication process.[43] A productive way to think about how those gatherings of objects that we call exhibitions exert influence can be found in Jane Bennett's term "vibrant matter." The aliveness of things and our relationships to them, she argues, form a "congregational agency."[44] In other words, it is the specifics of arrangement and interaction that call forth the power that we intuit objects possess, a power we cannot fully describe—or control.[45] In the case of exhibitions, this congregational agency is produced by all aspects of a display's design, the characteristics of the space (lighting, room temperature, ceiling height, flooring, etc.), the actions of the humans moving through it in any given moment, and so forth.

To think about exhibitions in this way requires analytical attention be given to how the embodied experience of the museumgoer contributes to meaning making. Here, both affect theory and sensory studies help to account for the complex interplay of sensory perception, emotional states, and cognition that shapes how humans come to "to know" something through their encounters with exhibitions, memorials, and other such spaces.[46] They participate, too, in the production of "belonging," the orientating of individuals to governing or collective bodies.⁴⁷ Indeed, greater consideration is being given within museum and public history scholarship to the contemporary role of affect within interpretation, design, and education and to multisensory modes of apprehension.⁴⁸ Although such investigations into museum exhibitions of the past are fewer, often due to lack of archival evidence, available works make clear that efforts to convey meaning through sound, tactility, movement, and other stimuli are by no means recent developments.⁴⁹

Among the issues that this work grapples with, in terms of the sensory and affective dimensions of such exhibitions as MoMA's *Wartime Housing*, which is examined in chapter 4, is the dearth of data from which to draw a composite of the "typical" museumgoer's responses. There is, too, the impossibility of accounting for perceptive differences among bodies that are as much socially constructed as they are physically individual.⁵⁰ Therefore, much of the analysis centers on how museums conceived of their audiences' embodied experiences and responses. It gathers this information broadly, from the profession's literature, and specifically, from curatorial documentation of the analyzed exhibitions. Where available, individual responses receive attention, but the analysis remains mindful that neither the paid critic nor the visitor pleased or peeved enough to register a documented comment with a museum is a sufficient stand-in for "the public." It must also be acknowledged that the white-run museum mainstream that constituted the majority of the field in this period typically made expansive, nonspecific pronouncements about serving the "the public" or "community" while excluding in consideration and practice groups based on race, class, and other prejudices.⁵¹

Things, too, are unruly subjects resisting tidy narrative containment. So, in analyzing the cultural work of the selected wartime exhibitions, attention is paid not only to curatorial ambitions but also to the possible ways in which these object gatherings worked—and meant—differently than their narrative frameworks. Another essential aspect of parsing the material rhetoric of the exhibitions examined in this book is to attend to the earlier-mentioned notion of museumgoing as civic ritual or performance. As will be argued, some war-era exhibits did more than materialize civic imaginaries; they functioned as occasions for public witness where visiting individuals as well as the host institutions could enact and affirm their belonging to those communities of belief and practice.

From Good Neighborhood to Home Front to One World at Peace

Chapter 1 details how arguments that museums should take a more active part in contemporary affairs intersected with changing ideas about how knowing through objects and meaning making through exhibitions occurred. Debates about the purposes toward which museums, their exhibitions, and the public should be directed saw some gravitating toward a material rhetoric of social instrumentality that favored thematic, storytelling frameworks, relevance to contemporary life, evident didactic aims, use of contemporary media, and, through multisensory appeals, an emphasis on the human-thing encounter as productive of thought, feeling, and action. These developments argue against the idea that museums' wartime work came chiefly as a response to the all-out cultural mobilization of the 1940s. To the contrary, by the end of the 1930s, an important if comparatively small segment of the field was already poised to increase museums' relevance by tackling topics important to daily life.

Thus, when the national call for hemispheric unity arose at the turn of the decade as a means to avoid war and defend the United States, museums across the country took up the cause. Chapter 2 describes how these new Good Neighbor initiatives built on museums' earlier involvements in Pan-American cultural exchange efforts. Likewise, government-museum partnerships normalized by the New Deal expanded when Nelson A. Rockefeller, on leave from his post as president of MoMA, stepped in to lead the new Office of the Coordinator of Inter-American Affairs. It is within this context that I examine museums' place in a coalescing wartime exhibitionary network of diverse interests working together and separately on loosely aligned agendas to shape public sentiment and behavior toward Latin America. Such examples as the Newark Museum's *Three Southern Neighbors: Ecuador, Peru, Bolivia* (1941–42) reveal the difficulties museums faced, from collections issues to racial biases, in materializing a hemispheric imaginary consistent with the stated aims of coequal transnational belonging.

Even as museums engaged in hemispheric unity efforts, they continued to debate how best to manifest their civic worth. Chapter 3 traces how the coming of war pushed into sharper relief the existing divide on whether purposive communications, so effective for winning audiences in the commercial and popular entertainment realms, could be used to good educational effect within museums. Those leaning toward the model of the museum as temple, as preserver of objective truths and humanity's highest accomplishments, argued the dangers of becoming propaganda organs. Others, aligning themselves with the model of the museum as social instrument, advocated for timeliness and active promotion of democratic cultural values. Both camps (and the many museums taking positions in between) saw themselves as serving their communities' wartime needs by contributing to social betterment, cultural stabilization, and morale.

Chapter 4 explores museums' part in defining the terms of home-front belonging while asserting their own places in the body politic. By examining the range of undertakings that institutions pursued, I illuminate the relations and strains within the wartime exhibitionary network. Against this backdrop, the struggles of progressive practitioners to reconcile their goals with those of multiple stakeholders and accepted modes of patriotic expression is analyzed through the Museum of Modern Art's *Wartime Housing* exhibition (1942), which was undertaken in collaboration with the National Committee on the Housing Emergency and the National Housing Agency. Because *Wartime Housing* involved message-driven manipulations of space, texture, light, sound, and photographic imagery, it is an apt example of the embodied ways of knowing and participatory democracy that the material rhetoric of social instrumentality sought to produce. By contrasting *Wartime Housing* with later efforts by the MoMA and other institutions, the chapter reveals how prewar investments in social reform ultimately gave way to narratives that reinforced social continuity on the domestic front.

Chapter 5 surveys examples of how US museums sought to prepare their publics for the peace to come by situating themselves as gateways to a new cosmopolitan citizenship. For progressives, the internationalist One World spirit of inherent human sameness and respect for cultural diversity seemed an apt match to prewar visions of what museums might accomplish in terms of civic good. By 1945, US museum professionals channeled these impulses at the global level. Figures from the early war's hemispheric unity efforts now assumed leading roles in the new Museums Division of the United Nations Educational, Scientific and Cultural Organization and the International Council of Museums. This chapter examines why, on the cusp of a seemingly promising peacetime agenda, American museums largely abandoned the social instrument paradigm and its accompanying material rhetoric. As shown through analysis of such exhibitions as the Art Institute of Chicago's *Art of the United Nations* (1944–45), the Wadsworth Atheneum's *What the Boys Send Home* (1945), and the Brooklyn Museum's *Clothing One World* (1947), implementation of internationalism's ideals ultimately reinscribed typological object arrangements and old underlying hierarchies of difference linked to colonial imperialism. Additionally, political reluctance to use internationalism to push for racial equity at home, rising Cold War nationalism, and Red Scare tactics that branded reform as subversive also played a part in dampening museums' enthusiasm for clear-cut involvement in the fray of civic life.

The concluding chapter of this investigation acknowledges the limits of socially progressive museum work as it was conceived in the 1930s and falteringly implemented during the war. It also makes the case for the importance of this fleeting experiment with the paradigm of the museum as social instrument, arguing that knowledge of this history can deepen understanding of the field's recursive debates over objectivity, neutrality, and civic purpose. Lastly, it urges that attention be paid to the ideals, conflicts, missteps, and ambitions that attended the period's development of a material rhetoric of social instrumentality. How might these early efforts to engage the sensory body, activate affective capacities, and harness the power of storytelling to assert museums' place as contributors to and resources for civic good invite new perspectives on social instrumentality through exhibition craft in our own time? And so it is with exhibition craft that this history begins. While much has been written of the field's long practice of borrowing display techniques from department stores, world's fairs, and corporate communications, particularly during the 1920s and 1930s, this literature does not give sufficient attention to the accompanying shifts taking place in how museums thought of meaning making from, through, and with objects. Likewise, these changes have not been adequately studied in the context of rising ideas about museums as active civic agents. The following chapter addresses these gaps.

Chapter One

TOWARD A MATERIAL RHETORIC OF SOCIAL INSTRUMENTALITY

> Educational approaches can be made through three sides of the individual—mental, emotional, physical. If all three sides are drawn out—through thought, feeling and action—the result is a balanced experience.
>
> —Laurence Vail Coleman, director of the
> American Museum Association, 1939

Early in 1939, newspapers, newsreels, radio programs, and other mass media recounted the gathering at Madison Square Garden of some twenty thousand American Nazis, including men, women, and youngsters decked out in party uniforms and regalia. As the months unfolded, the Golden Gate International Exposition transformed a New Deal–funded mound of dredged fill into a Treasure Island. To the east, the New York World's Fair touted the utopian Democracy of tomorrow, where social and technological planning would produce "a brave new world" of prosperity, leisure, "unity and peace."[1] Others of the time foresaw "a world trend from 'individualism' to 'collectivism'" if, in this "Age of Propaganda," socialist, communist, and other foreign politics took deeper root in the American psyche.[2] Meanwhile, throughout the country, projects aided by the Works Progress Administration (WPA) and other relief agencies took place within museums as laborers and artisans spruced up installations, catalogued collections, repaired facilities, debuted exhibitions, and even erected wholly new buildings and institutions.[3] These efforts could now be read against the newly published *The Museum in America: A Critical Study* by Laurence Vail Coleman, director of the American Association of Museums (AAM). By September, Britain and France had declared war on Germany, after its invasion of Poland. In December, and closer to home, a Nazi warship took harbor in a South American port after skirmishing with the British Royal Navy along the Argentinean and Uruguayan coasts.

Sandwiched between these events, members of the AAM convened at the end of June in San Francisco for their annual meeting headquartered that year at the Hotel St. Francis on Union Square.[4] This not only put attendees in easy reach of morning sessions at the San Francisco Museum of Art and the Golden Gate International Exposition's Pacific House, it also assured lodgers that all rooms, whether singles at four dollars a night or suites at twelve dollars and up, came equipped with a bath. The matter of how to make meaning with objects held pride of place at the conference, which took as its official theme "Interpretation through Exhibits." Accordingly, panels addressed such topics as "the didactic functions of muscum display," particularly as these related to engaging a modern public such as that being drawn to the exposition and its New York counterpart. Museum practitioners, true to earlier precedents, took a studied interest in the commercial displays and promotion tactics being deployed at both events and with aid of the Rockefeller Foundation produced two books on what they gleaned.[5]

Among the two hundred or so AAM members in attendance were those who envisioned museums not only as a social movement but as a social instrument that might more directly engage with the concerns of people's daily lives and in doing so strengthen American democracy. As earlier noted, the currents shaping this renewed strain of progressive museum practice included the influence of mass media practices, propaganda in its political and corporate manifestations, the adult education movement, Depression-era financial and social instabilities, museums' realigned perspectives on government support, and the specter of a new European conflict. Importantly, for this inquiry, the 1930s envisioning of museums as social instruments brought with it a reimagining of the material rhetoric of exhibition craft. That is to say beliefs about the ways in which objects possessed, embodied, and could communicate knowledge to the layperson underwent an important reconceptualization during this period.

As will be shown through the exhibition analyses taken up in the chapters that follow, display craft reflective of the social instrument paradigm typically favored thematic, storytelling frameworks, relevance to contemporary life, evident didactic aims, and an emphasis on the human-thing encounter as the dynamic locus of mental, emotional, and physical meaning making. Such work involved using any combination of text, sound, interactivity, photographs, film, and purpose-built didactic objects—together with collections materials (and sometimes without)—as narrative components that appealed to the physical senses as well as the visceral imagination. To be clear, this constituted a strand of exhibition craft, not the period's mainstream, and might best be characterized as a loose set of practices applied across museums of different disciplinary types. This approach had its critics as well as its champions, and, as appropriate to the topicality of its aims, manifested chiefly in temporary exhibitions rather than permanent galleries. Understanding when and why museums began to experiment with approaches that today seem unremarkable given their prevalence in contemporary practice is an essential starting point if one is to understand their deployment in the 1940s.

Object Knowledge

It is instructive to read the foregrounding of meaning making and instruction through exhibition craft at the AAM's 1939 conference within the context of changing ideas about how museums could reveal the meanings seen as inherent to natural and human-made objects. Victorian-era museums deemed artifacts and things of nature to be, in and of themselves, capable of self-evident communication to even the untrained, but careful, observer. Or, as one museum director put it in 1894, "All museum material should speak for itself upon sight. It should be an open book that tells a better story than any description will do."[6] The display modes designed to facilitate this "reading" of objects involved typological or synoptic categorization. These joined individual object meanings into aggregate, more complex concepts where nuances of order implied narratives of evolutionary, technological, and cultural progress—ideas rooted, of course, in the white, colonialist, male perspectives that then predominated the profession. Likewise, art galleries might use systematics of chronology, geography, or style to make collections' items legible.

By the mid-1920s, it is argued, a crisis of knowing through objects had arisen within the museum as university-based modes of advanced research, which did not rely on "object-based epistemology," edged most disciplinary museums out of the center of American intellectual life.[7] Losing status as sites for the generation of knowledge, museums turned more resolutely to public education as their principal mission.[8] This shift was neither rapid nor uniform, and some museums, particularly those focused on art, remained somewhat insulated by virtue of the nature of their research. Changing ideas in the 1930s about the nature and needs of "the public" also played a part in the push to reconsider how objects' meanings could be revealed.[9] Philanthropic organizations provided financial encouragement for museums to experiment with practices borrowed from public education, communications, and other fields. The Rockefeller Foundation's policies even treated museums as a type of mass medium.[10] Guided by the belief that commercial enterprises had better mastered the art of discovering and appealing to the common person's interests, the foundation's museum funding largely supported visitor behavior research, the study and development of exhibition techniques, and training programs for the professionalization of museum workers—all with an eye toward strengthening museums' stance in the marketplace of ideas. It is within this context that museums in greater numbers adopted the "storyline technique."[11] And indeed, museum literature of the 1930s abounds with advice similar to that of Carlos E. Cummings, director of the Buffalo Museum of Science and a part of the Rockefeller-funded initiatives, who proclaimed in his study of the New York and San Francisco fairs, "Today's Museums Should Tell a Story."[12]

The term "story" as used in this 1920s to '30s period of flux—which scholars have identified as museums' "communicative turn"—still described a variety of exhibition formats.[13] It could serve as shorthand for not-so-new methods of basic sequential display, particularly in science and art museums. Cummings, for example, conceived of entire floors within the Buffalo Museum of Science as each being a book further divided into chapters (rooms), paragraphs (cases), and so forth.[14] Within the field, and particularly to those studying museums' educational potential from the outside, such arrangements seemed ideal for communicating subjects across time and for the continued relating of progressionist narratives (including those rooted in ideologies of white racial and cultural superiority).[15] "Story" might also refer to object ensembles, such as the visual vignettes conveyed by period rooms within arts institutions or house museums, the "action" exhibits being championed by industrial and science museums, and the habitat groups of natural history halls. The communicative turn also owed a debt to earlier European museology and American academics for the field's widening interest in "culture history" or, as its German progenitors called it, *Kulturgeschichte*.[16] This approach, which Coleman described as "the interpretation of art, history, anthropology, and applied science—all together" now appealed not only to general museums, he reported, but seemed to be in growing favor among institutions under "the spell of Dana" or in the orbit of midcareer progressives such as Laura Bragg, who at the time of Coleman's writing in 1939 was some eight years into her second directorship, that of the Berkshire Museum in Pittsfield, Massachusetts.[17]

What separated storytelling rhetoric in service to the aims of the museum as social instrument from these older forms, which simply likened objects to words and groupings of them to textbooks, was the adoption of storytelling techniques from mass media as well as the integration of narrative elements into displays for purposes of didactic or persuasive education. Paradoxically, diminished faith not in objects but in words contributed to the idea that museums should not only learn to marshal the strategies of contemporary mass communication media but could also uniquely ground these other ways of knowing in material proofs. Thus, two important elements tightly tied to the material rhetoric of the social instrument paradigm were a sharper focus on the human side of the communications equation, specifically the embodied nature of reception, and the idea of foregrounding relevance to contemporary life and experience.

With regard to the latter, Arthur Casewell Parker (Seneca) emphasized that the next step, after analysis, in implementing a culture history approach to exhibitions, was to "begin the effort to unfold the story of what it all means to life and living today. . . . It goes without argument that people are interested in those things that touch their lives."[18] Parker, director of the Rochester Museum of Arts and Sciences in New York state, championed this line of thought in his many writings aimed at small local history societies, house museums, and municipal institutions like his own.[19] Parker, although not a degree-holding historian, brought to the subject an archaeologist's and ethnologist's interests in human-thing relations past and present.[20]

His 1935 book *A Manual for History Museums* detailed how contemporary relevance could be accomplished through simple, topical exhibitions. He instructed one to start by choosing a subject of interest to the community and then phrasing it as a question. Next, based on what one's collections held—or lacked—local developments over time could be shown through "well-arranged selections of objects, pictures, models, and miniatures, all fortified and made significant by informative labels written in a brief, interesting manner" so viewers might derive answers from the resulting exhibit.[21] He gave as his example a simple wall case display of five shelves called "Have Schools Improved?" The plan for such an exhibit should take into account its "emotional value," he counseled, but its chief aim "is to present a connected series of facts that make the past live again in the present—and to have the museum visitor react to this information."

The means to "touch" visitors' lives lay not only in making clear how the past bore on the present but also in engaging the senses both literally and imaginatively, as Parker's younger contemporary, the historian Edward P. Alexander, pointed out at the AAM's annual conference in 1936. Remembered today for his long career, which included the book *Museums in Motion*, first published in 1979, Alexander was in his late twenties when he addressed his colleagues assembled in New York City.[22] He suggested that even the most modest of institutions with budgets too small to employ dioramas and other methods of their big-city counterparts could achieve much with thematic arrangements. With sharp-eyed wit he castigated the antiquarian penchant for hagiographic materials of dubious origin by calling on historical society museums to extract the vintage fire engine that sat amid "tattered Civil War battle flags, splinters from Old Ironsides or Charter Oak, and a glass case containing two hairs from Washington's wig."[23] They should instead stage the truck with fire helmets, leather buckets, and other trade implements. A vintage print (or reproduction) of firefighting would suggest the artifacts' past lives of action while a label described their historic context vividly enough that observers imagined themselves manning the pump.

Alexander also recommended direct sensory appeal as a means to "enliven" local history institutions that lacked "but a few shovelfuls of dirt to sink into external rest."[24] Using (spare?) artifacts, volunteers could pare apples, grind meat for sausage, dip candles, and spin fiber. Motion, smell, and sound, "the whir of the spinning wheel and the thwack-thwack of the heavy batten of the loom," would illuminate objects' purposes as well as their place in larger processes.[25] It also made for a more vivid comparison between lives of the past and those of the present. The "alert" institution might do more than hold demonstrations; it might invite "the visitors to try it themselves." Similar strategies had earlier been employed to popular effect in the colonial kitchen of the Centennial International Exhibition of 1876 and, along more educational if not equally moralistic lines, at the Newark Museum beginning in 1916.[26] (That such activities are now stock-in-trade for "living history" museums makes it harder, perhaps, to appreciate their initial novelty.)

Configuring museum collections along these lines did not, Alexander asserted, represent an effort to compensate for opacity on the part of the artifacts. "The big objective of the historical museist is to provide flesh and blood for the bare bones of narrative history," he stated; "Words are still very deceptive and meaningless compared to actual objects."[27] Parker thought along similar lines: "It [history] must not merely be described by written words or by spoken traditions, though these have value. The fact is that the tangible has the advantage of the intangible when it comes to understanding."[28] That museum professionals argued for the communicative power of things is not at all surprising, but they were not alone.

Public school educators influenced by John Dewey's theories connecting pedagogy to the development of a progressive democratic society had long embraced the role of objects in learning. Museum-school partnerships in the progressive vein could be traced to the 1860s. By the 1930s, such efforts had come to include greater emphasis on instruction into adulthood as well as on visual-sensory education.[29] This mode of teaching referred to the use of visual aids, a popular catchall term for everything from three-dimensional models, miniature dioramas, and exhibitions to prints, magic lantern slides, and movies for history, geography, science, art, and other subjects. The production of such items—as well as the loan of collections materials—had received a boost from the various WPA museum extension projects in at least twenty-four states.[30] As a counter to verbalism (the overreliance on the spoken and written word to communicate unfamiliar subjects or abstract concepts), educators emphasized anew the value of "concrete teaching materials," of "the effective use of objects—specimens—models and museum lessons. . . . [to] enrich and vitalize subject matter."[31] Additionally, although the nature of the visual aids remained largely unchanged, aside from technological developments in film and photography, the period's greater focus on auditory and tactile encounters merited the addition of "sensory" to the older term "visual education."[32] In class, students could "see and handle materials which are being discussed, thus revealing such characteristics as three dimensions, coloring, weight, texture, etc."[33]

Proponents of adult education, aware of developments in visual-sensory approaches, listed both storytelling and sensory engagement as reasons to ally with museums.[34] Professor of political science Thomas Ritchie Adam, whom the American Association of Adult Education commissioned to produce two reports on museums, lauded "the grouping of objects around a simple story" as the distinguishing mark of the few institutions that excelled in visual education of the lay public through their exhibitions.[35] In the first of these books, *The Civic Value of Museums,* published in 1937, Adam also valorized the firsthand encounter with objects, human-made and natural, as a vital alternative to learning from "secondhand" sources, such as advertisements, books, and even museum lectures.[36] These, Adam maintained, were "hypnotic processes of education, allowing the individual to submerge his own reason to a common judgment."

The shaping of citizens into consumers by commercial interests posed, for the Adams of the age, a threat to the ideal democratic mind. Indeed, the 1930s marked what Roland Marchand has called a public relations craze. Many of the nation's largest firms made far more vigorous use of public relations than had previously been the case in order to combat anticorporate public sentiment and the New Deal government's efforts to reign in corporate autonomy. Through print and radio advertising, exhibitions at fairs, company magazines, and other promotional vehicles, they sought, Marchand argues, to direct the "economic education" of the populace in order to rebuild confidence in the capacity of industry to create personal as well as national well-being.[37] In part, the adult education movement represented a counterattempt to assert the authority of libraries, museums, and other cultural institutions in the public square.

In Adam's view, the antidote to the mind's manipulability lay in the body and its senses. Museums, therefore, represented ideal spaces in which to provide for such encounters—if they rose to the task:

> In the last resort, the museum can never achieve true educational rank until there is a concerted demand for the type of education that it alone can dispense. Adult education in a democracy must be something more than a continuation of classroom discipline or a benevolent type of mass propaganda. The leaders of this movement who are seeking to make a place for free minds in our technological culture might well consider organizing around the museum. Within its walls scientific and artistic facts, uncorrupted by authority or opinion, are available to all who are willing to make the effort to experience them through direct sensory perception.[38]

This remark deserves dissection, particularly for the apt way in which it encapsulates a continued tension within exhibition craft and meaning making with things. Quixotically, Adam and some of his contemporaries imagined and valued museum-displayed objects as "uncorrupted by authority or opinion." To rephrase this using more contemporary words, they believed that museums were neutral and that objects possessed a communicative agency impervious to the exhibition craft involved in their public presentation. Yet, at the same time, they urged continued exploration of new techniques to artfully, even dramatically, engage visitors' faculties. In essence, while object agency remained impervious to exhibition craft, visitors' interpretive capacities could be enhanced and directed by design.

Progressive-minded proponents of didactic exhibitions and directed meaning making in the museum saw this as consistent with the democratic ideal of the free-thinking citizen in that such work constituted a training of the mind's capacity to seek and engage with objective evidence in the literal, material sense. Here, US museums borrowed not only from the commercial sector but from the international avant-gardes as well. Dadaists, surrealists, Bauhaus, and other arts groups interested in mass media and cultural transformation pushed the capacity of exhibitions in the 1920s to engage patrons as active, sensing bodies rather than reduce them to mobile sets of eyes.[39] Techniques first deployed in Europe and brought to the United States in the 1930s and '40s by émigrés fleeing the encroachments of fascism and Nazism included unexpected juxtapositions, sound recordings, light effects, moving apertures that permitted or obscured viewing, and other devices that demanded more of visitors than the usual art gallery experience of gazing at well-ordered, static objects. The theories of vision and psychology underlying these experimentalist developments emphasized the idea that "'dynamic interrelation'" with the material world produced meaning.[40] That is to say, some creators of exhibition installations came to see meaning as residing neither solely in the objects nor in the humans regarding them but, rather, as being produced by the interplay between the two within museal spaces of encounter. This notion of the museumgoer being *within,* and therefore integrally a part of, the museum exhibition would continue into the 1940s and became part of the effort to prove museums' value as social instruments able to direct civic energies toward critical war issues. MoMA's *Wartime Housing,* analyzed in chapter 4, is, in its animating ideas and final design, a chief example of what one scholar has termed the "democratic surround."[41] Here, "democratic" is meant to define immersive installations that made use of multiple popular media forms, intended to promote active meaning making rather than passive reception, and, most importantly, stymied a facist-syle massification of the American mind by fostering individual and independent reasoning while also inspiring unity across difference to achieve common civic goals. "Unity across difference" is an apt summation of what efforts such as the Newark Museum's *Three Southern Neighbors* (discussed in chapter 2) hoped to achieve within the realm of Latin American relations, and later works sought to accomplish for postwar international accord.

Department Stores and "Fairs Sell Goods; Museums, Ideas"

Museums looked not only to mass media and the avant-garde but to the retail sector as well. Comparing museum exhibitions to department stores' displays, as well as those of expositions, did not mark a new state of affairs. Observers on both sides of the Atlantic had drawn these connections in the 1800s, well before John Cotton Dana's *The Gloom of the Museum* underscored museum failings in exhibition craft by pointing to innovations of commercial display that garnered public interest.[42] By the 1930s, ideas concerning the outfitting of exhibition craft to become a democratic medium of persuasive education was tightly bound to economic concerns about museums' continued viability as public attractions. Indeed, exhibition modernization as competitive necessity during this prewar period created the slipstream for experiments in social instrumentality. As Philip N. Youtz, the new director of the Brooklyn Museum, wrote in 1933, "To retain dingy, unattractive installations in the face of competition with modern commercial exhibits is certain economic suicide."[43] Youtz had previously worked in adult education, overseeing the fine arts program of the People's Institute of New York, a Progressive Era organization focused on instruction for the working class and immigrants. He came to the Brooklyn Museum fresh off a turn as director of the 69th Street Branch Museum of the Pennsylvania Museum of Art, a Carnegie Corporation–funded experiment in bringing museums to the people instead of the other way around.[44] Youtz argued that unless museums modernized exhibition craft as part "of an energetic policy of increasing the museum's service to the public," they would fail to prove their worth to communities in financial and social crisis and thereby have no case to make against cuts to municipal appropriations.[45] Based on his community experiences,

Youtz suggested that future museum buildings should be patterned after the modern sales emporium rather than the Renaissance palace if they wished to extend their public appeal.[46]

On the matter of the public's interest once inside museums, the field looked to such works as *The Behavior of the Museum Visitor* and other studies conducted by Edward Stevens Robinson, a professor of psychology at Yale University, in collaboration with AAM and Carnegie Corporation funding.[47] If, as Robinson reported, visitors spent barely six minutes in the galleries—lingering not even a minute before the object they found most compelling—the cause, one pundit said, was plain to see: "It is poor showmanship."[48] In their borrowings from the retail sector, museums considered both mind and body in shaping the patron experience—from nuances of lighting attuned to "the psychology of attention" to angled partitions, useful for moving and pausing visitors' amblings in a focused manner, to such creature comforts as better heating, ventilation, and cooling.[49]

Cooperative relationships among museums and department stores during the 1920s and '30s also helped set in place nodes of exchange that would function as a wartime exhibitionary network. The Newark Museum, the Brooklyn Museum, the Field Museum, the Metropolitan Museum of Art, the Museum of Modern Art, and others not only drew inspiration from flagship retailers in their cities but also collaborated with them on exhibits and invited store executives to sit on their boards.[50] For their part, stores sometimes engaged museum staff to design special shows, borrowed from museum collections to augment displays, and even turned over their windows to promote museum exhibits or membership drives.[51] The stores benefited, too. Such alliances helped establish their status as the commercial mavens of good taste while cultural enticements offered free of charge drew patrons and won favorable publicity.[52] Such interminglings further normalized exhibition as a craft of persuasion.

Another change in museum practice that retail as well as mass media methods helped to encourage was the mounting of temporary shows, which the WPA had also embraced. Frequent, shorter-run exhibits were necessary, one observer noted, because "the rapid changes in the pageant of modern life have educated the public to look for novelty and new experience."[53] One hope for temporary exhibitions was that they might encourage repeat patronage much like a change in cinematic presentation did at the local motion picture theater. Not only that, the press had little interest in even the best-written copy if it dealt with an older display; only new exhibits made the news, a fact that increasingly-public-relations-conscious museums could not dismiss. They also could not dismiss, at least not lightly, trustees who in their capacity as businessmen saw themselves as Edsel Ford did: able to "sense the pulse of the public perhaps to a greater degree than the somewhat absorbed and sequestered professional [museum] worker."[54] This sensitivity, as Ford acknowledged, came through consultation with on-staff experts in display, merchandising, public relations, advertising, and other increasingly specialized domains within the corporate sector. He credited trustees (like himself) as driving the adoption of presentation practices responsible for the "breaking down of barriers between the visitor and the new museum." Not all trustees received credit for being forward-looking, however. Low, for one, listed them as conservatives who, alongside directors and curators, proved just as likely to impede museum efforts to popularize museum fare and reach outside accustomed elite circles.[55]

Perhaps the display forum best known for breaking down barriers between institutions and the public remained the exposition.[56] Exhibition craft occupied center stage in public as well as professional media in 1939 when the Golden Gate International Exposition opened in February and the New York World's Fair in April. Years in the making, these two events have been described by scholars as efforts to reassert a narrative of national technological and social progress that had been rendered threadbare by the Great War and the Depression.[57] In fact, Robert Rydell argues that the many interwar expositions held in Europe and the United States despite economic, political, and social turmoil spoke to an ongoing faith in exhibition culture as a forum for the material and symbolic assertion of national ambitions.[58] In preparation for the fairs, large corporations turned to the emerging ranks of public relations experts for advice on how to win back consumer confidence that, like the economy, had crashed.[59] Companies were told that specialists skilled in "visual dramatization" would be essential to the success of any display at the 1939 expositions; likewise, "interpretive showmanship" would be needed to ensure that the masses walked away retaining at least an impression of the "story of industry."[60] Many firms, for the first time, hired industrial designers for the task and sought to provide fairgoers with participatory, even immersive, experiences. A major difference between exhibits at the US fairs of the 1930s and those that came before was their selectivity in communicating a central idea and their emphasis on perceptual novelty.[61] These lessons would not be lost on museums.

In the summer of 1939 the Buffalo Museum of Science and the New York Museum of Science and Industry (NYMSI), which dubbed itself "a laboratory of modern exhibition practice," undertook studies of the world's fairs aided by a two-year grant from the Rockefeller Foundation. Cummings, director of the Buffalo Museum of Science, and Richard P. Shaw, director of the NYMSI, oversaw the activities of their respective teams.[62] Cummings, whose museum work included involvement in exhibitions for the World's Columbian Exposition in Chicago (1893), the Pan-American Exposition in Buffalo (1901), and the Century of Progress International Exposition in Chicago (1933–34), had ample experience with his subject. The grant included preparing experienced museum professionals to make observations and collect data; the window displays around Fifth Avenue served as their training grounds.[63]

Described as "idea sourcebooks," the two volumes resulting from the studies differed significantly in character.[64] *Exhibition Techniques: A Summary of Exhibition Practice Based on Surveys Conducted at the New York and San Francisco World's Fairs of 1939,* published by the NYMSI, strove for an impartial, scientific tone in its descriptions of the more notable features of the 136 corporate displays surveyed. Abundant illustrations of praiseworthy strategies and quantitative data from visitor surveys rounded out the package. The volume's authors hoped not only to inspire their museum colleagues but to also guide industrial executives, advertising and public relations groups, educators, and others in the "dramatization of ideas, developments, services, products, etc."[65] This ambition reflected the close ties—too close, critics said—between commercial interests and the industrial and science museums of the age.

In contrast, *East Is East and West Is West: Some Observations on the World's Fairs of 1939 by One Whose Main Interest Is in Museums* is the work of a raconteur sprinkled with anecdotes, wry asides, wordplay, photographs of some thirty-odd displays, and, to capture the theme of each chapter, drawings by the author's daughter. Numerous callouts, such as "Fairs Sell Goods; Museums, Ideas," crystallized Cumming's core points for those seeking quick navigation through the book's 382 pages.[66] Cummings's stylistic approach perhaps suited his main and repeated point: exhibitions ought to tell a story. The uncredited author of *Exhibition Techniques* concurred: "An exhibition is a short cut to knowledge. It is a form of expression, used to project ideas by the display of objects" to "tell the story" with "order, simplicity, unity, progression."[67] Summarizing one of the study's chief conclusions, the researchers stated, "It was evident throughout the fair that the most successful exhibitions were the ones presenting their material in the form of a story done in a simple and popular fashion."[68] Success, by the study's criteria, consisted of first attracting a person's attention and then communicating a "main idea" such that each individual not only grasped that idea but also made some connection between it and their "daily life and well-being."[69]

The notion that museums dealt in ideas conveyed through storytelling received pushback on several fronts.[70] Critics advisedly rejected as a wasted effort the wholesale reordering of museum floor plans, which treated galleries as sequential chapters of the the larger "text," charging that the resulting "reading" proved far too subtle for the rank and file. Others targeted the overreliance on labels, charts, and other museum-prepared visual aids. Museums should be showcasing their collections, *not* materials created solely for the purpose of exhibition, warned objectors. In this and other areas of practice, industry and science museums could be trusted by fans and critics alike to put the boundaries of new material rhetorics to the test. Observers of the time acknowledged that these, along with health and safety museums, often led the field in new display tactics, particularly those inviting interaction or explaining processes, *but* they did so at the expense of original, collection-worthy objects and by taking on education, or diffusion, as their "social purpose" rather than "the *increase* of knowledge through investigation."[71] Critics also decried the uncomfortably close ties that the NYMSI, the Chicago Museum of Science, and similar institutions maintained with trade associations and industry in terms of funding, use of corporate-made exhibits, and the conducting of visitor research for the benefit of exhibit makers in business as well as museums.[72] "Their neutrality has already been compromised," wrote Adam, "and their future choice lies between the educational task of critical exposition and the propagandistic role of science fairs."[73]

The use of story in history museums, that most narrative of disciplines, also presented gray areas for debate. "This method of display has its values and its dangers," wrote Coleman. "It is thoughtful and awake. It can narrate—which is an important point for history museums. But also it falls easily into making what is little more than an illustrated book—big and cumbersome and looking like an exhibit, but really a book all the same."[74] Of a still greater danger, he warned, "This practice can lead on to indoctrination. It gets away from what museums are for—to give evidence, primarily." Cummings, too, urged that adaptation of commercial display tactics and a storyline framework not lead to compromise. He underscored that a wholesale borrowing of marketing values along with techniques was to be avoided. "When we enter the realm of museums, however," he counseled, "we can only tolerate the firm position that any statements involved in the story should be not only the absolute truth but should be told in such a way that no misinterpretation or confusion is ever possible."[75] That, he admitted, was not so easy given the unpredictable nature of visitor interpretation. The wide range of ages, backgrounds, and attention spans tromping through museums made it "hard to put over a story with precision."[76] The issue of where truth lay—in the object, in the research and ideas the museum wanted to convey, in the panoply of individual beholders, in mass consensus, in the gallery docent's remarks, or somewhere in between them all—seemed newly problematic the more one learned about the craft of commanding attention. Cummings, while declared for absolute truth, referred frequently to the development of museumgoers' attitudes as being a more important goal than the "simple cold-blooded attempt to teach facts."[77]

By shaping visitor attitudes, he largely meant creating receptivity to engage and retain what was presented; however, he also allowed for a more penetrating agency on the part of the well-crafted display. The study of the fairs, he noted, had provided "quite a number of illustrations of the practical application of the theory of mind-control or subjective guidance, if the term suits you better . . ."[78] Such observations convinced him that, for museums, "one of the greatest possibilities of development in the future lies in taking advantage of every legitimate method to mould the mind of the visitor into a proper state to assimilate what is placed before him."[79] Indeed, the field's deeper struggle to re-envision exhibitions as vehicles for social instrumentality lay not in whether they should provoke "thought, feeling, and action" but in the degree to which these energies could or should be directed toward a clearly evident purpose.[80] As Coleman put it, "An exhibition of symbols—conveying what somebody thinks about something—is a break with custom," and, on such topics as housing, industrial relations, or government, he said, could be "taken as indoctrinating or merely informative, according to predilection."[81] Lest there be any confusion about *his* predilection, Coleman reminded readers, "The most conspicuous rock to avoid is persuasive teaching. The museum's work is to lay before the senses what will furnish the mind with information and wisdom and the perceptions with power and skill. But to influence action directly is not its task."[82]

Parker disagreed. Objects stood for "ideas and facts," and museums of the modern educational sort functioned as "value-distributing institutions."[83] This notion repeats throughout his writings. In fact, Parker's first index entry under the letter "I" in his *Manual for History Museums* is "Ideas more important than specimens."[84] When planning exhibits, no matter how small the museum's space or staff, he advised, "The idea in mind is of first importance, for ideas and not merely impressions of specimens or 'relics' are the values that the visitor and student carry away. *The objects shown are merely tools in the visualization of ideas.* With ideas in mind as the function of the institution, one may work and plan for the materialization of ideas."[85]

One example of ideas for action during this period was the *Housing Exhibition of the City of New York* (1934), which argued for architectural design as an essential tool for amelioration of substandard urban living conditions.[86] This joint effort of the Museum of Modern Art and the New York City Housing Authority harkened back to the work of Progressive Era institutions, such as the Harvard Social Museum, the American Safety Museum (where Coleman briefly served as director), and the Municipal Museum of Chicago.[87] Although social museums as a genre had waned by the late 1930s, their brief tenure provided models for those wishing the broader field to be a force for civic good and, even, social change. While some institutions, such as the Safety Museum, held artifacts related to their areas of focus, most relied on evidentiary photographs, charts, maps, and models as the substance of their work and exhibitions. For this reason, mainstream practitioners did not see social museums as museums at all since they prized communication and intervention over collection and preservation. Their exhibitions, organized by government agencies, professional associations, museums, and other civic groups, sometimes in cooperation with one another, tackled such topics such as child welfare, city planning, health, worker safety, and other problems of modernity.[88]

Perhaps most well-known is the *International Tuberculosis Exhibition* of 1908–9, which debuted at the United States National Museum (now the Smithsonian Institution), showed in modified form at the American Museum of Natural History, and earned public and professional acclaim.[89] It even featured a few bona fide objects, including "wet specimens" of infected animal and human organs, which made a memorable impact.

While social museums, as a distinct institutional type, may have been fading from the scene, their favored display techniques received new attention from those seeking exhibition formats suited to the ideals of the museum as social instrument. Inspiration during the 1930s came from new technologies for affordable photographic enlargement, exhibition work by the WPA, the aforementioned influence of European installation design techniques, and the work of sociologist Otto von Neurath as instituted at the Museum of Society and Economy in Vienna.[90] His aspiration to create a universal pictorial language suited the goals of museum and adult educators seeking to widen public reach and take on social issues. By the late 1930s, American sociologists such as Francis McLennan Vreeland, who was involved with DePauw University's social museum and worked with the WPA researching the effects of unemployment, championed the value of "picture-symbols."[91] In addition to conveying complex data, relationships, and processes more simply than text alone, they offered a remedy to the "undemocratic and class-restricted" emphasis on prose that limited who could access knowledge on pressing social issues.[92] Coleman knew of Neurath's work and was not impressed; he deemed such presentations *"predigested"* and underscored that "charts are not exhibits."[93]

As earlier stated, the museological trend acknowledging the power of story to organize and communicate meaning through objects happened alongside a lingering suspicion of verbalism, which is one reason Neurath's theories gained traction in the United States. Writers and scholars of the 1930s became "obsessed with the idea of language gone awry," the belief that "propagandistic language, machine-age conditions, and human susceptibility to magical ways of thinking had made human language increasingly useless as a problem solving tool."[94] Those who brought discussion of semantic theory into popular channels spoke of the need for concrete referents, the mooring of expression to the tangible. Alexander, for one, noted, "Words are still very deceptive and meaningless when compared to actual objects."[95]

Museums provided an obvious and abundant source for such anchors of meaning, a fact that some pundits emphasized when making the case for museums' potential to assume a more prominent role in education and social issues. Youtz, underscoring museums' claims to communications tactics now being leveraged by others to better advantage, noted, "The development of movies, illustrated periodicals and newspapers, advertising, and store window displays all prove that the visual method of the museum is the most potent means of education that has been found."[96] Further, he argued, "Visual education can be developed by progressive museums to a point where it will make them the leading educational institutions of the country." That proponents of the exhibition-as-story would push material rhetoric in a direction reliant on verbal frameworks, while at the same time arguing for material rhetoric as an antidote to verbal mutability, highlights a core tension within this development.

The idea of a material rhetoric crafted to the purposes of relating a story that touched on present concerns required greater acknowledgment that museums did more with their objects than *share knowledge* (a putatively objective act); they also *made meaning* (a subjective act) with them. In other words, the interpretive function now came into sharper relief. Of course, museum artifacts and specimens had always been embedded within metanarratives, guiding logics meant to order experiences and perceptions. From the seemingly erratic arrangements of *Kunst- und Wunderkammern* to the ordering taxonomies of the Linnaean system, an ideological disposition had always framed how thing-based information might best be communicated through arrangement and presentation. These metanarratives of organization coevolved with the sociopolitical orders of their day, as numerous scholars have shown. Now, however, the expressed emphasis on a material rhetoric of story made the relationship between the guiding logic of arrangement and the objects to be arranged seem less stable—not to mention less clearly rooted in the objects themselves. Within such a framework artifacts and specimens might now function as characters or even plot devices. For example, Cummings noted that placing less interesting items, such as a model of a mine shaft, at the end of an exhibit created an "anticlimax" when one had seen real gold nuggets at the outset.[97] While this example still exerts the primacy of the authentic specimen over that of the simulacrum, it points to fluidities and, therefore, more expansive opportunities for uncertainty in composing meaning. So, the matter of how museum objects should and should not be displayed constituted more than a logistical concern. It represented struggles not only over the production of meaning but also over the purposes toward which those meanings, museums, and the public should be directed.

Through Thought, Feeling, and Action: The Mind-Body Appeal

As previously described, visual education by the 1930s frequently encompassed engagement of the other senses. Here, some argued, museums possessed resources that set them apart from other schools of learning. "Man has been endowed with the five senses of touch, taste, smell, sight, and hearing," wrote the director of education for the Carnegie Museum in 1938. "In the museum *now,* we often find that more attention is being devoted to the use of man's various special senses than is the case in the college or university," he observed. "There is the lecture to be *heard* and the specimens singly (or in series) to be *seen*. They are often available to be *touched* or *handled,* sometimes to be *smelled* and sometimes to be *tasted*."[98] Admittedly natural history museums offered more possibilities for such encounters than most. That said, designers of exhibitions traded ideas about how even small installation choices could, in today's words, stimulate the visceral imagination and prompt affective responses. For example, in addition to the usual practical concerns associated with selecting the color of a fabric or paint to be used as a backdrop (complementarity with the displayed artifacts, ability to conceal nail holes, propensity to fade or show dust, etc.), the savvy craftsperson now considered emotional tones, too. Black, one expert claimed in 1940, had "a depressing effect on the average person" and would likely produce "a vague feeling of dejection."[99]

Likewise, the relation of optical effects to somatic perception gained notice. The same expert counseled against the use of horizontal lines in small rooms or areas with low ceilings, as the accompanying physical sensation would be "stifling." Consideration of the sensing body more often focused on means to heighten the verisimilitude of encounters in the museum through illusion and stagecraft. This trend had multiple origins, a long history, and by the 1930s remained most evident in habitat or nature groups of natural history museums.[100] While not universally loved by curators, these uncanny works of science, art, and artifice found favor with administrators for their public appeal.[101] Art, history, and general museums had habitats, too, from the period rooms of the American Wing at the Metropolitan Museum of Art to the structures and streets of Colonial Williamsburg to WPA-produced dioramas.[102] All invited museumgoers to step either literally or imaginatively into a world beyond their own, be it the jungle, the past, or the inner workings of a coal mine.

The words of Waldemar Kaempffert, first director of the Chicago Museum of Science and Industry (CMSI), capture this development as it emerged in his field during the 1930s: "All the art of a stage director is invoked to tell a technical story. Yet this is no technical Coney Island. The dramatic is introduced not for its own sake but as a means to an educational end."[103] The CMSI, he noted, strove to "vivify teaching."[104] This meant buttons to push, levers to pull, machines put in motion, and senses engaged. The museum's much-vaunted Coal Mine exhibition, opened in 1933, exemplified this philosophy. The curious entered by squeezing into a miners' cage, rigged to simulate a five-hundred-foot drop down a narrow shaft. Of the experience Kaempffert wrote, "Real? It is impossible to distinguish reality from illusion here.... There is a blast of cold air and a musty smell—both inseparable from coal-mining. Ears, eyes, nose, skin—every sense proclaims the coal mine."[105] Once deposited "underground," museum adventurers continued their travels by train, exploring the operations, safety features, and technologies of a simulated Illinois mining operation. Corroborating Kaempffert's assertion of the exhibit's realism, Coleman noted that museum guides carried spirits of ammonia to revive guests who "fall victim to illusions of depth and dangerous passage."[106] Even to this day, the CMSI touts the verisimilitude of this still-functioning exhibit, enticing would-be-visitors to "Step on the hoist and ride down into an experience with atmosphere so real, you may start wondering where to punch your time card."[107]

Museums also experimented with sound, from the precorded narrations of "talking labels" to explain exhibition contents to more atmospheric uses of music and of what might today be called environmental soundscapes. The latter uses, some thought, might increase museumgoers' receptivity to an exhibition's theme if strageically deployed. The American Museum of Natural History, for example, had featured a live African music performance in proximity to habitat groups from the continent in order to "vitalize the scenes" for viewers.[108] Even the oflactory received attention in the museum studies of the 1939 world's fairs. The researchers noted the ability of scent to heighten one's connection to a distant place, as in the case of the orange blossom fragrance used in the Florida Building at the New York World's Fair. It could also inspire a fuller-bodied appreciation of displayed objects, as demonstrated at the Golden Gate Exposition's Redwood Empire Building. Here, strategic use of heat encouraged pungent release of the towering conifer's natural oils from hewn timbers.[109]

The interest that the museum field of the 1930s paid to ideas about sensory experience as an additional conduit to immersion and understanding dovetailed with its attentions to the potential of storytelling, sentiment, and modern media forms for didactice purposes. In terms of what this all meant for museum professionals, who on the brink of the 1940s sought not only modernization but a material rhetoric suited to the aims of social instrumentality, perhaps Coleman stated it best: "Educational approaches can be made through three sides of the individual—mental, emotional, physical. If all three sides are drawn out—through thought, feeling and action—the result is a balanced experience."[110] The remaining chapters of this book focus on the adaptation of material rhetoric to the aims of social instrumentality and what happened to museums' more progressive impulses once the nation went to war.

One outcome of not connecting museums' wartime history to developments and concerns of the 1930s has been the too-easy dismissal of all civic engagement as only so much propaganda or as arising solely out of wartime conditions. Museum workers, opinion leaders, and the public alike paid great attention to propaganda in the 1930s.[111] Concerned with its uses during the Great War and in the rising field of advertising, scholars studied it, isolationists decried it, and imaginations endowed it with exaggerated powers. By 1935, some five thousand books dealt with the subject, whereas barely a dozen on the matter had been published in 1924.[112] The populace's susceptibility to government propaganda during the Great War seemed, in the eyes of some observers, to reveal democracy's vaunted "rational public" as being a naïve phantasm.[113] Debates ensued as to whether this public deficiency could be remedied through standard means of public education or whether it required strategic intervention from experts and "symbol specialists" operating outside corporate and government sectors. These latter methods, some thought, aligned well with the vision of the museum as social instrument.

In teasing out the distinctions that American museums of the period made between pursuasive and propagandistic exhibition craft, it is important to remember that the term "propaganda" itself described a wide range of practices and did not always carry negative connotations. Across museum publications in the 1930s and even early '40s, authors frequently used the word "propaganda" in its older, ecclesial meaning: to disseminate or propagate. This value-neutral use typically referred simply to the contemporary public relations and communications strategies being embraced by museums. The field was not blind to propaganda's darker meanings, of course. This self-awareness is revealed not only in 1930s' debates over whether objects or ideas took precedence for museums but also in the consternation that would soon accompany discussions of what museums ought and ought not do during war.

Even when taken to mean persausive communication of an ideological bent, the word "propaganda" still held status as a type of modern tool that, in responsible hands, could be used both productively and democratically to educate a populace. For examples of propaganda's misuse, museums could look to the state-run exhibitions of fascist Italy and Nazi Germany—the two most famous of which each drew crowds in the millions, underscoring American fears of the media-produced mass mind.[114] In the case of *Mostra della Rivoluzione Fascista* (Exhibition of the Fascist Revolution, 1932), an avant-garde installation marking the tenth anniversary of Benito Mussolini's ascent to power, recognition of its import came chiefly to US museums with hindsight. Of its 1932 debut, the *New York Times*, relying on a stringer, simply described the exhibit's environs as striking in their "ultra-modern style" and its contents as "principally of a historical character."[115] A few years later and closer to home, an exhibition of contemporary Italian art sponsored by Il Duce's government elicited much commentary on modernism's artistic value but rather less on the politics behind its propaganda-as-diplomacy tour, which included museums and other venues in eleven US cities (January 1935–May 1936).[116] Noted one critic of the Los Angeles Museum showing, "The merits or demerits of Italian Fascism are the Italians' worry, not ours. But Italian art produced under and sponsored by Mussolini's government has broken the chains of a long decadence to emerge strong, Mediterranean and modern."[117] Germany's *Entartete Kunst* (Degenerate Art, 1937) and the intended headline event *Große Deutsche Kunstausstellung* (The Great German Art Exhibition), on the other hand, drew more immediate critique and disdain for their politics. These shows had been preceeded by others of a similar vein *and* some four years of repressive Third Reich cultural policies, which included the ouster of museum professionals judged to be unacceptable in their tastes or ancestry. This, plus the arrival of many artist-émigrés to the United States, made propaganda in this case, perhaps, easier to see.[118] Once the United States entered the war, these Axis exhibitions took on more ominous, cautionary value. Likewise, the word "propaganda" steadily lost its other meanings until it became synonymous with ideological content designed to manipulate the masses.

A New World Beckons as the World of Tomorrow Fades

Not long after Cummings, Shaw, and colleagues wrapped up their exposition research, Europe's fast-widening war cast its shadows over the utopian World of Tomorrow and Pacifica's dream of unity. Cummings made brief reference to "the present turmoil on the other side of the Atlantic" in his volume, noting only that he agreed with the publicists of the New York World's Fair who declared that only knowledge and education, particularly in the area of science, stood between "'civilization and catastrophy.'"[119] It was after each research study had ended that the fairs adapted their offerings to reflect the world's new realities. In New York, exhibitions soon appeared on the theme of "Peace and Freedom" to promote American support for European relief efforts, allied friendship, and admirable modes of wartime citizenship.[120] In San Francisco, fair organizers introduced a series of "Peace Days" on the theme "Keep America Out of War," and, like their eastern counterpart, increased efforts to emphasize "the spirit of neighborly co-operation" with Latin America.[121] For its part, once Britain and France declared war on Germany, *The Museum News* began carrying regular reports on the activities of museums in the allied nations. Readers learned of policies promoted by Britain's Museums Association, from air raid precautions, education for children relocated from cities, and safeguarding collections to cooperation with the Ministry of Information and development of more frequent temporary exhibitions addressing issues connected to the war.[122]

Yet, even before the fairs of 1939 had opened their gates, an alternate imaginary rooted in the New World of the Americas had already begun to coalesce. Pan-American trade and cultural initiatives of the 1920s and '30s, in which some museums had been involved, now took on the posture and importance of a national defensive strategy. So, by the time 1940 arrived, some in the museum field were already seeking to take an active part in contemporary concerns and, by doing so, reassert their potential as social instruments capable of producing civically beneficial modes of thought, feeling, and action within their communities. With this impulse came the complementary drive, inspired by the effective use of narrative forms in mass media, to fashion exhibitions into more compelling tools of popular education. The advent of new, highly publicized national agendas—first hemispheric unity as a means to avoid war, and then the war itself—simply focused these interests on the very things a growing number of museum professionals had been seeking: relevant issues of importance to their local and national publics.

Chapter Two

MATERIALIZING THE GOOD NEIGHBORHOOD

The Exhibitionary Network and Hemispheric Citizenship

> The example of the Newark Museum should be followed by other institutions in the cities of North, Central and South America as a valuable means of converting theoretical Pan-Americanism into a practical, tangible reality.
>
> —S. E. Durán-Ballén, Ecuadorean consul general, New York

Three days into the new decade, President Franklin D. Roosevelt used his January 1940 address to Congress to argue for the necessity of increased spending on munitions for American defense. The request found disfavor among many in and beyond the Capitol Building. Certainly, for isolationists and pacifists who tuned in to any of the major radio networks that carried the president's speech live or who read it reprinted in full in newspapers on January 4, it seemed a menacing step away from neutrality. "But," urged Roosevelt, "there is a vast difference between keeping out of war and pretending that this war is none of our business."[1] In fact, it was business through trade with the countries of Central and South America that constituted Roosevelt's second defensive front. Here, he emphasized the dedication that his administration had given to "the policy of the Good Neighbor" since he first took office in 1933.[2] The "unanimity of ideals and practical relationships" of which the president spoke had not been left solely to commerce, of course, as events elsewhere that month proved. On January 17, the Virginia Museum of Fine Arts forged "a new link in President Roosevelt's good neighbor policy" with its ambassador-studded unveiling of an exhibition of Argentinian art.[3] On the West Coast, the *Mexican Cultural Arts* exhibit, featuring silverwork, pottery, and other items organized by the history department of the Los Angeles Museum and counting the Mexican consul among its sponsors, was one of three shows drawing record-setting crowds to Exposition Park.[4] And, on the very same day as the president's address to Congress, the director of the Newark Museum and Library, Beatrice Winser, began a yearlong correspondence with Sumner Welles, undersecretary of the Department of State and a chief adviser to Roosevelt on Latin American affairs. Her goal: to marshal funding for what eventually became the two-part exhibition *Three Southern Neighbors: Ecuador, Peru, Bolivia* (1941–42).

The federal re-embrace of the Good Neighbor policy in the 1930s set in place the framework around which the wartime exhibitionary network of display and exchange among museums, government agencies, businesses, and media firms first coalesced. Sometimes working together, sometimes separately, these agents shared loosely aligned agendas that instantiated the supranational imaginaries of "Latin America" and that of the hemispheric "Good Neighborhood." Art exhibitions, such as the Museum of Modern Art's *Twenty Centuries of Mexican Art* (May 15–September 30, 1940), curated in collaboration with Mexico's National Institute of Anthropology and History, constituted museums' primary contributions to cultural diplomacy both at home and abroad during the 1930s and '40s.[5] This fact reflects art museums' status as the period's predominating type and the belief, rooted in object-based epistemology or knowing, that artworks "spoke" a universal language, making them the ideal cultural ambassadors.[6] Exhibitions deploying a material rhetoric of social instrumentality stood in the minority. They, and to some degree even the more conventional exhibitions of art, speak to how active participation in hemispheric unity initiatives constituted, for some museums, an opportunity to showcase their importance as social instruments capable of building public competency on important contemporary issues. Putting social instrumentality into practice, however, involved complex navigations of political waters, public and institutional interests, unexamined racial biases, and the exhibitionary network itself. *Three Southern Neighbors: Ecuador, Peru, Bolivia* provides a glimpse into this work.

Foundations of Wartime Exhibitionary Network and Hemispheric Unity Work

The early 1940s proved to be a busy time for Latin American diplomats, US government officials, and others invited to speak at a long run of hemispheric unity event openings across the United States. Teddy Hartmann, a consul general of Bolivia, was among those who spoke at the Newark Museum's 1941 unveiling of *Three Southern Neighbors: Ecuador, Peru, Bolivia; Part*

II: Viewing the Present (October 1, 1941–February 1942). He underscored that when it came to creating neighborly bonds, "The Americas know each other very little. The task of making them better acquainted is in the hands of its intellectual institutions and business men."[7] His Ecuadorian counterpart, Dr. S. E. Durán-Ballén, observed, "The example of the Newark Museum should be followed by other institutions in the cities of North, Central and South America as a valuable means of converting theoretical Pan-Americanism into a practical, tangible reality."[8] Months later, at a rather different opening, Nelson A. Rockefeller, head of the Office of the Coordinator of Inter-American Affairs (OCIAA), reported, "Displayed here are examples of the richness of the New World's resources; fruits of American labor, skill and ingenuity; the promise of a future rich in peace and production which we of the Americas will share with sane and cooperating nations and with which we will insure civilization for our posterity in a free world."[9] His praise went to Macy's Latin American Fair, a marquee event at the retailer's flagship store in New York City (January 17–February 7, 1942). Rockefeller spoke again, this time in Spanish and English, at the Toledo Museum of Art to kick off *Chilean Contemporary Art,* an exhibition organized in collaboration with and funded by the OCIAA. "To win the struggle," he said, "we need more than diplomatic and political cooperation between governments, more even than economic cooperation between our industries and productive agencies. We need a feeling that we are neighbors—intimately and personally neighbors—both in the crisis we face and in the stake we have in a better future."[10]

The US Department of State, which inspired the Newark show, and the OCIAA, which backed the Macy's and Toledo events, saw such cultural initiatives within US borders as achieving two aims. Domestically, they would educate US Americans about their southern compatriots and set forth the terms of becoming a hemispheric citizen. And when publicized abroad, the exhibitions would signal to the other republics that overtures from the United States now came in a spirit of reciprocity rather than self-interested imperialism. As the speakers at the Newark and Macy's openings emphasized, culture and commerce *together* would bond the nations by quite literally materializing—making "tangible"—the imagined Pan-American community of Good Neighbors.[11] Here, museums as keepers of the artifactual markers of shared cultural, political, and economic interests played an important role. As the remarks in Toledo foregrounded, it was the emotional ties between remote members of the far-flung community that the human-thing encounter as a surrogate for direct human interaction among neighbors could catalyze.

Spurs to the development of new governmental apparatuses devoted to inter-American affairs included fears that German and Italian liaising in South America might lead to the establishment there of Axis air and submarine bases. Defense strategists also counseled securing access to the continent's raw materials to mitigate war-related trade and supply disruptions. Such had been the atmosphere in the previous decade, when in 1936 the Inter-American Conference for the Maintenance of Peace met in Buenos Aires, Brazil. The accords it endorsed included promises to promote Pan-American cultural relations through exchange programs. Toward this end—and animated by the belief that government involvement would focus and speed work traditionally handled by private, corporate, and philanthropic entities—the Department of State eventually formed a Division of Cultural Relations (DCR).[12] Forces in opposition to the idea questioned whether marrying culture to statecraft followed too closely along fascist lines. The DCR declared itself dedicated to fostering partnerships, not to producing propaganda (which meant promotional material, generally, as well as darker forms of suasion).[13] Given the DCR's limited prewar budget, this largely proved true.[14] It gave guidance to those already active in inter-American exchange and served as an information clearinghouse for the growing number of private and public organizations, such as museums, seeking to become involved.[15]

In 1940 another new agency came on the scene: the Office for Coordination of Commercial and Cultural Relations between the American Republics. Created by the Council of National Defense and with Rockefeller at the helm, it became the Office of the Coordinator of Inter-American Affairs in 1941.[16] Its varied works abroad ranged from projects in health, agriculture, and industrial infrastructure to dance, music, and sports programs, art exhibitions, and mass media offerings in print, radio, and motion pictures.[17] Rockefeller, who had toured Latin America in 1939, is credited as the driving force behind the OCIAA's creation. The experience is said to have convinced him that European countries, including Nazi Germany, had firmer ties to the southern continent's local cultures than did the United States.[18] Other scholars have detailed the deeply entwined nature of Rockefeller's corporate, cultural, philanthropic, and political interests in Latin America, including how these shaped the Museum of Modern Art's involvement in hemispheric unity programs.[19] For example, the OCIAA appointed MoMA trustee and executive vice president John E. Abbott to chair its all-volunteer Advisory Committee on Art. The committee (which replaced and was similar in composition to an earlier panel of the DCR) made proposals to the OCIAA's Cultural Relations Division, helped shepherd approved projects to completion, and interfaced with the DCR on Latin American exhibitions and exchanges. Other panel members included George C. Vaillant, associate curator of Mexican archaeology for the American Museum of Natural History, and several museum directors, including MoMA's Alfred H. Barr, Laurance Roberts of the Brooklyn Museum, Juliana R. Force of the Whitney Museum of American Art, the Metropolitan Museum of Art's Francis Henry Taylor, and Grace L. McCann Morley of the San Francisco Museum of Art.[20] Rockefeller's own experience in foundation and museum work made such alliances a logical means of expanding the OCIAA's capacity to pursue cultural diplomacy.[21]

Some have characterized the OCIAA as favoring mass media channels, corporate communications' philosophies and metrics, and the achievement of near-term results tied to national defense objectives.[22] The policies of the DCR, it is said, reflected an old-guard internationalism favoring longer-term processes of intellectual and cultural exchange, particularly among the more highly educated, as the best path to accord.[23] That said, both agencies engaged paid staff and volunteer advisers from various private and public sectors, including academia, industry, the media, and cultural institutions. Both endorsed exhibitions, particularly of art, as vehicles for education and diplomacy not only abroad but also in the United States, which is the focus here.

In spirit and in aim, stateside hemispheric unity efforts from the perspectives of the OCIAA and DCR constituted a form of performative repair. Through internal memos and public statements, both agencies acknowledged the damage that US imperialism, from military incursions to trade policies, had done to inter-American relations. "Latin Americans will not lend support to the United States," read one OCIAA memo, "unless they are convinced that our own citizens have a sincere interest in them."[24] Building domestic commitment fell to the OCIAA's Division of Inter-American Activities in the United States, which took as its mission the "Credo for the Individual U.S. Citizen." Like its complement, "The

U.S. Credo for the Individual Citizen of Latin America," the domestic version advanced four articles of faith necessary for allegiance to the Good Neighborhood. Among its goals: "to diminish any form of discrimination shown in the U.S. against citizens from Latin American countries."[25] (Racism not only undermined diplomacy, it gave Axis propagandists material to exploit.) The Credo read:

I. I believe that Latin America has much to offer me not only economically but also socially, esthetically, and spiritually.
II. I believe that the Axis wishes not only eventually to conquer Latin America but also more immediately to use certain of the Republics as bases from which to attack the U.S.
III. I believe that active cooperation from Latin America in all ways is essential if the U.S. is to win the war.
IV. I believe that, therefore, Latin America should be assisted by the U.S. in order to enable her to assist us and also herself.[26]

Evident in this document is the era's embrace of market-oriented tactics designed to systematize the art of persuasion—tactics popularized by such works as *Propaganda: Its Psychology and Technique* (1935), authored by Leonard W. Doob, PhD, a former classmate of Rockefeller.[27] Also present is the line that modern communicators sought to draw between propaganda aimed at massification of the public mind and that useful for the propagation of ideas in a democracy. The credos' titles and articles emphasize the individual actor and position belief as a rational outcome of having engaged with the proffered public media communications. These came in diverse forms, from textbooks and museum exhibitions to lectures, concerts, movies, and radio programs created and distributed through a cooperative domestic network of government agencies, civic groups, educators, and nongovernmental organizations.[28]

Some in museums saw the work of illuminating transnational economic, political, and security interests as an opportunity to showcase museums' ability to serve the public by providing the knowledge it needed to understand complex contemporary issues. Likewise, promoting cross-cultural accord fit well with the more progressive view that museums held potential to transform society in useful ways. The field also had its own experiences with Pan-Americanism and multiparty collaboration from which to draw.[29] In 1924, for example, the American Association of Museums (AAM) had approached Leo S. Rowe, PhD, director of the Pan-American Union, about working together to develop closer relations between museums in South and North America. After learning that the Carnegie Institution of Washington already had such plans underway, although more narrowly focused on archaeological exploration and exchange as museums' "chief ground" of common interest, the AAM formed a committee on Pan-American Cooperation with representatives from each group.[30]

The effort stalled as the AAM worked to secure its own financial and organizational footing. Finally, in 1928, a three-thousand-dollar award from the Carnegie Endowment for International Peace allowed the AAM to undertake its earlier plan to send a delegate to South America to "study museum problems, to invite cooperation, to spread an understanding of our attitude and to demonstrate our sincerity through actual service."[31] The AAM's director, Laurence Vail Coleman, traveled to Argentina, Brazil, Chile, Uruguay, Peru, Ecuador, Bolivia, and Paraguay in pursuit of these tasks.[32] During the four-month journey he met with museum and university professionals, US foreign service workers, and local government officials, including a few presidents.[33] He gathered ideas for projects that would appeal to "agencies interested in international cooperation and understanding" and also material for the AAM publication *Directory of Museums in South America* (1929). The volume's pragmatic mission was to set out the terrain of possible collaborating institutions for all concerned with "international relations in education, art, science or history."[34] It acknowledged the imperial origins of the continent's oldest museums and noted that a number of newer national museums arose from centennial celebrations of independence.

The year after the *Directory*'s publication, the Department of State appointed Coleman to the US National Council of the newly formed Inter-American Institute of Intellectual Cooperation, which had grown out of a resolution adopted at the Sixth Pan-American Conference.[35] Aspirations for this effort flagged when Congress, faced with more pressing matters, failed to provide it a budget.[36] Still, despite the worldwide economic collapse, and to some degree because of it, leaders on both American continents continued seek improved relations. With the establishment in 1930 of April 14 as Pan American Day, museums counted among those "giving expression to the spirit of continental solidarity and to the sentiments of cordiality and friendly feeling" among the hemisphere's republics.[37] By the mid-1930s, the AAM proudly reported that an international relations survey had credited museums for their part in fostering foreign exchange and educating US citizens about "other peoples."[38]

The Newark Museum and Library also had its own history of cultural and trade diplomacy that director Beatrice Winser (1869–1947) referenced as she rallied support for what would become *Three Southern Neighbors: Ecuador, Peru, Bolivia*. Called the "busiest woman in town" for her efforts to increase the museum and library's usefulness to the community throughout the rocky 1930s, Newark-born, Columbia College–trained Winser had joined the Newark Public Library in 1889.[39] Active in the community, her appointment to the Newark Board of Education in 1915 made her the first woman in the city's history to sit on a governing body.[40] That same year, under John Cotton Dana's tenure, she became the museum's assistant director and secretary. On Dana's death in 1929, she assumed leadership of the conjoined institutions.[41] One of the librarians under her charge, Julia Sabine, later remembered her boss as "not a large woman, but [one who] had a commanding presence which, along with her deep voice, could seem intimidating to those who did not know her."[42] Staff and others, Sabine recalled, could depend on Winser's "sense of justice and her quick response to people."

When Winser first approached the Department of State in January 1940 in hopes of securing funding for the Newark Museum's plans to launch a major contribution to the work of hemispheric unity, she frankly and frequently underscored its foreign relations track record through exhibitions on Colombia (1918) and China (1922). More than once, she sent along materials produced in conjunction with these efforts. Both exhibits, more so than the museum's more ethnographic national showcases, had highlighted international trade. Winser referenced these to emphasize the advantages of partnering with the very same museum that had "presented to this country an Exhibition of the Republic of Colombia, at a time when Colombia was not feeling very friendly to the United States."[43] Not only had Colombia's president lunched with staff and "expressed himself as highly pleased with what the Newark Museum had done," but the State Department, too, had "praised the exhibition and stated that it would be glad to have other museums do what the Newark Museum had done to aid in the comity of nations."

The 1918 discord to which Winser referred concerned debates over whether hemispheric unity during the Great War meant remaining dedicated to neutrality, as Colombia wished, or following the United States in its April 1917 declaration of war against Germany.[44] President Woodrow Wilson's administration used the implied threat of embargos to maneuver Colombia and similarly minded countries into a position of wartime solidarity with the United States.[45] The Newark Museum had touted *Colombia: South American Republic* (also called *The Newark-Colombia Exhibit*) as "An exhibition of the country, people, products, resources, transportation and imports and exports, suggesting to the business men possibilities of after-the-war trade with South America."[46] *Colombia* had earned praise not only in the press but also from Rowe (then assistant secretary of the US Department of the Treasury). He lauded it for having come "at a most opportune time" and wished that "similar exhibits for all Latin American countries might be arranged in different sections of the United States."[47]

President Wilson also endorsed *Colombia*, calling it "a notable international work" that "ably advanced . . . an enduring structure of mutually beneficial intercourse between the two countries."[48] Newark Museum publicity highlighted the president's telegram, resulting in such headlines as "Wilson Endorses Colombia Exhibit."[49] What the press did not mention (and perhaps did not know) was that the museum had proactively solicited the president's remarks. Trustee Richard C. Jenkinson, a businessman appointed to head the New Jersey arm of the US Fuel Administration, a wartime agency, had asked this favor of Wilson. In delivering the telegram to Winser (then the museum's assistant director), Jenkinson wrote, "Mr. Dana, the great advertiser, will know how to do this up brown so as to help Newark and the Museum."[50] The utility of such recommendations lay not only in their publicity value but also in their function as bona fides during an exhibition's planning stages as it sought cooperation and artifacts from foreign diplomats, individuals, corporations, and other museums.

The Newark Museum's inspiration to create a new Latin American exhibition likely came from the Department of State itself. In late 1939, staff member Julia Sabine attended the Conference of Inter-American Relations in the Field of Books and Libraries. State hosted this and similar convenings for arts, music, and education to solicit ideas from nongovernmental organizations and encourage their participation in cultural diplomacy.[51] (Attendees paid their own way.) Winser informed Welles that the museum wished to respond in a timely fashion to the call for Latin American initiatives and sought advice on which countries to single out for attention. She imagined treating no more than five nations, asking that they be on friendly terms with the United States and have stateside representatives willing to help obtain material for display. Welles suggested Ecuador, Peru, and Bolivia, noting only that the three had "certain similarities in their ethnic and cultural characteristics."[52]

This assessment left aside the pressing political realities behind the recommendation. As the long-standing border dispute between Peru and Ecuador inched closer to military confrontation, the prospect of an inter-American war gave the United States cause for concern; so too did the fact that both countries had hosted military missions from fascist Italy in recent years.[53] In the corporate sphere, German interests not only limited US economic inroads but, as in the case of Deutsche Lufthansa affiliates in Peru and Ecuador, also represented a potential defensive vulnerability.[54] As to Bolivia, the United States hoped to reduce German influence there, curb the economic nationalism that had led to the 1937 expropriation of Standard Oil's holdings, and secure access to tin, a material already in short supply just four months into Europe's war.[55]

From this point, Winser and Welles danced around the elephant in the room: funding. He wanted details before referring the proposal on to the Advisory Committee on Art. She, hoping for financial support, withheld details but reminded him that the exhibition would not be about the countries' arts alone but also "their education, commerce, natural resources, etc., etc."[56] Her hope for a contract, while not unfounded, did fly against the odds. A miniscule portion of the DCR and OCIAA budgets went to exhibitions, and the lion's share of that went to just a handful of institutions.[57] Only when Welles rebuffed her request for a letter of endorsement did Winser finally deliver a three-page plan for complementary exhibitions in the library and museum.[58] By January 1941, Winser had State's endorsement in hand and final surety that this marked the extent of its support. Welles wrote, "The Department is especially desirous at this time of encouraging enterprises such as yours, which tend to reinforce the bonds of friendship among the American Republics and which, at the same time, inform the people of the United States concerning the civilizations and economies of the countries to the south of us."[59] Applying the lessons of *Colombia*, Winser used Welles's letter to garner advice, artifacts, and, later, publicity from others. She also used it, along with repurposed language from her Welles correspondence about *Colombia,* to approach Nelson Rockefeller and the OCIAA.[60] But all she netted there was a referral to the Pan-American Union.[61]

Early War Marks a Hemispheric Heyday

No token effort, *Three Southern Neighbors: Ecuador, Peru, Bolivia* consisted of two halves and for its ten-month span was the museum's major exhibition. *Part I: Reviewing the Past,* which opened on Pan American Day in 1941, focused on the pre-Colonial and Colonial periods. Debuting in October, *Part II: Viewing the Present* emphasized contemporary culture and commerce. It cost just over five thousand dollars to produce, drew some 55,585 visitors during its first two months, and ran through February 1942.[62] *Three Southern Neighbors* as a whole coincided with what would prove to be the high-water mark of the exhibitionary network's hemispheric unity efforts. In February 1941, at a museum gathering for educators from the various republics, MoMA announced it would be working with the federal government to facilitate Pan-American exchange through exhibits of art, architecture, and design and, through its film department, the selection and translation of nontheatrical motion pictures into Spanish and Portuguese.[63] John Hay Whitney, speaking in his dual capacities as MoMA president and chairman of the OCIAA's Motion Picture Division, told the assembled and radio broadcast audiences, "We conceive of the function of a modern museum as something quite different from that of a static peepshow of antiquity."[64] MoMA's press release after the event spoke just as strongly about the museum's active role in current affairs; its headline read, "John Hay Whitney Announces Museum of Modern Art Will Serve as Weapon of National Defense."[65]

Other museums working directly with federal agencies on stateside activities included the American Museum of Natural History (AMNH). With help from the OCIAA, it received the popular mural map series that Mexican artist Miguel Covarrubias had painted for the Golden Gate International Exposition's theme building, Pacific House.[66] The AMNH also lent collection materials to a OCIAA-funded traveling exhibition series, *Latin American Art* (1941), the pre-Columbian and Colonial parts of which the Brooklyn Museum organized. The San Francisco Museum of Art managed the contemporary section under director Morley's guidance.[67] Morley (1900–1985), who held a doctorate in French literature and art from the University of Paris, taught briefly in her disciplinary area at Goucher College in Maryland until she became one of a group of instructors sponsored by the Carnegie Corporation to attend a summer training in 1929 at Harvard's Fogg Museum.[68] This connected her to Paul J. Sachs's museum professionalization program and, as Morley put it, to "this great wave of Fogg-trained people who went out across the country to museums."[69] That tide carried her to the Cincinnati Art Museum, where she assumed the position of general curator in 1930. By 1934, back in the state where she had been born, Morley was founding director of the all-but-collectionless San Francisco Museum of Art.[70] Her burgeoning support for Latin American contemporary art at the museum, as well as her ability to speak Spanish, soon put her in charge of organizing a showing of Central and South American paintings for the Golden Gate International Exposition.[71]

The work that Morley and colleagues from the AMNH and Brooklyn Museum put into the *Latin American Art* tour dovetailed with the Brooklyn Museum's own exhibition, *America South of U.S.* (November 13, 1941–January 2, 1942). Publicized by the Brooklyn Museum as "One of the most comprehensive Latin American exhibitions to be held in the current program in conjunction with the promotion of friendly Inter-American relations," the effort benefited from OCIAA funding that sent Herbert Joseph Spinden, head of the museum's Department of American Indian Art and Primitive Cultures, on a six-month trip to Argentina, Peru, Bolivia, and Chile.[72] While there, he lectured and gathered artifacts not only for the exhibit but for the museum's collections as well.[73] Roberts, the museum's director and member of the OCIAA's Advisory Committee on Art, had suggested the plan, noting that Spinden's time south would benefit OCIAA relationship building as well as the upcoming exhibition.

Materials from *America South of U.S.* not only toured the United States after the Brooklyn showing but also became the nucleus of the museum's new Latin American galleries. These opened in 1943 and supported a program designed to introduce local elementary and junior high school teachers to Latin American history and culture. Such instructional efforts by museums not only occurred during special exhibits but continued after as well, extending the research conducted and the message of unity into the community. Some 12,500 school children went to the Newark Museum specifically to see *Three Southern Neighbors*. Staff also organized a traveling version to send out to classes and provided teachers with materials to aid in correlating the exhibit with schoolwork. For its part, the AMNH offered free courses to elementary school instructors on how to use its exhibitions and visual aids to teach about the hemisphere's other nations.

Pan-Americanism also took center stage in Columbus, Ohio, at the American Association of Museum's annual conference, where more than three hundred museum professionals, from twenty-five states, Canada, and China, gathered in May 1941. A general session on defense and hemispheric unity opened the gathering "on a note of interest more intense than usual."[74] The talks (later published in *The Museum News*) called for museums to become more involved in the shaping of "cultural rapprochement."[75] Indeed, attendees passed a "spontaneous resolution" that conference papers on museums' part in hemispheric solidarity be called to the attention of the OCIAA's Nelson Rockefeller. In these papers, such figures as Morley, Whitney, Charles H. Sawyer (director of the Worcester Art Museum), and Philip R. Adams (director of the Columbus Gallery of Fine Arts) explored both the possibilities and difficulties associated with Pan-American efforts.

Morley lamented having too few US museum workers with expertise in Latin American cultures or fluency in Spanish or Portuguese. Having such qualifications herself, she became an indispensable figure called on by the OCIAA and others to provide advice as well as lead inter-American art projects. With humility, she emphasized that she knew enough to realize that her grasp of the arts, cultures, and peoples of South America was "superficial" compared to the "great complexity of the subject."[76] She also cautioned attendees to remember that the term "Latin America" was but a glib convenience erroneously suggesting commonality where mindfulness of specific histories, geographies, and lifeways was essential.

Sawyer critiqued the shortcomings of government-led exchange exhibitions. After attending the State Department's 1939 Conference on Inter-American Relations in the Field of Art, Sawyer said that he and others had left "with something of a feeling of futility at the inadequacy of the solutions advanced" and at the DCR's inability "to take real leadership or suggest means of financing the various types of activity proposed."[77] He offered a kinder assessment of the fledgling but by comparison cash-rich OCIAA, saying it had "begun to assume that necessary leadership—to initiate, plan, and finance these activities." With depleted coffers and uncertainties about economic resurgence, Sawyer, Winser, and other museum leaders were rightly concerned about how to fund inter-American efforts if government support proved more a matter of spirit than of scrip.

Drawing on his recent visit to Guatemala, Sawyer also urged government agencies to aid museums in ascertaining the specific interests of the countries to which exhibitions would be sent and to better define who in each nation the United States sought to court. Here, he counseled that they be designed for the masses, not only the governing elite. His thoughts on how to design didactic exhibitions sent abroad echoed display strategies discussed for stateside use. Sawyer emphasized, "If, with the experience we are constantly accumulating with modern exhibition techniques, we could prepare dramatic, visual exhibitions illustrating the developments of this country in industry and public works, we could prepare a legitimate propaganda display which would be tremendously effective and which could reach with a minimum number of words and language difficulties a far larger percentage of the population than any traditional exhibition of oil paintings or sculpture is likely to reach."[78] Lastly, he urged, "We need to take advantage of all the technical knowledge and experience in display available today in the museum, advertising, and commercial world."[79]

Adams, who presented "A Plan of Inter-American Cooperation," noted that the United States remained "over insistent on our own importance" when formulating exhibition plans and content.[80] He proposed pairing thirty "of the many less cosmopolitan cities" in the United States with counterparts across Central and South America. Through correspondence each pair would discover shared interests during a planning year; then they could develop for both cities twelve or more months of museum programming in history, science, and the arts.[81] This, Adams thought, even if started with only ten municipalities, would move cultural diplomacy beyond the "pallid generalities" of which Morley warned to a new state of affairs: that of tenderness and affection. Here, Adams veered into masculinist, colonialist stereotypes as he invoked the *Carte de Tendre* to map the contours of this geo-emotional terrain. US culture workers became "shrewd gallants" wooing their feminized "quarry" in order to progress from "the city of 'new friendship'" to a more intimate, interpersonal neighborly unity.[82]

In choosing a *Carte de Tendre* to represent hemispheric unity, Adams fittingly conflated the meanings of "state" as a bounded political entity *and* as an affective condition of being. The Good Neighborhood's perimeter would be defined not only by continental borders but by bonds of affection, too. In the words of his time, Adams spoke of museum exhibitions' power to provide, on both continents, moments of transformative human-thing encounter. "Surely," he wrote, "it is possible that, in a small way, should the tangible evidence of the lives and ideas of an unfamiliar land be physically, and personally, present for a time in our midst, people, not humanity and not mankind, but simply people, might be helped to speak cross the distances, and through the darkness."[83] It is this notion of the embodied encounter that *Part II* of *Three Southern Neighbors: Ecuador, Peru, Bolivia* strove to provide.

Exhibitionary Tourism: Performative Consumption and Affective Encounters

From the outset, Julia Sabine and Margaret Jarden, chief organizers of *Three Southern Neighbors,* envisioned *Part II: Viewing the Present* as a "'Travelogue'" that situated the museum visitor as a vacationer from the United States touring the three Andean nations.[84] Jarden, who by 1958 would hold the title of director of exhibitions for the museum, likely took lead, while Sabine assisted and also marshaled the library's contributions to the effort. The exhibition's prescribed travel sequence took the visitor-tourist on a counterclockwise path through the partitioned galleries (figure 1).[85] First came maps and charts providing a geospatial orientation and brief historical overview of the twenty republics south of the United States. Next came samples of local currency, newspapers, and common Spanish phrases. The exhibit brochure was bilingual as well. "Thus equipped," explained a guide to the exhibition, "the visitor becomes the 'traveler' and proceeds on his journey," a nine-day, 2,800-mile sea voyage from New York, through the Panama Canal, and into Ecuador's chief port, Guayaquil.[86] From there, the traveler progressed "from the coastal plain, up into the Andes, and over toward the Amazon, through the jungle area."[87] Along the way, this virtual tourist beheld "Flora, fauna, Indian life, remains of Inca civilization, unusual scenery, historic spots of Spanish occupation, modern engineering feats . . . curious customs of the countries; points of common interest as well as points of difference . . . as though the visitor to the exhibit were actually a visitor to the countries."[88]

Materializing the Good Neighborhood 55

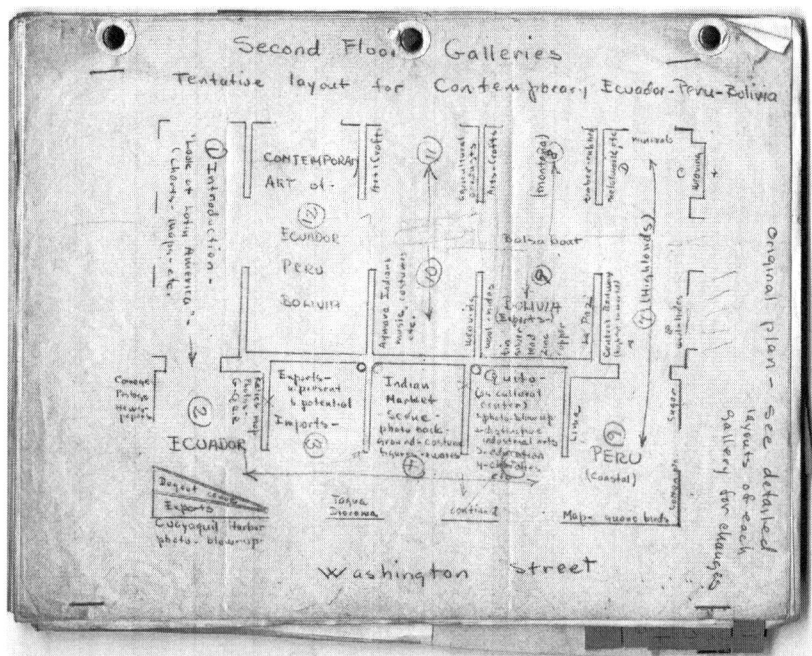

FIGURE 1. Structured as an imaginative journey through three nations, the initial floor plan (shown here) as well as the final installation for *Three Southern Neighbors: Ecuador, Peru, Bolivia; Part II: Viewing the Present* began, as many trips do, with an investigation of maps and local currencies before departure (section 1). The sightseeing, which managed to integrate a commercial tradeshow into the itinerary (section 3 and figure 2), culminated in a visit to an "art museum" (section 12) showcasing contemporary artists from each country. From "Original Plan" for *Three Southern Neighbors: Ecuador, Peru, Bolivia*, 1941, page 1. Folder: Latin American Exhibition, 1941—Jarden's Working Plans. Exhibition files, box 54. Archives of the Newark Museum.

The traveler also encountered the Andean republics' exports, "especially as they relate to the life of the people of Newark, the tanning materials which are used in Newark industries, the fruits that Newarkers eat, the coffee they drink, the rubber, the minerals, the oil that they may be using every day in their lives."[89] The tour concluded with a selection of contemporary art from the three countries. The exhibition script, with its vivid descriptions of the scenes that would be created through the assembled photographs, cultural artifacts, natural specimens, and life groups, demonstrates the curators' desire to craft a surrogate for the firsthand encounter, to emulate bodily immersion in another culture. In contrast, the first installment of *Three*

Southern Neighbors, which emphasized the nation's shared cultural histories, had been presented as a conventional art gallery–style installation.

Three months after the Newark Museum opened *Part II: Viewing the Present,* Macy's kicked off its twenty-one-day Latin American Fair.[90] The event, which Macy's described as being both a sale and an exhibition, offered buyers of every budget a stake in the hemispheric order. One might go home with "a letter written by Cortez [sic] in 1524 (Macy-priced at $33,499) or a contemporary earthenware ashtray (Macy-priced at 14¢)."[91] Distinguishing itself from competitor Gimbel's concurrent *Ancient Arts and Crafts of South America,* Macy's crowed, "This is no museum exhibit confined to ancient arts. It is a thrilling, vital exposition of Latin America *today* . . . its craftsmanship, its contemporary arts, its living cultures." The OCIAA had aided with supply chain logistics, publicity, and the furnishing of dignitaries, including First Lady Eleanor Roosevelt, for the opening gala.[92] MoMA contributed, too, with four of its staff sitting on the fair's nine-member advisory board.

Macy's reported that more than 825,000 people had attended the fair during its three-week run.[93] It was, in many respects, the culmination of government efforts to enlist major retailers in promoting stateside consumption of finished goods produced in South America.[94] It also harkened back to museum-retailer collaborations of the industrial arts movement, which sought to shape the aesthetic tastes of producers and consumers alike. The Metropolitan Museum of Art, for example, had partnered with Macy's in the late 1920s.[95] In terms of hemispheric unity, other museum-retailer collaborations included MoMA's *Organic Design in Home Furnishings* (September 24–November 9, 1941) and its companion show at Bloomingdale's. At the OCIAA's suggestion, the design competition's domestic focus had expanded to include entrants from Latin America.[96] (The chairman of MoMA's Trustee Committee on Industrial Design, Wallace K. Harrison, also served as the OCIAA's director of cultural relations.) A consortium of other department stores from Boston to Los Angeles joined in Bloomingdale's promise to commission goods from the winners.[97] Commenting on the resulting exhibit's Pan-American virtues, Harrison invited speculation on what would have happened "if Hitler had been one of its Judges."[98] "One-half the Competition would have been ruled out because the competitors were not of Nordic blood," he said, "and an announcement would have been put out that Americans, North and South, were degenerates and had no place in the new order."

The Gimbel's event, which Macy's had hastened to distance itself from, marked that store's centenary and a collaboration with Hammer Galleries for an exhibition and sale of pre-Columbian and Spanish Colonial artifacts, reputedly worth $2 million.[99] It included items previously shown at the Brooklyn Museum, Tulane University Museum, and the Newark Museum. The airing via "short-wave good neighbor broadcast" of speeches and musical performances given at both the Gimbel's and Macy's events underscores, again, that the involved parties sought to produce occasions for witness, occasions to demonstrate the "sincere interest" of northern neighbors in their counterparts to the south.

Just as the Newark Museum reminded visitors of the ways in which Latin America, through its goods, was already woven into the quotidian fabric of their lives, so too Macy's emphasized "things" as sites of encounter. To imagine a United States without Brazilian coffee or cacao for chocolate, to "picture a child's world without banana splits or a bar without that perfect synthesis of north and south, Rum and Coca Cola," was to conjure sensory deprivation.[100] Materializations of the hemispheric imaginary supplied (to the degree different institutional constraints allowed) an orchestrated multisensory fullness through spaces coded either as generically Latin American, in Macy's case, or more carefully nation-specific, as in Newark's creation. That both took as their framework an imaginary journey through the Good Neighborhood is no coincidence.

A core tenet of hemispheric cultural diplomacy was the supposition that direct encounters between US citizens and the cultural products, if not the people, of the other nations of the hemisphere would best facilitate attainment of a sensate knowledge productive of sympathetic bonds. In other words, physical or embodied knowledge acquired through the senses would be more likely to inspire "neighborly" behavior rooted in emotion as well as understanding. For museum professionals interested in social instrumentality, the notion of educating the public through efforts that engaged the mind, the emotions, and the body reflected still-new ways of thinking about how visitors might not only come to understand through exhibitions but how they might also be encouraged to put their learning to use out in the world.

With European travel increasingly curtailed in the late 1930s, corporate and government interests alike encouraged tourism to Latin America. In part, the government hoped to weaken German- and Italian-owned stakes in commercial air and sea ventures as a means to prevent their possible conversion to military uses. An increase in US tourism would also demonstrate that Yankee dollars could support neighboring economies through purchases other than raw materials. Even as war conditions began to impede inter-American transit, the travelogue became a pervasive trope; it appeared in radio dramas, such as *Pan-American Holiday* (1942), documentaries, and even a book series, *Good Neighbor Tour* (Pan-American Union: 1943), intended for use by civic groups wishing to embark together on "an imaginary visit to the republics of Latin America."[101]

As a surrogate form of travel, exhibitions did something these other media did not: they allowed for embodied immersion in and a sensory encounter with the hemispheric imaginary. In this, they echoed international expositions' illusion of containing entire nations within one border, thereby enabling denizens of the host country to travel unfettered through tamed foreign spaces. This constructed the hemispheric citizen as the beneficiary of ideologies promoting the inter-American system. Through this dual-citizenship, US Americans gained a self-sufficient zone of safety, material abundance, and cultural invigoration. At best, the promise went, the New World would flourish while Europe again descended into war; at worst, its collective resources, technologies, and manpower would see it capably through armed conflict. This two-sided proposition flourished precisely because it held out peaceable internationalism and preparative strategy in proportions enough to appeal to isolationists, interventionists, and the in-between.

Tourism, as a set of embodied practices such as shopping, museum-going, wandering, photo taking, eating, and so forth, contributes to a relational negotiation of the tourist-self and the local-other.[102] From its appropriating gazes to more literal forms of intake, touristic practice is a consumption of place that is also productive of it.[103] Thus, the dynamic of secondhand tourism offered by *Three Southern Neighbors,* Macy's Fair, and similar efforts was as productive of the hemispheric imaginary as the installed sights and sites themselves. These spaces not only functioned akin to world's fairs in miniature, they often took inspiration and substance from them as well. For example, among the much-mentioned attractions at the New York World's Fair were the Brazilian Pavilion's aviary and coffee sampling bar. These were echoed in the "gorgeously plumed tropical birds" inhabiting Macy's jungle and in its "sidewalk café" that treated shoppers to hot brew.[104] In contrast to the International Style pavilion's careful negotiation of a cosmopolitan national identity, however, Macy's twenty-republic pastiche offered, as Lisa Crossman notes, a romanticized, neocolonial vision of the exotic Other.[105]

For its part, *Three Southern Neighbors* incorporated novel diorama techniques used at the New York World's Fair and described in *Exhibition Techniques* (1940).[106] In the gallery where a seventeen-and-a-half-foot-long photograph montage of Guayaquil's harbor welcomed new arrivals, the curators deepened the illusion that the museum-tourists had just disembarked at their first port of call by arranging artifacts at the foot of the panorama. These consisted of the "principal exports one might see piled up on the dock," along with a twenty-one-foot-long dugout canoe that gestured to the unseen "Indian" who had transported tagua nuts and other goods downriver.[107] Such tableaux enhanced the corporeal nature of this secondhand tourism by extending photographed scenes into the material, chronologic, three-dimensional space of the viewer. Others have argued for tourist photography as "a technology of world making" that participates in the creation of what Edward Said termed "imaginative geographies."[108] Exhibition practices that materially extended the bound space of the photograph into the observer's bodily sphere amplified this productive capacity. The world-making power of the resulting space lies, as scholars have theorized, in its being an encounter between the local and the distant that is "at once imaginative and physical."[109] But whose eyes constructed the tourist gaze offered up in the photographs used by Newark, Macy's, and others in the exhibitionary network?

The Newark Museum's installation used photographs liberally. Some contextualized specific artifacts; others enabled the museum-tourist to encounter the architecture, people, and environs of current-day Ecuador, Bolivia, and Peru. They came largely from the publicity arms of businesses with stakes in South America. The W. R. Grace and Company, for example, provided photographs it had commissioned to promote hemispheric travel via its passenger ships and Pan American–Grace Airways (Panagra). E. I. du Pont de Nemours and Company also furnished images, many originally intended to give *La Revista Du Pont*, a Spanish- and

Portuguese-language version of the corporate magazine, a local touch for distributors, dealers, and consumers in Latin America. Macy's, which hosted a travel bureau at its fair, also worked with the W. R. Grace Company as well as Ask Mr. Foster and the United Fruit Company. The retailer boasted of its "emphasis on photographic treatment," which included at each of the fair's two entrances identical friezes composed of some fifty photographs of the people and places of the twenty nations represented within.[110] Macy's also enticed visitors to act the tourist, "to photograph Latin America in replica" as part of a store-sponsored contest.[111]

The influence of World's Fair exhibition craft also extended, in Newark's case, to repurposed display materials. The museum negotiated to take on loan (and, in a few cases, purchase) materials from the Pavilion of the Republic of Ecuador. These included export goods, a relief map, Indigenous "costumes," oil paintings, and the national flag.[112] For Jarden and Sabine this proved to be a stroke of luck, as they had found securing artifacts that matched their plans to be more difficult than anticipated. The United States had relatively few Latin American collections at the time; so, as hemispheric unity efforts proliferated, curators' loan requests frequently received regretful replies from other museums, corporate contacts, diplomats, and private collectors who reported that the requested items were already part of current or planned exhibitions.

Despite some disappoints, the Newark Museum secured loans from such colleagues as the AMNH, the New-York Historical Society, the Textile Museum in Washington, DC, and the US National Museum (Smithsonian Institution). Still, when Winser caught word that the New Jersey State Museum in Trenton had plans underway for its own Latin American exhibit, she promptly sounded out whether the two organizations might be "duplicating" or "interfering in each other's exhibits."[113] Trenton's curator reminded Winser that it was a crowded field, emphasizing, "I strongly feel that every community should endeavor to become better acquainted with our neighbors to the south. As you most likely know, the Museum of Modern Art is planning an extensive Pan American exhibition for this spring; and the Philadelphia Arts and Crafts Guild is to open a Latin American display soon, etc."[114]

Part II: Viewing the Present also emphasized trade relations, extending the Newark Museum's long-standing practice of working with local industry. So lenders also included firms such as the Button Machinery

Company, which imported Ecuadorian tagua nuts to produce its wares. It contributed samples of vegetable ivory in various stages of refinement as well as photographs tracing the nuts' journey from harvesting in Manta to the final inspection of buttons in Hoboken.[115] The American Smelting and Refining Company of Perth Amboy, New Jersey, provided materials related to its silver, tin, and lead mining concerns in Peru and Bolivia. Attentiveness to the conduits that provided display materials to museums is more than a matter of dry logistics. It reveals how trade circuits established in earlier decades of US corporate colonialism and economic imperialism not only persisted but flourished during this period and on into the war.[116] The W. R. Grace and Company, for example, was arguably one of the first US-based multinational corporations with interests in several Latin American countries. Behind its newer ventures in the tourist business lay its textile mills, sugar plantations, munitions shipments, and other deep entanglements in Peru's political and economic affairs.[117] So, even as the imaginary of the Good Neighborhood promised repair of these rifts through a new mutuality, it was through the existing arteries of informal empire that artifacts for exchange as well as enclave flowed north into retail outlets and into Pan-American exhibitions.

Another instability in the imaginary's narration was the embodiment of US hemispheric belonging in the figure of the tourist, a trope predicated on attraction to difference and novelty rather than neighborly familiarity. Indeed, representations of contemporary life in the other republics seldom depicted commonalties among the Americas' educated and better-off classes. They favored instead picturesque exoticism, ethnic difference, and what some have called a nostalgic attraction to primitivism born of US desires for a simpler social order free of corporate infiltration.[118] There was more to it, however. One thing that the emphasis on Indigenous and mestizo cultures provided was grounds for arguing a shared rejection of European imperialism. For example, in a 1939 address to a Pan-American symposium convened in New York to promote hemispheric unity as a safeguard against war, the Brooklyn Museum's Herbert Spinden commented on the destruction of Indigenous cultures, remarking, "With the discovery of America, Europe succumbed to the temptation of conquest. Columbus, Cortez [sic], Pizarro, who have been glorified as great adventurers, were in reality kidnapers and robbers."[119] Placing the spotlight on European imperialism made it easier, of course, for those in the United States to continue to minimize and "forget" their own national past and ongoing brands of imperialism. In similar fashion, a 1941 review of Brooklyn's *America South of U.S.* noted, Colonial-period Latin American folk art stood as a "symbol of democracy" because the "arts of native folk bent to those of the strange aristocratic masters but did not break."[120] This common history of resilience was, in Spinden's words, "at once the best propaganda and the best social cement that democracy can have."[121]

Such bald enthusiasm for propaganda is a reminder that the term held a broader meaning then than now. Spinden could have been crowing over the publicity and bonding value revealed in the exhibit's material truths just as much as he was pleased by the power of democratic, or "white," propaganda, which was also seen as rooted in truth, unlike the deliberate falsehoods of the "black" propaganda churned out by the Axis. Museum workers incorporating modern communications techniques into exhibition craft hoped to construct compelling educational experiences better suited to the information needs of a complex world. Instrumentalists had the added aim of moving a better-informed polity toward social good. Consider, for example, Macy's and Newarks' shared invocation of the marketplace as the hemisphere's meeting ground—a tactic MoMA had used, too, in 1940 by setting up displays in its garden that looked like vendors' stalls for the *Twenty Centuries of Mexican Art* exhibition.[122] Macy's described their market as a space that "bubbles with activity and hums with cheerful chatter," so compelling the shopper-tourist would "want to stop and talk with the charming mannequins in gorgeous native costume that stand under the trees."[123] However, when it came to the widespread, repeat purchases the government hoped to stimulate, US shoppers largely proved satisfied with one-time "souvenirs" to mark their experience. Appeals to charity followed next. "The vanity and whimsy of American women may be catered to through the array of Latin-American products at the Macy Fair," reprimanded one author, "but for thousands of Latin-American women the display means new hope, a chance to earn the money they so sorely need to buy the bare necessities of life."[124] Here, the veil of fantasy lifted to reveal the inequities of hemispheric citizenship.

The Newark exhibit, with its inclusion of manufactures dependent on Latin American materials, more carefully argued the entwined realities in its community of local and distant markets. The stay in Guayaquil included an overview of Ecuador's history, governance, topography, and climate.

The museum-tourist's next stop had all the appearance of a trade show, emphasizing that this trip, at least, was as much business as pleasure. Here for inspection were Ecuador's current and potential exports to the United States as well as the manufactures it imported. It was with this broader sense of transnational commerce in mind that the journey continued to Quito, by way of the "Indian Market Fair" patterned carefully after those in Otavalo, Riobamba, and Ambato. Fragrant with tanned hides, bundles of straw, and the wooly skins of llamas, goats, and sheep, the scene was meant to be perceived as "crowded, noisy and richly colorful."[125] (Efforts to add a taxidermied pig and geese to the scene for additional realism came up short.) Life-size figures in Indigenous garb sat "under the shade of their umbrellas with their wares spread out on woven mats before them, while others appear to be engaged in the inevitable process of bargaining before buying."[126]

Set within the journey's full itinerary, the marketplace was meant to be read against its Andean context—and in tandem with the different crafts and arts, clothing and textiles, cities and villages, and agriculture and animals associated with specific regional geographies and cultures of the three countries. Supporting programming included weekly exhibit tours, motion pictures, recorded music, and radio talks. Ultimately, the curatorial team sought to replicate what it saw as intelligent tourism: "Because we believe that the greatest understanding between peoples can only come through personal contact with people in their own environment, and because the opportunity for travel is open to only a few, we would like to present a graphic picture of the principal facts concerning these countries that a traveler would acquire as he travels from place to place."[127]

Evident, too, however, in both planning and outcomes, are unexamined biases. While the exhibit's Ecuadorian marketplace conjured an image of tourists and locals alike bartering in a highly localized, seemingly timeless setting, publicity photos contextualized the North American consumer quite differently. One, featured in the museum's monthly members' magazine, shows a woman, an actual or staged museumgoer, standing in the gallery dedicated to US-Ecuadorian trade (section 3, figure 1) and positioned so she occupies a metaphoric international crossroads (figure 2).[128] Her purchase decisions are ordered by access to economic statistics and executed with awareness of the role she plays in the larger geopolitical transactions of her international community. This, of course, also

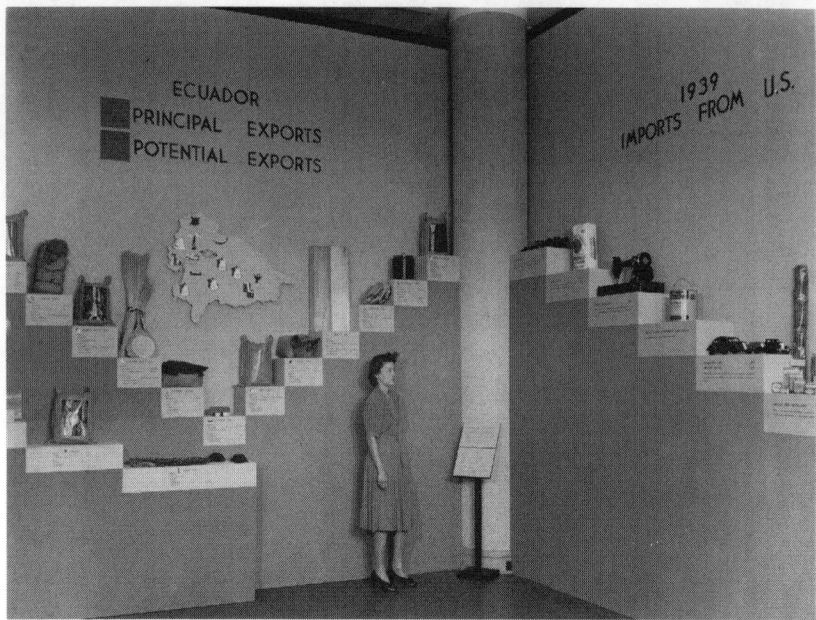

FIGURE 2. In contrast to shoppers in the localized markets representing South America, the US consumer stands here at the nexus of international trade, underscoring the necessity of informed, participatory consumption to the building of neighborly bonds. From "Ecuador Imports and Exports, *Three Southern Neighbors* exhibit," Exhibition photographs 1940–1941, Box 33, Folder 9479: October 1941, *Three Southern Neighbors*. Archives of the Newark Museum.

represented the type of intervention that museum social instrumentalists hoped their educational efforts could achieve: a well-informed citizen capable of discerning how the activities of daily life might contribute to a better society, in this case by contributing to the cause of peace, security, and amity.

Stereotypes also slipped through good intentions in descriptive text. "Indians of eastern or tropical Bolivia tend to be idle and complacent," read the members' bulletin, compared to the "virile, hardworking folk" of the Altiplano, who, aligning more favorably with Euro-Western types, "have been compared to the highland Scot in the obstinacy with which they wrest a living from the stony soil."[129] Exhibition planning also revealed chauvinism. Richard Foster Howard, director of the Dallas Museum of Fine Arts, cautioned Winser:

> We have found that any of the Latin American people are likely to be very charming and polite and say "Yes" and then never do anything.... I think the only sure way to get anything from Latin American countries is the way the Museum of Modern Art did—to send several representatives down with ample funds and political connections and live there until the show is complete. As I said in the beginning, I am sorry to be discouraging, but everybody has had the same experience. The only successful shows of Latin American objects have been the result of a long visit by an energetic competent North American.[130]

In other correspondence to Winser, Jarden ended the account of her and Sabine's visit to the Peruvian consul general with this gratuitous assessment: "As a person the Consul is very Latin, stocky stout, voluble, excitable and I imagine very irritable."[131] Such characterizations mirrored broader public opinion. In 1940, when presented with a list of nineteen adjectives and asked to choose which most aptly described the peoples of Central and South America, 47 percent of US respondents selected "lazy," while "efficient" ranked last, at 5 percent.[132] Other list-topping descriptors were "quick-tempered" (49 percent), "emotional" (47 percent), and, at number one, "dark-skinned" (80 percent).

Issues of race and class also surfaced in the curators' meeting at the Bolivian consulate. The representative's response to their question of whether he knew any Bolivians in New York who had "costumes, etc?" perplexed them.[133] Jarden wrote, "[He] seemed to regard it as a bit odd to expect a consul to know the whereabouts of a native costume. Asked us if we thought a US consul in Europe, if asked for a Mohawk Indian costume, would know the whereabouts of one." Their visit to the Ecuadorian consulate also underscored the gulf between North and South American conceptions of how Latin republics should be depicted. The Ecuadorian official there argued, perhaps sarcastically, that his countrymen would want to show a grand, new $100,000 building they had constructed, but in the United States, with many $200,000 buildings of its own, "an Indian child by the roadside might have more appeal."[134] As others have observed, US ignorance of ethnic, racial, and class dynamics in the varied republics, as well as its focus on indigeneity and difference, proved frustrating for diplomat-class Latin Americans who wished to focus on a shared cosmopolitan identity.

Input also came from the Columbus Gallery of Art's Philip Adams, who by the summer of 1941 was working closely with the OCIAA's Committee on Art. At Winser's request, he came to see *Reviewing the Past* and plans for *Viewing the Present*. He reportedly praised the museum for "doing pioneer work" ("as we know," commented a staffer), deeming it one of the few reliable sources on Latin American culture along with the Brooklyn Museum and Grace McCann Morley.[135] Others in the exhibitionary network, however, faulted *Viewing the Present* for its emphasis on the "primitive," which they found "interesting and picturesque" but "misleading in a way."[136] The complainants, a long-time staffer and writer with the *Pan-American* magazine and her companion, further emphasized,

> There is such wide-spread ignorance in this country of anything in South America, and a misconception to the effect that they are all Indians and "natives", etc. . . . [that we feel] that one should strive to point out the fact that they, in truth, lead lives very much like our own, wear like clothes for the most part, have huge cities and industrial centers, and so forth. Of course, we both realize that this particular theme is not picturesque or particularly colorful, but a combination of this with the Indians might give a more comprehensive view of South America. . . . Of course, everyone loves to see the exotic and what is different from our own, but I think you see what I am driving at. Please do not interpret this as a disparagement of your exhibit, which I think is grand and far the best I have seen . . .

A hand-written rebuttal on the letter objected that the exhibit *did* feature photos of cities and "white people in modern dress." Word of the exhibition did reach at least one of the featured nations. Quito's newspaper *El Comercio* praised it as a "unique exhibition" that contributed in "a genuine way" to "the high and noble purpose of inter-American knowledge."[137]

Hemispheric Citizenship, Interrupted

By the time *Three Southern Neighbors* closed, the United States was at war. During the 1941–42 fiscal year, an estimated one million people in the United States had seen an OCIAA-supported exhibition, be it a simple tabletop display in a library or community center or one of the few more elaborate museum efforts. This compared to roughly 1.6 million who had seen an OCIAA-backed film.[138] However, dismantling of the government infrastructure built to support Good Neighbor initiatives had already begun in order to direct resources to new fronts. Even in make-do mode, the OCIAA reported in 1944 that it continued to receive "favorable comments on the usefulness of exhibits and requests for more."[139] Also that year, the government allocated funds to establish an Inter-American Office at the National Gallery of Art and began to transfer the agency's remaining efforts there.[140] In 1948, when government subvention ceased, the museum shuttered the operation.[141]

The withdrawal of government support from Pan-Americanism did not surprise those more deeply invested in cultural internationalism. Their concerns had earlier been voiced in *The Museum News*. "Are these efforts to be interpreted as the results of a special international situation which may change tomorrow, or as representing a real foundation for the future of the three Americas," worried one author writing from Uruguay. "Will these efforts cease when peace arrives? Will they change with a change in government?"[142] Noting the American penchant for "quick results," he cautioned, "But understanding and friendship, if they are to be durable and not created as mere emotion for a short, particular moment require patience and sympathy." Others, writing later and attentive to the emerging talk of a global postwar community, rightly predicted it would "render a mere continental system superfluous."[143]

Good Neighborhood–inspired exhibits, either self-initiated or taken on loan, continued but now numbered among efforts increasingly focused on allied nations, home-front concerns, and, later, battle zones. That was true for the Newark Museum, where *Look to Latin America for Design* (1942) and *Our Neighbor Republics* (1943) rounded out its hemispheric work. True to the premise of social instrumentality, exhibition topics shifted to issues of greater contemporary interest and concern. That said, Pan American Day each wartime April continued to bring forth a flowering of museum events nationwide, at the encouragement of the Pan-American Union and the dwindling OCIAA. One of the last such affairs to be reported in *The Museum News* of the forties was the Rochester Museum of Science and Arts' *Parranda Pan Americana* (April 13–30, 1945).[144] This community-wide celebration and exhibition involved high school and college students of Spanish, the local Good Neighbor Group, the Rochester Civic Orchestra, and invited speakers. Department stores also turned their attention to new fronts. Macy's, for example, coordinated exhibits addressing such matters as the army's use of camouflage and how to find wartime substitutes for hard-to-find or prohibited goods.[145] None matched the scale and ceremony of its Latin American Fair.

Some have argued that the contract system employed by the cultural relations arms of the OCIAA and Department of State shrouded the government's role in steering stateside cultural policy. Among museums, at least, independent hemispheric unity efforts far outnumbered those funded by government and, more to the point, regardless of the financing source, museums routinely publicized how their hemispheric unity initiatives aligned with federal entities and policies. The MoMA, which reportedly fulfilled thirty-eight government contracts (for overseas as well as domestic work) totaling $1,590,234 by the end of World War II for the OCIAA as well the Office of War Information, the Library of Congress, and other agencies, routinely announced its alliances in its members' bulletins and press releases.[146] If anything was obscured by the government, even to collaborating museums, it might have been the deeper particulars behind the recommendations that the agencies made when putting forth certain countries as ideal candidates for stateside programming.

Exhibitions and events such as those put on at Newark and Macy's also functioned as sites of public witness where visiting individuals as well as the host institutions could enact and affirm their belonging as citizens of the Good Neighborhood as well as the United States. For participating museums, the hemispheric unity campaign provided a nationally visible forum within which to demonstrate their civic value as social instruments well suited to educating adults about complex modern issues. For institutions such as the Newark Museum that embraced contemporary thought on exhibition craft as a communicative medium, it also provided opportunity to field didactic narratives that understood human-thing encounters to be productive of changes not only in intellectual and emotional understanding but in action as well. Museum work in this area also demonstrates the ways in which the still-broad term "propaganda" carried positive valence when understood by its museum practitioners as persuasive education directed toward a perceived common good.

As to the "public" part of the witness, this describes those who, as a result of such exhibitions and related work, beheld museums not only as repositories but also as active agents in current affairs. It also includes the act of visitors regarding themselves and their fellow museumgoers as participants in a civic-minded event. While others writing of museums have used the term "virtual witnessing" to describe how visitors within an immersive exhibition can feel transported to a past time and place, less attention has been paid to how some museum interpretations of current, still-unfolding events can also encourage a witnessing dynamic.[147] Here, it is useful to look at scholarship that conceptualizes witnessing as an act of exchange that engenders an obligation to testify to the thing experienced.[148] The more emotionally powerful the recipient perceives the encounter to be, the more likely they are to feel compelled to witness to that encounter, to share that experience with others. In terms of the members of the public who partook of such events, the time spent self-educating in the museum or shopping in the department store; discussing what one had learned, felt, and experienced afterward; showing off purchases; trying a new recipe; or seeking out news on hemispheric issues—all might give testimony to one's curiosity about, if not allegiance to, the state of the Good Neighborhood.

While the impact of museums' hemispheric unity work on local sentiments and international cultural relations remains difficult to gauge, efforts that adopted the trope of the touristic encounter constructed a witness dynamic that situated Latin American good neighbors as foreign rather than fellow. This dissipated the possible unitive and generative dimensions that had interested participating museums in diplomacy work, leaving them instead as not-fully-aware contributors to an unequal hemispheric belonging structured by consumer capitalism and economic imperialism. The institutional component of witnessing still held, however. Museums made visible their value in the marketplace of ideas and information through the ability to materialize, in ways mass media truly could not, the New World to which their local constituencies were called to belong. Hemispheric unity efforts also extended the cooperative (if not always like-minded) relationships within the exhibitionary network that continued not only into World War II but into the economic and cultural imperialisms of the Cold War as well.[149]

Chapter Three
WAR COMES TO THE MUSEUM

> An exhibit now being prepared on Japan and the Indies is aimed, not at patriotism, not for propaganda, but towards understanding. Why? Because we want to have the reputation for honesty in 1942 as we hope we had in 1941.
>
> —Robert T. Hatt, director of the Cranbrook Institute of Science, 1942

Even as US museums undertook hemispheric unity efforts as their civic contribution to cultural understanding and maintenance of peace, on at least one side of the globe, they kept an eye on developments in Europe. After the fall of Poland in September 1939, the American Alliance of Museum's weekly members' bulletin, *The Museum News*, began publishing regular updates on the wartime trials faced by European institutions. Topics ranged from the removal of collections for safekeeping and museum closures to staff departures for military service and new policies guiding museum participation in war emergency service. Hopes that the United States would remain the "Great Neutral" strained in 1940 as Paris fell and Italy entered the war. Back at home, the initiation of peacetime conscription by the Selective Training and Service Act set a somber mood. Throughout 1940, *The Museum News* continued to encourage members to keep track of developments in adult education and to purchase their three-volume set of the 730-page-long *The Museum in America: A Critical Study* for $7.50 postpaid.[1] By June, some 350 AAM members had gathered in Detroit for the annual meeting, which included transportation provided by the Ford Motor Company to and from all events not held in the headquarters hotel. These included a tour and luncheon at Greenfield Village as well as a tea at the Grosse Pointe home of Edsel B. Ford. The Museums Association, the AAM's British counterpart, which had been on war footing for nine months at this point, sent their US colleagues a telegram, which when read at the conference's opening session sent up a thunderous round of cheers. "Greetings to American colleagues," it read. "Our associations are linked by the same ideals. Long may these be defended."[2]

By March 1941, the Lend-Lease Act authorized provision of arms to Britain and other nations deemed critical to US defense. A month later, *Part I* of *Three Southern Neighbors: Ecuador, Peru, Bolivia* opened at the Newark Museum on Pan American Day, April 14. By June, advice on how to prepare US museums for the possibility of war now mingled in the pages of *The Museum News* with continued updates on hemispheric unity work. Reports of museum exhibits being newly provided to US Army bases filling up with conscripts began appearing too. By year's end, on a Tuesday morning, the Honolulu Academy of Arts would open its doors according to its usual schedule and welcome a dozen or so visitors to it galleries just two days after Pearl Harbor had been bombed.[3] Staff there and at the Bernice P. Bishop Museum had moved swiftly in the hours after the Pearl Harbor attack (and during their normal Monday closure) to put their emergency plans into play, starting with removal of selected collections materials to safer locales and followed by swift rearrangement of the galleries.

As earlier noted, US wartime involvement began not with Pearl Harbor but with the political, economic, and cultural mobilizations involved in constructing the hemispheric imaginary of the Good Neighborhood. Likewise, the nation as home front began forming in thought and policy as Americans in many fields, including museums, focused on preparedness for war. In this transitional period, the imagined communities of the "Good Neighborhood" and the "Home Front" coexisted, the first waning as the other waxed. The growing reality of war gave urgent, new context to continued debates about whether—and how, exactly—museums should function as social instruments. Those who envisioned museums as guiding lights to help citizens navigate a complex world saw war-related exhibitions as a path to public relevance. The more traditionally minded, particularly within the arts, placed greater value on the idea of the museum as a spiritual haven removed from current events so that it might better provide a refreshing pause from contemporary realities. Each version of the museum founds its place and neither existed in purity of form. Even reticent institutions, sometimes pressured by internal and external forces, eventually made some concession to wartime topics over the course of the conflict. Here, lectures, films, and other educational programs on defense gardening, first aid, nutrition, civilian morale, and profiles of the allied nations presented turnkey means to be of service. The more contentious issue now set before museums was the matter of determining the proper role of exhibition craft as means to engage wartime issues.

Looking to the British Example

By early 1941, *The Museum News* carried regular notices of bomb damage to British museums along with reports on their wartime activities. Museum boards in the United States began preparations to safeguard their holdings against the possibility of air raids, while at the federal level the Committee on Conservation of Cultural Resources drew up plans for the emergency care of collections and buildings.[4] The AAM, too, published advice on the topic.[5] In cautiously anticipating the worst, the AAM looked often to the example of the Museums Association, now weathering its second great war. Ralph H. Lewis, a field curator in the Museum Division of the US National Park Service, surveyed the *Museums Journal,* the Museums Association members' publication, and offered a summary of what he saw as the core policies most relevant to the field in America. These were: "1. insistence on the importance of museums," "2. gearing up museum services to meet war-time cultural needs," "3. cooperation in war measures," and "4. contribution of men."[6]

The first of these policies constituted institutional self-defense and called on the field to emphasize that "the regular functions of museums in preserving, increasing, and disseminating culture are so vital to society that they should be maintained in spite of the exigencies of war. This is more than an article of faith for museum workers; according to the policy it is an idea to be stated publicly and clung to in the face of opposition."[7] Indeed, the AAM urged member institutions to prepare to defend their importance by resisting efforts to have their facilities taken over by the military, local government, or others for emergency war use—even if such a policy came "dangerously close to arousing public opinion against museums."[8] While this counsel may seem overcautious for mainland museums far from theaters of war, some communities did call on municipally and state-funded museums to step up. For example, the US Navy temporarily displaced the Fine Arts Gallery of San Diego, the Museum of Man, and the Natural History Museum from their Balboa Park sites, which it used for supplementary hospitals.[9] In Britain, where most museums were government-subsidized, the Museums Association's president had to argue their wartime importance before Parliament when requesting that they not be closed or commandeered for military use. In the United States, this argument, the AAM agreed, would need to be made to the public, moneyed donors, and local officials rather than Congress—save for the few federally funded museums, including those of the National Park Service.

Throughout the war, US museums did make the argument for their importance in a variety of ways, from creating lounges for off-duty service personnel to mounting war-related exhibitions and programming to asserting the restorative value of time spent wholly apart from the anxieties of the day. They adjusted public hours to match factory shifts, waived admission fees, gave meeting space to community groups, and, "in cooperation with war measures," observed blackout regulations as well as supported war bond sales, scrap metal salvage drives, and other civic duty initiatives. Their curators, scientists, and other specialists lent expertise to the military, from designing camouflage and gear for bomber pilots to authoring navigational and field survival guides.

Such efforts were in keeping with the second policy provided in Lewis's accounting: "Gearing up museum services to meet war-time cultural needs." This topic, more than any other, reanimated the field's debates about the relationship of museum work to current affairs. The fiscal crisis and attending social disruptions of the 1930s, as well as a progressive spirit of social instrumentality, had led some to argue that museums needed to demonstrate their relevance more clearly or risk loss of both their cultural status and financial viability.[10] The prospect of war intensified discussions of how far from traditional practice the field ought to move in terms of directly engaging with civic issues through the medium of exhibition craft. Lewis and other proponents of demonstrative involvement noted:

> Exhibits are excellent means of teaching food conservation or war gardening practice. Museums are well equipped to illustrate the culture of allied countries, and to display objects and pictures showing the work of the armed forces. Direct cooperation between museums and morale officers to provide special service for soldiers probably falls in this category also. While perhaps not a major contribution to the war effort, museum cooperation in these matters can be very useful. At the same time it benefits museums by counteracting to some degree any unfavorable impressions created under the first-mentioned policy [of resisting

government or military impingement on museums' facilities and normal operations].[11]

Lewis argued that if the British experience in two successive wars was any indicator, US museums should view the new responsibilities of wartime as "exceptional opportunities" to meet their communities' needs; doing so ably would earn "a rich endowment of public good will." *What* exactly the public needed and *who* exactly constituted "the public" remained abstractions to be sorted out at the institutional level.

As much as the US museum field looked to the British example, it offered no lessons from its own responses to the Great War. AAM publications from the late 1910s contain but a few scattered reports of state commissions formed to collect posters, diaries, letters, and "relics" so that future generations could write the war's history. These notes also foregrounded museums' provision of specialized expertise to government, military, relief, and industrial entities.[12] Just a few exhibitions earned mention. *Minerals and Munitions* at the American Museum of Natural History (AMNH) in 1918 had illuminated war-essential natural resources.[13] At the Chicago Historical Society, a display of empty flour and potato sacks embroidered with symbols of international unity expressed the gratitude of Belgians for the war relief programs supported by Windy City residents. Some museums offered educational programs on war topics, and a few, lacking staff and funds, found it necessary to close for the brief duration of America's involvement. War service earned its place as a topic at AMM's 1918 annual meeting, alongside education, industrial relations, and installation problems.[14] Six months later Germany surrendered, and the field moved on.

Global Concerns and Alliances

While hemispheric unity work served as the dominant nexus for the exhibitionary network's efforts during the early 1940s, its security-minded ethos also supported museum-government exhibitions more directly concerned with war preparedness. *Can America Be Bombed?*, a touring display created by the Science Museum of the St. Paul Institute that debuted in April 1941, is one such example.[15] Designed as the first in a series of shows on national security, the exhibition received four thousand dollars for materials from the state of Minnesota's defense council, with twenty-four thousand dollars in labor for research, design, and fabrication activities provided by the Minnesota Art Project of the Works Progress Administration. The exhibition was intended to teach a public that still harbored isolationist sentiments about the nation's vulnerability to air attack and, in the subsequent units, about the need for land and sea defenses.[16] The project, initiated around 1939–40, took some two years to prepare. To more accurately communicate geospatial relationships, the museum had created spherical, concave, and convex map displays and giant hinged globes that could be opened and separated for wall-mounted, side-by-side display of the hemispheres. The St. Paul Science Museum even translated its exhibition design innovations into a short-lived wartime industry. One customer, the US Navy, contracted the museum to produce blackboard-surfaced globes for use as training aids.

After Pearl Harbor, the federal government funded duplication of the exhibit series so that it could be sent "throughout the land" and seen by a larger public newly and acutely interested in the topic of aerial bombardment.[17] On December 22, by which time *Can America Be Bombed?* was already on tour, *Time* magazine pronounced the St. Paul institution to be the "War-smartest museum in the U.S."[18] Meanwhile, the exhibition on view back in the science museum's own Minnesota galleries was the second in defense series, *Strategic Elements of Naval Warfare*. Although the show had opened five months earlier, staff now hustled to keep its variety of custom-made globes (some of which were at least six feet in height, and most of which could be spun or swung by visitors) up to date with developments in the Pacific. The museum workers, *Time* said, "were busy designing 'thrust arrows'" to indicate reported naval activities. They also had to update materials for *Can America Be Bombed?*. All prior calculations of possible flight ranges had assumed that pilots would reverse course based on the fuel reserves needed to return safely to their base of operations. As *Time* put it, "Until the Japanese crisis they had never considered the range of planes sent to die with their victims."

The director of the Science Museum of the St. Paul Institute, Louis H. Powell, PhD, who designed many of the innovations that made the outsize globes moveable and reconfigurable, later wrote with pride of the exhibition's widespread popularity and value as an education medium. "Not only was it displayed elsewhere within and outside the state," he said, "but it made museum history by surmounting the traditional barriers that separate art and science museums and appearing in leading museums of both kinds—the Buhl Planetarium [in Pittsburgh], the New York Museum of Science and Industry, the Toledo, Cleveland, and Minneapolis art museums, and the Albany Institute of History and Art."[19] Powell further noted, "Replicas of several of the units appeared in the rotundas of the office buildings of the House and Senate in Washington."[20] Lest he appear boastful in his assessment, Powell explained, "I mention these facts to establish the thought that here was something different and valid in a museum approach to the setting forth of elementary facts of geography for the benefit of the general public."

In addition to defense-minded educational efforts, exhibitions promoting kinship with America's allies did (true to Lewis's predictions) proliferate during the war, but here, too, the building of sympathetic bonds had begun before Pearl Harbor and concurrent with hemispheric unity work. These early efforts, which sometimes took place in conjunction with war relief fundraisers, roused US sympathies for embattled civilians in Britain, France, and the growing list of European nations invaded by Axis troops. Their affective tone urged charitable sympathy rather than the mutual dependence that undergirded Pan-Americanism. In this work, museums cooperated with aid societies and, through foreign embassies, with the various countries' information offices to create or take on loan exhibitions. Some carried pointed political messages, casting human suffering as the outcome of appeasement. The Museum of Fine Arts in Boston, for example, hosted a showing of contemporary British war cartoons in 1940 that exposed "the chicanery of Hitler, the bombast and cunning of Mussolini, the weakness of Chamberlain, the subterfuge of Japan, the mystery of Stalin."[21] Others, such as *War Comes to the People: A Story Written with the Lens* (discussed in chapter 4), which opened at the Museum of Modern Art (MoMA) in December 1940, wrapped the sympathetic impulse for the European plight into a cautionary tale for US isolationists to ponder.[22]

Once the United States entered the war, narratives that had constructed Allied nations first as victims of the Axis and then as casualties of indecisive political will were displaced by themes familiar from hemispheric unity initiatives. Cultural sharing as the root of common cause moved to the front. For example, the Toledo Museum of Art, which had received federal funding for its Good Neighbor effort *Chilean Contemporary Art*, devoted much of its 1942–43 season to *Art of Our Allies*. The museum's director announced the series by observing,

To the end of broadening our acquaintance with the cultures of our friends—and thus a museum wartime activity—we have arranged a series of showings for next season which will include Australian Art, Contemporary British Crafts, British Paintings and Prints, Chinese Art, Russian Paintings, and Dutch Paintings. We are also working on other projects pointed in the same direction. We believe that such exhibitions will give us, just as did the Chilean Contemporary Art of last season, a better basis for understanding the nature and mentality of peoples with whom it will be our pleasure as well as our duty to collaborate for a better and safer future.[23]

As noted, foreign government agencies often made available exhibits and materials for these Allied friendship displays. Such was the case with the Toledo Museum of Art's aforementioned British and Dutch shows, which were marshaled by the British Council and the Netherlands Information Bureau, respectively. Similarly, MoMA joined forces with the National Gallery (London) and the British Ministry of Information on *Britain at War* (May 22—September 2, 1941). This exhibition included examples of camouflage and other military work being undertaken by England's artists and designers; it also featured artists' impressions of the Great War and of current scenes, including Dunkirk and the Blitz, captured in a range of media. After its New York showing, versions of the exhibit toured to other US cities and Canada.

As with efforts to promote a sense of hemispheric belonging, cultivating affinity for Allied nations did not develop spontaneously or evenly across different classes of Americans. Aware of this, the US Office of War Information undertook a 1943 study of public sentiments toward the British. They wanted to determine whether Axis propaganda, which "scoffed at the concept of cultural kinship" between the two nations and blamed the empire for manipulating the United States into fighting its battles, had increased the number of Americans who already held such beliefs.[24] In general, even those who took a dim view of Britain, describing it as a classist, imperial bully affording little opportunity to the common man and likely to default on its war debts, found favor in the Brit's fighting spirit and the people's "ability to 'take it.'"[25] The fact that popular media, including exhibitions such as *Britain at War*, had earlier focused on portrayals of British grit no doubt aided in this later consensus.

US museums also made their "contribution of men"—and women—to the armed forces, Red Cross, and other war-critical fields. This left many institutions understaffed and a few temporarily shuttered. The dwindling of WPA funding and then, in 1943, its cessation exacerbated budgetary losses. With men exiting their positions in greater numbers relative to female staff, women had new opportunities to step into more prominent roles—some at institutions to which they had already devoted years of service. Such advances came, however, with a host of new operational burdens and often without pay raises reflective of their expanded duties or commensurate with men's salaries. It is fair to say, based on my differently focused examination of archival records, that to truly understand the shape of the field during the war, a museum history devoted to women's experiences, accomplishments, impacts on practice, and postwar trajectories is needed.

While much of what Lewis augured describes the general contours of US museums' wartime work, his statements did not anticipate a primary tension within the field: sorting out whether, under war conditions, social instrumentality through exhibition craft would set museums more firmly on the path to civic relevance or steer them away from the truth of things. After December 7, 1941, such musings over the possible impact of war on US museums became moot. The AAM urged reasonable precautions based on geographical location to assure the safety of collections, staff, and visitors; it also exhorted members to remember the duties "from which they must not retreat":

> Now is the time to show what faith we have in the usefulness of our institutions. Surely no museum should close its doors or put itself practically out of business by extensive evacuation of collections or by sand-bagging and other digging-in to the point of becoming comparatively useless to the public. Any exhibits removed should be replaced by other and more timely exhibits. Temporary exhibitions and educational efforts that bear on subjects of the day or on parts of the world in which the public is most interested at the moment can have more than ordinary attention. . . . Museums have always made notable progress in times of disturbance. They have great opportunities now.[26]

This notion of a silver lining to wartime disruptions became a recurring theme. It echoed pronouncements of the 1930s that had cast the Depression's upheavals as opportunities for museums to exert their value as social instruments.[27]

While patriotism and the continuing mission to prove their social worth provided incentive for museums to adopt wartime programming, the need to attract the public played a role as well. Declining attendance had been both a worry and an impetus to change at the end of the 1930s.[28] The nation's entry into war may have exacerbated this trend. Chicago's museums, for example, reported a 20 to 30 percent decrease in attendance for the first four months of 1942 compared to the same period the year before.[29] A report by the Museum Council of New York City also showed sizable declines in attendance compared to 1941. The Brooklyn Museum had some 142,000 fewer visits, representing a 27 percent decrease, and the Metropolitan Museum of Art's attendance shrunk by 13 percent as it realized a loss of nearly 132,400 visits.[30] The American Museum of Natural History saw a visitation shortfall of 14 percent, while other cultural institutions, such as the Brooklyn Botanic Garden, the New York Public Library, and the New York Zoological Garden, saw decreases ranging from 5 to 32 percent. One of the two museums cited as enjoying an increase in attendance was the Museum of Modern Art, which claimed over 5,300 additional visits in 1942 compared to 1941.[31] MoMA, which is the focus of chapter 4, bucked the downward trend while *Road to Victory: A Procession of Photographs of the Nation at War* (May 21–October 4, 1942) was in the galleries. Some eighty thousand people, 29 percent of the year's total attendance, reportedly came to see that exhibit.[32]

Serving on the Psychological Front

By the time of the AAM's annual meeting in May 1942, many museums had already made an initial response to the war through special exhibitions and programs. Just as "Defense and Hemisphere Solidarity" had provided the programmatic focus in 1941, the "Wartime Duties of Museums" now fostered sessions on "public service and the positive side of emergency work."[33] The AAM reported than more than two hundred attendees from twenty-six states and "5 parts" of Canada had convened in Colonial Williamsburg, Virginia, a site that added "a keynote of patriotic and professional interest" to the conference.[34] This meeting would prove to be the AAM's last during the war, as travel and other restrictions prevented the membership from formally gathering again until 1946.[35] More than seventy speakers, representing the different disciplinary types of museums and specialists working within them, presented on the wartime duties topic. Several of the papers reached wider audiences as *The Museum News* featured them in issues over the next year and half.

Concerns voiced at the meeting included how to operate, let alone meet new public needs, with tightened budgets and staff made leaner as personnel left for military duty or higher wages in war-related industries. The causes cited for flagging museum attendance included reduced leisure time owing to war-related work and volunteerism and reduced visitation from outlying areas due to rubber and gasoline restrictions. Some directors expected a "certain amount of neglect, perhaps even scorn" from the public given that museums' usual cultural functions would seem of secondary importance during the war.[36] Others, however, noted that many places of recreation, from golf links to racetracks, still attracted patrons in substantial numbers. This meant, they said, that the fault also lay with museums whose "lack of promotional planning and poor showmanship" had failed to draw the public to their doors.[37]

A poll of fifty museum directors conducted prior to the conference confirmed that obtaining public support was a chief concern of leadership. The poll had been fielded by famed public relations counsel and author of the book *Propaganda* (1928), Edward L. Bernays, who the AAM had invited to speak at the annual meeting. His address, "The Museum's Job in Wartime," touched on the survey's top worries, which he summarized as: "(1) the matter of inadequate contributions and inadequate membership, and (2) the problem of getting people to use the museum and to recognize that attendance at museums is something they should do."[38] Then there was the matter of how to maintain interest once the public, in its various ages, backgrounds, and requirements, got through the museum's doors. To set the stage for his advice to museums on how to improve their public standing while also weathering the war, Bernays said, "The exigencies of total warfare demand that every institution in the democracy re-examine, re-evaluate itself to find its place in a democracy under these wartime conditions, and to fit itself effectively into the peace that will follow the war."[39] Because the field had little to offer the nation's economic and military campaigns, museums' place, he argued, was on the "vital internal psychological front."[40] Here, a peoples' belief in common goals, in each other, in shared sacrifice, and a shared future could be created through reason, authority, factual evidence, persuasion, emotion, and tradition (i.e., collective memory).

Museums, as their first duty, Bernays argued, stood fully equipped to support national morale through exhibits. In any disciplinary field, factual evidence, combined with appeals to emotion and tradition, could build morale *and* modify attitudes. Their second duty would be provision of "constructive escapism" to refresh the spirit and "give rise to clarified thought and action."[41] Fostering democratic individualism constituted their third function. On this score, Bernays noted, "This war is being waged in part to emphasize the value of the individual man, the creative spirit of the individual, as opposed to the mass spirit of the state. Creative man thrives in a democracy, is thwarted, frustrated, and suppressed by Fascism and Nazism." As to the larger aim, gaining publicity and public support through such work, Bernays counseled that each museum must first have clear objectives and, second, undertake a study of its community in order to understand localized interests; only then might both wars be won.

As in the 1930s, debate continued over the matter of whether an exhibition that educated with a purpose and social action in mind constituted too great a departure from standards of objective museology. Indeed, depending on where one stood on the issue, terms such as "propaganda" and "showmanship" carried quite different meanings. For avid proponents of popularizing museums, showmanship meant adapting proven mass communications and publicity techniques not only to attract adult patrons in greater numbers but also, more importantly, to transform their curiosity into the desire for knowledge and new understanding. Storytelling, a hallmark of the material rhetoric of instrumentality, served to encourage the public to drink from the deep, clear well of museums' object-based knowledge. Proponents also continued to emphasize equipping citizens to evaluate information, reject fifth-column enticements, and make reasoned, independent decisions that conduced to the collective good of the democracy.

Writing on this subject in 1941, Ned Burns, head of the National Park Service's museum division, had noted, "The dry and technical facts of history and science can be given a truthful presentation without loss of their inherent dramatic possibilities."[42] In this view, story was not so much imposed on artifacts as teased out of them. "The unique value of the museum as a teaching and inspirational medium lies in the fact that it presents objective evidence," Burns wrote. "No copy, reproduction, or facsimile can equal the power of the original."[43] This made exhibitions as storytelling vehicles quite unlike "the books, periodicals, lectures, radio programs, and motion pictures which reach our people in a constantly increasing volume."[44] Historic sites, such as those under Burns's watch, added outdoor experiences into the bargain; these provided a "double-barrelled opportunity to couple physical and mental recreation with inspiration and the imparting of sound knowledge."[45] Here, the sensory nature of embodied encounters, such as walking across a battlefield or crouching to enter a pioneer's log cabin, could provoke a visceral, affective response, "a feeling akin to acquaintance and participation," he said.

Viewing, too, might produce such effects *if* museums employed good showmanship. After clarifying that he used "this term in its finest sense," Burns noted that the basics of good showmanship meant attentiveness to such practical (but neglected) details as tidy, uncrowded, well-lit arrangements accompanied by well-worded, legibly printed labels and, where useful, communication through symbols. The real keys, however, were to humanize the story being told and to facilitate the "telling power" of museum artifacts.[46] This conception of exhibition craft as scaffolding that enhanced object "telling power" resonates with Jane Bennett's theories on vibrant matter, in which object agency is a relational production of human-object encounter. Looking beyond the plethora of founding father sites and battlefields under his care, Burns also envisioned applying this approach to cultural and economic histories as well as to the lives of poets, writers, inventors, and scientists.

Burns, who approached civic need from a federal vantage point and through the prism of sites rooted in national lore and identity, argued that objective evidence relayed with showmanship would inspire patriotism rooted in truth and able to withstand the "peddlers of honey-coated venom" who undermined public morale. A year later, L. Hubbard Shattuck, director of the Chicago Historical Society, echoed these sentiments as he pointed to the example of France, where, in his view, the people's loss of faith in democratic principles had preceded—and facilitated—its shockingly swift collapse. For this reason, Shattuck argued, fortification of morale constituted history museums' primary role in wartime, not only for the public good but for that of museums as well. "If they are to survive," he said, "they must justify their experience as a vital element of community and national life. Our danger comes not alone from enemy military force, but also through propaganda directed toward our civilian disintegration. It is against these negative forces of internal disruption that historical museums must strike a most effective blow, and thus assist in the uniting of our people in the common national cause."[47] However, two obstacles stood in the way. The first concerned inconsistencies in how various agencies at the federal, state, and municipal levels viewed and classified museums. Classification had direct bearing on visitation, funding, and other operational necessities. To underscore the importance of this issue, Shattuck gave as an example an adverse ruling by the State Rationing Administrator of the Chicago Metropolitan region that had explained why his own institution had seen an unexpected drop in visits by school groups. Whereas revised tire-rationing regulations continued to permit the use of buses to ferry children and teachers to and from schools, their use for fieldtrips to any sort of museum was now prohibited. One can almost hear Shattuck's spitting fury in the following line from his AAM conference paper: "Permit me to emphasize that museums have been classified as recreational rather than educational institutions, and are placed under the same restrictions as amusement parks and other purely recreational centers."[48] Shattuck called on the AAM to study and publish guidelines to advocate for proper recognition of museums "as centers of learning rather than amusement" and urged his peers to work with local government, civic groups, and national authorities to make clear museums' "patriotic as well as educational usefulness."[49]

The second challenge was poor exhibition craft. Shattuck, like Burns before him, took the view that displays lacking in "dramatic or living value" also lacked in purpose and thus failed to earn the attention of a critical, even suspicious, utilitarian-minded public whose rising generations, in particular, had no time for "pleasant mustiness."[50] The shades of distinction practitioners saw between deceptive propaganda and that based in objective truth permeates the speech. For example, while eyebrows today might be raised at Shattuck's declaration that history museums "should become the shrines of true Americanism" in their communities, he states with equal certainty their duty to present "the virtues as well as the failures of the past." Not only did Shattuck's address reach a wider audience through *The Museum News*, his home institution also made it available as a ten-page booklet.[51]

At the same meeting, Albert Eide Parr, director of the American Museum of Natural History in New York, spoke on the matter of how, in his field, patriotic usefulness and educational usefulness fit together. He agreed that museums had a "stupendous responsibility to the future of democracy" but noted that the very need to debate and define museums' wartime duties revealed "the painful anxiety and uncertainty with which we search for our proper function in the national struggle for a better future."[52] Certainly, all museum folk with expertise applicable to the war effort should give it, but the redirection of usual museum functions, he said, needed a guiding credo. Parr offered his own, which he described as born of late-night scrutiny and daytime testing: to serve through war-related "special research" when called and "in problems of morale," to build relations with US allies, and to provide "educational preparation of the public mind for the problems of peace."[53] Natural history museums, for example, could foster knowledge about the world, its peoples, climates, and natural resources.

As with his compatriots in history, Parr saw propaganda as having more than one nature. As to its dark side, he warned, "the museum, should, of course, carefully refrain from presenting anything but the known facts, and should not make themselves into organs of propaganda for some particular theory or point of view, however much it might be favored by the museum staff."[54] This did not, however, preclude museum fare from contributing to cultural diplomacy, an area in which he felt that the "propaganda potential of museum" had been "miserably neglected so far." In particular, he thought natural history specimens were underutilized good will ambassadors. Unlike the rarified art exhibit, which might be as likely to create "displeasure as pleasure," public dissatisfaction at exhibitions in his field was "as rare as dodo," Parr crowed with no small amount of bias.[55] The displeasure revealed in this remark is Parr's own over the preeminence of art in government-supported hemispheric unity efforts.

Art museums, which as a category had been less inclined to employ a material rhetoric of social instrumentality within their galleries before the war, now voiced reticence about the need to change intrinsic practices involving the public. This sharpened the prior decade's tussles between curators and the newer ranks of purpose-trained museum educators over control of public education, exhibition, and the ideological functions of collection objects. Trends in display craft that emphasized culture history at the expense of an aesthetic focus had, for example, been a development some feared populist education and civic instrumentality would only exacerbate. "The task of art museums in war time as in peace time is to provide spiritual refreshment through the resources of one of the realms of the spirit—to minister to the inalienable right to the pursuit of happiness, in the enjoyment of 'living breathing form,'" said Fiske Kimball, director of the Philadelphia Art Museum, to his colleagues.[56] Furthermore, once art museums had taken necessary measures to safeguard their most valuable treasures, they should, he said, "Go right on doing essentially what we have been doing, not for the sake of 'business as usual,' but because what we were doing is still the right thing to do."[57]

Kimball's words stand as a clear rebuttal to Lewis's earlier article in *The Museum News*. Lewis had stated that museums most certainly should carry on their ordinary work, but, he said, "This does not imply 'business as usual.'"[58] Kimball did concede, "All museums with programs worth their salt have always tried to pay attention to actuality, to timeliness, in exhibitions, in activities," and he trusted that this would continue. Even as the war progressed, Kimball remained steadfast in his view that art museums served their publics best when remaining above the fray of civic affairs. In 1943 he wrote, "A world in flames has confronted art museums with an alternative: of making frantic efforts to serve, for the most part badly, purposes for which they are ill adapted, or of continuing calmly to serve well their characteristic purpose, as a haven of serenity, peace and rest. We have not hesitated to choose the latter, and the public—whether of war workers, or of men on leave from the services, or of relatives who must wait in anxiety—seems to have ratified the choice."[59]

The vice director of New York's Metropolitan Museum of Art, Horace H. F. Jayne, took a similar view, flatly stating, "As a general topic 'the Art Museum in Wartime' is, in the full sense of the word, a dreadful one. It is rather like that of 'the Church in Wartime.' I can imagine any preacher being rather appalled when asked to answer the question 'what is your church going to do in the war?'"[60] Imagining art museums as quasi-sacred spaces underscored that while they existed in the world, they were not fully of it; they looked chiefly to eternal rather than ephemeral concerns. The Association of Art Museum Directors outlined these spiritual functions in a release issued after Pearl Harbor that ran not only in the profession's publications but in daily newspapers as well. The thing enshrined by art museums was no less than the spirit of freedom itself; collections, no matter their contexts, now constituted "the visible activity of free minds."[61] The valorization of individual creativity stood in opposition to the mass mind of

Nazism and fascism. As a civic paradigm for art museums, this reinforced that their existing states of arrangement and function already supplied the communion and communication necessary to "fortify the spirit on which Victory depends."[62] Certainly, other museum types, especially those focused on history, also claimed to enshrine essential civic values for public benefit, but they professed a greater openness to making relevance, or at least relationships, to current affairs more explicit in their presentations.

Also from the Metropolitan Museum of Art's ranks but carrying a rather different message was Theodore L. Low, whose book *The Museum as a Social Instrument* was already causing a stir.[63] His words to meeting attendees were no less rousing. "Today we have the collections which our predecessors formed," he said. "We can thank them for them and we can build soundly on what we have. But it is time that museums should stop the emphasis on collecting and become social institutions in practice rather than in imagination."[64] For Low, this meant widening the scope of museum's adult education initiatives so that they reached beyond the small circle of current partakers whose educational, social, and financial attainment made them an elite minority. As for exhibitions, aside from the one or two a year that might fruitfully be created by an art museum's curators for a small coterie of experts, Low thought the bulk of these should come under the direction of educational staff who, after all, were "closest to the public pulse."[65] Museums' wartime task, Low told his assembled colleagues, was to admit their shortcomings as *public* organizations and to set in place policies that would finally realize the field's long-standing claims to be "social institutions operating for the greatest good of the greatest number."[66] Not long after the meeting, Low entered the US Army, serving two of his three years in India. On his return stateside in 1946, he became director of educational activities at the Walters Art Gallery and held the position until his retirement in 1980.[67] After his death in 1987 at the age of seventy, colleagues recalled him as "a kind of evangelist for the cause of art and public education. He was a real Jeffersonian Democrat, believing in education as the salvation of the people."[68] Low's obituary included a quote from *The Museum as Social Instrument* and noted the importance of that 1942 work.

Arthur C. Parker, another voice for museums' social instrumentality and now eighteen years into his directorship of the Rochester Museum of Arts and Sciences, also presented at the conference. Following the Great War and through the "social groping" of the Depression, museums had been growing, Parker said, "with a new emphasis upon service and participation in community life."⁶⁹ However, he continued, so long as museums' place in civic life remained unclear outside and even inside the field, museums would not be taken "seriously as a part of the social and political structure" of the country. Parker, who had informally polled colleagues about what their museums planned to do with regard to the war, reported some of their responses. With these, he underscored that war-related exhibitions could be vehicles for timely public education *and* also remain faithful to disciplinary standards. The Cranbrook Institute of Science in Bloomfield Hills, Michigan, for example, emphasized that "in a manner consistent with honesty," its new exhibit on Japan and the Indies was "aimed not at patriotism, not for propaganda but towards understanding. Why? Because we want to have the reputation for honesty in 1942 as we hope we had in 1941."⁷⁰ Similarly, the North Carolina Historical Commission noted its exhibits of the war would be "designed to spread ideas and information, and not to arouse Rah-rah patriotism."⁷¹

Just as the profession had initially been wary of accepting federal funds in the 1930s for concern that such largesse might invite government influence over museums' affairs, it remained mindful now of the political uses to which the Axis had put museums, art, and culture. The AAM's acting president, Clark Wissler of the AMNH, warned, "There are examples in parts of the world of how museums may be used by government for direct propaganda. The spectacle is not inviting. . . . The curator should watch his step. Trustees and public officials are the most likely pressure groups for propaganda objectives. They have power to force the curator's hand. Let us hope that the museum of the future escapes the hard fist of political and social propaganda so that it may continue to be a place of intellectual freedom."⁷² One of Wissler's concerns related to this was who, exactly, had greatest control over the development of a museum's chief educational instrument: the exhibition. "The expected evolution of new types of showmanship in museum exhibitions," he warned, "will tend more and more to separate the functions of the curator and the educator."⁷³ The result? Scientists, curators, and others on the research side of the house would provide lists of facts, with the educators deciding on selection, treatment, and the interpretive act of writing labels. While Wissler did not see this as a happy outcome, he did advocate strongly for updating exhibits to keep pace with the production of knowledge.

As to how the AMNH, after its hemispheric unity work, went on to engage wartime topics, *Animals and the War* (1943) is an example. In part this exhibit provided a straightforward history of mammals pressed into military service, from Hannibal's elephants to contemporary uses of reindeer, dogs, and camels.[74] An additional set of painted vignettes drew parallels between "the weapons of animal warfare" and "the unending race between offensive weapons and defensive measures" that characterized the new world war.[75] The spitting cobra's "blinding spray of venom" functioned like a flamethrower, the octopus's ink served as a smoke screen, and the so-called "four-eyed" fish's double-focus ocular lens mirrored the submarine's ability to detect enemies both above and below the ocean's surface. Such analogies stretched humorously thin in a few labels, such as that likening two desert lizards taking cover from a hawk to quick-witted persons escaping aerial attack by dashing to an air raid shelter.

Also worried over what Wissler called the "illy defined border zone between scientific honesty and salesmanship" was colleague Margaret Mead. Writing for a wider audience, Mead observed,

> During the last few years museums have been criticized as old-fashioned, out-of-date, lacking in verve and splash and modernity. The critics have called many of the exhibition methods stuffy and conventional and have lamented the slow and careful pace to which museum staffs have held in the modernization of exhibits. The high-pressure salesmanship of modern advertising has been recommended to us. We have been urged to think more of influencing the moods of our visitors and less of fidelity to our materials. Those who seek to find among the American people the enthusiasm for national ends which is so essential, find that again and again they are faced with cynicism and apathy, in people who feel they have been over-propagandized, over-sold. The tricks of the propagandist have been labeled and displayed, the machinations of the advertiser are known to everyone, the public is dishearteningly canny, suspicious of every means of communication open to those who would fire the imagination of the people with the importance of the present hour. Dishearteningly suspicious they are—except of museums. Because the staffs of museums have insisted on saying: "Is this true?" instead of asking: "Will this make a hit?"—they have kept the people's trust."[76]

The scholar Fred Turner has connected Mead's thoughts on museums, exhibition craft, and propaganda to her work as a member of the National Committee for Morale, which sought to forge communicative works that could lead to an embrace, both reasoned and heartfelt, of national common cause.[77] It is also he who coined the earlier-mentioned term "democratic surround" to describe the immersive, multimedia environments influenced by new psychological theories about the culturally determined nature of national character. It is important to note that Mead's thoughts on the museum as medium also reflect the field's ongoing concerns with the matter of social instrumentality through exhibition craft, concerns that, as shown here, predated and also informed museums' wartime activities.

So, what of the more progressive, albeit narrowly so, aspirations of the museum as social instrument envisioned in the 1930s? Certainly, practitioners continued to share their success stories, many of which had been supported by the WPA, on in to the 1940s. For example, Frank L. DuMond of the Grand Rapids Public Museum reported on what might today be called a community-engaged exhibition. Speaking of how a withering 87 percent budget reduction inspired ideas "so obvious we wondered why we hadn't thought of them before," DuMond talked of forming a committee of city and nearby community residents to develop an exhibition and programming on their shared Dutch heritage.[78] Here, the material rhetoric of social instrumentality resided not so much in the resulting display as in the network of relationships coalescing through and around "family heirlooms" during the exhibit's making. The intergenerational effort, DuMond observed, instilled in youth a sense of pride in their heritage, where previously they had been ashamed of their elders' "Old-World ways and dialect."[79] The seniors benefited, too, from a renewed sense of their value as community builders. It also inspired other ethnic groups to approach the museum. The popularity of the affair not only helped rescue the museum from threat of closure but also aided it in securing a new purpose-built home, where community-involved work continued on a more modest, sporadic scale through the temporary exhibits program.[80]

Two exhibitions of the early war period that exemplify social instrumentality in their design *and* intent are *The Great Idea* (January 14–February 26, 1942) and *Wartime Housing* (April 22–June 21, 1942). The first appeared at Vassar College's Social Museum and was produced by students under the direction of faculty, some of whom also served as the museum's staff.

Following the tradition of social museums, *The Great Idea* conveyed its message about the country's racial and religious demographics through maps, models, photographs, and statistical charts rather than with collections' artifacts in the traditional sense. Although the exhibit's contents did not make explicit reference to the war, its title, taken from Walt Whitman's "By Blue Ontario's Shore," made clear the type of national unity its creators sought to encourage:

> For the great Idea, the idea of perfect and free individuals,
> For that, the bard walks in advance, leader of leaders,
> The attitude of him cheers up slaves and horrifies foreign despots.[81]

News of the exhibit ran in the *New York Times* under the headline "Racial Freedom Shown at Vassar."[82] Like other reviews, this one noted the exhibit's connections through Vassar personnel and alumni to the National Conference for Christians and Jews. Another accounting made plain the idea that campus and public visitors should take from display: "From the first 'we' to the final appeal for religious freedom, *We need the Catholic, We need the Protestant, We need the Jew*, the exhibit built up in the spectator a compelling sense of personal pride in this composite nation which is creating 'out of diversity, Strength' and of personal challenge in the economic, social, religious, and psychological barriers which hamper individual development and limit national greatness."[83] Whereas *The Great Idea* emerged from a social museum, a short-lived genre already on the wane in the United States when Vassar founded theirs in 1937, *Wartime Housing* hailed from an institution very much on the rise: the Museum of Modern Art.[84] Both efforts also marked the carrying forward into the war years of earlier traditions of using social documentary photography in exhibitions to direct civic action and reform, as will be explored through the next chapter's analysis of the making, form, and mixed aims of *Wartime Housing*.

As 1942 wore on, few museums could ignore the war's impact on day-to-day operations, particularly if they were situated along the coasts. Museums followed blackout procedures, canceled galas that now seemed ill-timed, and hosted films and presentations on civilian defense. They moved collections off-site and equipped themselves with axes, steel helmets, flashlights, and first aid kits; established air raid procedures; and stocked Foamite and dry ice should the need arise to battle chemical fires ignited by incendiary bombs. In addition to such defensive measures, museums did, as noted, mount a flurry of exhibitions and other programming related to wartime topics. Based on the evidence reviewed, few developed cohesive or farsighted visions about their role on the home front. Most proceeded on an ad hoc basis as fluctuations in staffing, finances, internal politics, and institutional interests dictated. The Museum of Modern Art, dubbed Uncle Sam's strangest recruit, proved the exception in terms of its government ties, prolific output, and receipt of federal commissions and funding. Still, most museums did enter the cultural fray as a means to demonstrate their wartime worth—some whole-heartedly as an aspect of their social instrumentality, others as token interruptions to a sense of mission largely unruffled by war, and most taking positions somewhere in between. Even those institutions whose leaders had voiced the gravest misgivings at the 1942 AAM conference eventually offered up war-related programming of some fashion. Not infrequently, these efforts came in the form of circulating exhibitions created by their less reticent peers.

It may not seem unusual, in retrospect, that museums played a part in the all-out cultural mobilization of World War II. After all, war themes inflected all manner of media, from films and radio programs to advertisements and songs to art and design. What has been lost in museum histories of the period, when it is not altogether ignored, is how those in the field viewed, debated, and staked out their modes of wartime participation in relationship to their sense of public mission. The heady task of reconciling mission, aspiration, and new modes of public communication fomented division and discussion. Revealed in these debates is the dilemma that the adoption of the storytelling approach to exhibition craft posed for the field—a dilemma compounded by museums' didactic aims *and* the goal of some to foster better-informed democratic decision making by becoming an audible, authoritative voice in the competitive public square of media communications.

Together, these aims foregrounded the rhetorical nature of exhibition craft, setting this aspect of museum work on more obvious shared footing with other communicative acts, from educational persuasion to "black" propaganda, designed with influence in mind. In other words, moves to embrace the storytelling paradigm drew back the museum's curtain of objectivity; it forced discussions about the gray areas of subjectivity involved in human-thing meaning making—on both the curatorial and public sides of the exhibition as site of encounter. The reasons for describing this shift as a development in material rhetoric are two. First, taken in its classical sense, rhetoric provides a useful framework for analyzing how the various, multiple elements in the period's storytelling exhibitions integrated appeals to the audience's logic (logos), emotions (pathos), and desire for credible expertise grounded in (what were perceived as) right values (ethos). Here, one can see the parallel to Laurence Vail Coleman's 1939 statement that described well-balanced approaches as those that sought to address the museumgoer-as-learner in their mental, emotional, and physical capacities so that "thought, feeling and action" might be directed toward the common good of informed participation in civic matters. The second reason for using rhetoric as an analytical lens through which to examine the relationship between exhibition craft and social instrumentality more specifically is that, as other museum studies scholars have shown, rhetoric encompasses not only the creation and content of the communications but the experiencing of it as well.[85] And it is to this, the experiencing of the home front not as an individual passage but as a shared civic identity and state of belonging that we turn next.

Chapter Four

WITNESSING WAR FARE

The Construction of Home-Front Citizenship

> Geared as your program is to the war effort, you manage to elevate the stark realities of today into something quite awesome and beautiful. . . . The present is easier to bear and the future looms up brighter because of what the Museum of Modern Art is doing for Society.
>
> —Parent of a serviceman and renewing member of the Museum of Modern Art, October 1943

After the attack on Pearl Harbor, institutional responses to the many questions around how museums should or should not engage with the current events of war rapidly moved from the realm of idealistic pronouncement to the reality-born and compromise-shaped facts of practice. In much of this work and across a range of topics, museums made tangible the new imagined community of the Home Front. Media of all types routinely placed home, hearth, and family at the emotional heart of wartime appeals. This comes as no surprise. Issues of politics and identity are often refracted through the lens of the domestic sphere, conflating the private family and its concerns with larger issues faced by the imagined national and international families. Museum exhibitions, with their ability to materialize the normally private domestic sphere as a collective, public site, served as spaces within which belonging to the national family could be both performed and witnessed. Through such work museums also asserted *their* belonging within the body politic.

Exhibitions that dealt with home-front issues did more than contribute to "the maintenance of national morale," as the National Resources Planning Board, other agencies, and the field itself hoped would be the case.[1] They also taught and reinforced particular ways of performing, or embodying, home-front citizenship, often through habits of material use and consumption. Sometimes accompanied by live demonstrations or movies, such exhibitions configured belonging through the purchases one did or did not make, the way one washed clothes and maintained old appliances, planted a Victory garden, cooked vegetables, or saved toothpaste tubes for salvage. *The Homemaker and the War* (1942), held at the Chicago Museum of Science and Industry in conjunction with the Westinghouse Electric and Manufacturing Company, promised to immerse female museumgoers in "the best ways to do all that is expected of them as patriotic housewives."[2] *Home Front Homes,* an exhibit by the Carolina Art Association shown at the Gibbes Memorial Art Gallery in Charleston, South Carolina, offered its community "practical ideas on how to furnish a home comfortably and attractively in wartime at low cost with old furniture ingeniously used, wartime substitutes, space saving devices, and color harmonies."[3] The exhibition's centerpiece was a prefabricated house of the sort designed for defense workers. It was erected within the gallery and furnished for use by an imaginary couple, Mr. and Mrs. R. U. Worthy, and their three children. To the north, in Pittsfield, Massachusetts, the Berkshire Museum organized a program for newcomers drawn to its county by war production jobs. In addition to introducing the area's educational, recreational, and scenic opportunities—and the museum itself—the event also encouraged recent arrivals to meet each other as well as the public officials in attendance.[4]

Other efforts included the Brooklyn Museum's *The Consumer Front: Essential Wartime Economics* (1942) and *Inventions for Victory* (1942–43). The latter, like the Museum of Modern Art's *Useful Objects in Wartime under $10* (1942–43; the fifth installation of the *Useful Objects* series), featured home goods in line with the standards of the Conservation and Substitution Branch of the War Production Board. After all, the agency urged museumgoers, "If the Axis civilians can part with many peacetime luxuries, for the sake of their soldiers, we think American civilians can do that job better, too."[5] The bonds of home even extended to reviving American-Soviet friendship for the good of the war effort. The Office of War Information's photo-narrative exhibition *Two Allies—One War—One Peace,* which showed at the New York Museum of Science and Industry in 1943, featured an installation of two kitchens, one American and one Soviet. Here, on this common ground, despite the vast geographic and ideological distances separating the two, each ally shared the plight of mealtime under rationing.[6] (Ironically, it would be in another kitchen, one featured in the 1959 American National Exhibition in Moscow, that leaders of the former allies antagonistically debated whether capitalism or communism best serve the common man.[7])

For practitioners and museums entering the war period guided by notions of social instrumentality, engaging with such contemporary realities was not a dilemma but a duty. However, without the bedrock of established practices on which to build, each undertaking stood as an experiment in discovering how to develop a material rhetoric of social instrumentality. The aim, as Laurence Vail Coleman had phrased it in 1939, was to construct a balanced experience that addressed museumgoers' mental, emotional, and physical capacities for knowing—and to do so in a fashion true to the objects displayed and true to democratic principles of civic education, whereby individuals would come away inspired to think, feel, and act for greater social goods.

The difficulties of striking that balance are exemplified in the Museum of Modern Art's *Wartime Housing* (April 22–June 21, 1942), an exhibition undertaken in collaboration with the National Committee on the Housing Emergency and the National Housing Agency. The making of *Wartime Housing* illuminates how the rekindled spirit of social reform struggled to persist by seeking openings within both the public's and the museum field's rising sense of national duty. Ultimately, the strategy proved an uneasy fit, with messages of reform yielding to visions of social continuity. *Wartime Housing*'s material expression is illuminating, too. Similar to social reform exhibitions of the Progressive Era, it consisted solely of photographic reproductions, charts, and models, all of which had been created (and, in some cases, remediated) specifically for—or, more precisely, *as*—the exhibition. Here, the rhetoric of social instrumentality as a simultaneous appeal to mind, body, and emotion is richly evident in the exhibition's deployments of space, moving and still images, light, sound, textures, and other elements. Described as an "exhibition in 10 scenes," *Wartime Housing*'s stated purpose was to educate communities and decision makers about the urgent need for worker accommodations, to present modern architecture as the socially progressive solution, and to provide practical guidelines for meeting long-term as well as immediate civic needs.[8]

"Propaganda for Freedom"

In 1939, MoMA celebrated its tenth anniversary by moving to 11 West 53rd Street, the facility it still occupies today (although in considerably altered and expanded form). Via radio address, President Roosevelt marked the occasion by dedicating the building "to the cause of peace and the pursuits of peace."[9] His speech also made clear, however, the museum's role in the ideological war already underway. Individuality, creative artistic expression, and democracy, he argued, flourished in common soil. MoMA's mission to bring through its expanded definition of art and its circulating exhibitions the best of cultural production to "all of the American people" placed the museum in opposition, Roosevelt argued, to nondemocratic conditions that would have life turned into "a routine," society into "a regiment," and the world itself into "a stereotype." Allan Wallach has termed this span in MoMA's history its "utopian moment."[10] Certainly, MoMA's aims to influence modern aesthetics not only in the sphere of the fine arts but in the commercial and civic realms, too, resonated with calls to remake museums into social instruments. It echoed, too, of course, Progressive Era museums' interests in shaping mass manufacture and consumption.

Because of its emphasis on contemporary works and embrace of cinema, photography, architecture, and industrial design as artistic forms, MoMA saw itself, in the words of its founding and wartime director, Alfred H. Barr Jr., as "untypical in its field and in much of its work."[11] The museum certainly proved unique in the number of war-related exhibitions it produced, the extent of its financial involvement with the government side of the exhibitionary network, and in having a ready-made program for circulating exhibitions. The latter sent thirty-eight different wartime exhibitions, twenty-three of which had first shown at MoMA in fuller form, to factories, hospitals, army camps, and United Services Organization centers, as well as to the colleges, museums, and community sites that routinely sought out its offerings.[12] Some exhibits also went abroad, occasionally with financial support from the Office of War Information (OWI). While a number of museums provided recreation lounges, classes, and other programs for service personnel, MoMA went beyond the norm here, too, thanks to Abby Aldrich Rockefeller, a MoMA founder and mother to OCIAA head Nelson A. Rockefeller. She spearheaded development of the museum's Armed Services Program. This effort not only made museum space and special events available to the Allied Nations' personnel on leave in New York but also brought art displays and supplies to domestic military installations and promoted arts therapy. This latter focus evolved into "the child of Mrs. Rockefeller's imagination," the War Veterans Art

Center, which endeavored to reorient returning combatants to civilian life through therapeutic and prevocational arts programs.[13]

In addition, like other museums, MoMA had begun materializing the Home Front imaginary simultaneous with its contributions to the Good Neighborhood. Consistent with its mission to influence contemporary design, MoMA hosted and exhibited the winning results of two competitions, *Posters for National Defense* (July–September 1941) and *Image of Freedom* (October 29, 1941–February 1, 1942). The Treasury and War Departments endorsed the first effort, providing thematic prompts, serving as judges, and, for some winning entrants, purchasing reproduction rights. The second competition, focused on photography, also sought to bring the work of the best contemporary American artists "convincingly to the attention of government agencies who need and are commissioning these services."[14] MoMA itself provided such services and in fiscal year 1940–41 posted its first income from government appropriations for the various film and other projects it managed. Only foundation grants ($96,997) and members' dues ($80,358) exceeded the $62,062 brought in by its hemispheric unity and beginning home-front projects.[15] By 1943, John E. Abbott, the museum's executive vice-president, claimed, "We estimate that the museum staff devotes 32 per cent of its time to these wartime services."[16] In fact, so ambitious was the scope of MoMA's wartime involvement that fuller treatment of it would constitute a book-length effort. Here, however, a sketch sufficient to place *Wartime Housing* in context and to spark other researchers' curiosity must suffice.

Enthusiasm for wartime programming among MoMA's staff varied over time as well as according to individual temperament and situational demands. Julian Street Jr., secretary of the museum, proposed in 1940 that MoMA might assist in forming a Government Bureau of Industrial Design. Its function would be to equip the nation's wartime presence and publicity efforts with greater consistency and aesthetic appeal. As far as Street was concerned, the United States had already lost the branding and image war to the totalitarian states. Commenting on two recent images in the *New York Times,* Street lamented, "One is an impressive picture of German parachute troups [sic], the other a pathetic demonstration of the U.S. Army at war games in Louisiana showing a gawky recruit carrying a portable radio-telephone set which looks like a sack of potatoes and at his side another soldier who resembles one of Walt Disney's seven dwarves.

The latter is obviously making a fake telephone call and looks very embarrassed about it."[17] Other sins included the inferior visual quality of everything from posters and stamps to housing projects and the placement of insignia on military airplanes.

Among those taking a less ebullient view of wartime entanglements was Barr. Certain missions, such helping European artists immigrate to the United States, gained his direct involvement. Others met with skepticism about their appropriateness to the museum's mission. When Abbott asked in 1940 whether the museum ought to take on an exhibit of donated artworks to be sold for the benefit the British war relief effort, Barr replied, "I do not think the Museum as an institution should sponsor any kind of charitable or benefit undertaking, whether sale or exhibit, ball or football game."[18] This sentiment, perhaps swayed by Mrs. Rockefeller's involvement, did not preclude later fundraising in support of the museum's Armed Services Program. In June 1942, an exhibit and auction of works donated by trustees and friends took place in the member's penthouse, raising some fifteen thousand dollars for the program.[19]

In staking out an ambitious program of wartime engagement, MoMA ran counter to the consensus opinion among more traditional art museums. Fiske Kimball of the Philadelphia Museum of Art had articulated that view best in his AAM address, which affirmed that museums would best serve the public by undertaking their "business as usual."[20] Kimball later asserted, in the museum's annual report, that the public had "ratified" his institution's choice to remain "a haven of serenity, peace and rest" by avoiding, for the most part, "frantic efforts" to put on war-related programming.[21] This caught MoMA's attention. A 1943 letter to Nelson Rockefeller with accompanying minutes from a meeting of the board of trustees, quoted precisely this passage from Kimball. It also offered a stern rebuttal, citing a higher rate of membership renewals and increased attendance as evidence that MoMA's members and the public had also "ratified our choice" to "seriously but by no means 'frantically'" serve the war effort.[22] As further proof of public ratification for MoMA's choice, the letter quoted correspondence from a renewing member. This parent of a son serving overseas had been "again and again" to see *Road to Victory*. "Geared as your program is to the war effort," they wrote, "you manage to elevate the stark realities of today into something quite awesome and beautiful. . . . The present is easier to bear and the future looms up brighter because of what the Museum of Modern Art is doing for Society."

As measures of worth, membership numbers and attendance figures provide an imperfect yardstick. In terms of yearly attendance, the museum reported steady increases from 314,445 in 1943 to 415,926 in 1944 and 473,026 in 1945. The rise in renewals and new members that brought the final tally for 1943 up to 4,880 came after two successive years of decline from 1940's peak of 7,309 members. Membership did continue to build thereafter during the war, reaching 9,382 by September 1945.[23] As to what membership meant, one patron sending in his fifteen-dollar renewal fee wrote that even though his business as a designer and wholesale distributer had been ruined by the war, "The activities of the Museum must be carried on and if my humble contribution helps to do so, it makes me very happy."[24] Another member praised MoMA for keeping "abreast of the need for meeting the demands, intellectual and spiritual, of this time of war, when so many cultural organizations are falling by the wayside."[25]

Of MoMA's many efforts to meet the demands that war posed to the public, *Wartime Housing* is, in some respects, typical of the museum's many wartime exhibits that employed a photo-narrative format. What makes *Wartime Housing* unique is its focus on inspiring and facilitating social action on a long-term public good. It stands, too, as an example of the general difficulties practitioners faced in working out how to adapt storytelling approaches to exhibition craft and of the more particular issues associated with the photograph as object.

Wartime Housing and Social Instrumentality

"To see an exhibition as ugly as Sin, as shocking as a Coney Island horror house, small-town mayors, housing officials, clubwomen and school kids trooped into Manhattan's Museum of Modern Art last week," reported *Time* magazine in May 1942.[26] The show that inspired this flamboyant prose went by the comparatively staid title *Wartime Housing*. The museum had, according to *Time*, "caged and displayed the 'Housing Crime.'" The crime in question concerned the shortage of adequate emergency housing for workers and their families. Even before Pearl Harbor, the hopeful had flocked to emerging centers of wartime production in search of employment only to find themselves living in overpriced substandard accommodations located impractical distances from job sites and lacking sanitation or, worse yet, in tents, flophouses, railroad cars, automobiles, and even grain bins.[27] By 1939 the magnitude of the problem merited mention by President Roosevelt in his dedication of MoMA's new facility. He called housing "the great social art . . . which by its very nature is one of the most formidable challenges to a democracy" and declared it a vital national interest worthy of museums' attention.

At the start of World War II, housing emerged as a critical defense, economic, and social problem. And that problem was sizeable. An estimated fifteen million or more civilians crossed county lines in search of work, including, by some accounts, eight to twelve million whose move brought them to a new state.[28] The more than sixteen million individuals who entered the service were on the move as well. Many cities were ill prepared to handle the influx. Not only was adequate housing in short supply, basic services were taxed beyond capacity as well. The "hot bunk" system, in which a single bed was rented to several workers, all pulling different shifts and, therefore, requiring use of the bunk at different hours, was common in the manufacturing boomtowns created by the war industries. Rural poor and nonwhite in-migrants typically suffered the worst conditions.

Concern for the migrants' welfare and fears of social chaos motivated reformers. Many communities, however, balked at providing wartime housing. They still remembered the Great War's aftermath when factories closed, workers left, and wartime housing projects became ghost towns or slums. Established residents also viewed in-migrants from differing racial, regional, and class backgrounds with prejudice. Temporary solutions held appeal, as these might prevent outsiders, particularly the poor and nonwhite, from settling down for the long term. For the government and corporate interests involved, proper housing served as a means to ensure factories met production quotas for munitions, ships, planes, and other implements of war. Insufficient housing threatened the war machine because it limited the available labor pool, reduced worker efficiency, sapped morale, and led to high turnover rates.

While federal policy responses navigated between the shoals of need, prejudicial community resistance, and private sector interests to encourage construction of public housing for defense workers, progressives within the architectural field saw opportunities to collectively design a better society, from the family unit on up to the local and, ultimately, national aggregate of communities. Indeed, as Andrew Shanken delineates in his account of the Modern Movement in the United States during World War II, many of the factors that birthed this "culture of planning" within the architectural field of the 1920s and '30s are those that shaped aspirations for the museum as social instrument.[29] Through work and association with MoMA, more so than any other museum, architects of this vein also became participants in the exhibitionary network and often brought their own government and corporate connections into the mix, as *Wartime Housing* demonstrates. The Farm Security Administration (FSA) and other government agencies engaged such leading International Style and modernist architects as Eero Saarinen, Richard Neutra, George Howe, Oscar Stonorov, Louis Kahn, and Vernon DeMars to work on projects around the country—projects that, in various stages of completion, would be featured in the MoMA exhibition. *Wartime Housing* brought together individuals interested in advancing New Deal–style, socially progressive visions of cooperative community housing in order to lay the cultural, political, and literal foundations of postwar social revitalization with others less invested in such aims.

The gathering of like minds began in March 1941 out of the hope that stalled agendas for low-income and collective housing could ride the coattails of the nation's push to provide public housing in support of wartime production. An ad hoc citizens group, calling itself the National Committee on the Housing Emergency (NCHE), formed to study possibilities and promote action. Just months later the NCHE approached MoMA about organizing an exhibition with the tentative title *No More Ghost Towns*—a clear reference to communities' lingering fears over ending up with ill-constructed, surplus housing once military production ceased as had happened after the last war.[30] Although not a government agency, the group held political clout. Its cofounder, noted reformer Catherine Bauer, was not only a member of MoMA's Committee on Architecture and Industrial Art but had published a well-regarded tome on architecture for social change, coauthored the Housing Act of 1937 (which encouraged government subsidies for local public housing agencies), and served briefly as director of information and research for the US Housing Authority (USHA).[31] The equally passionate NCHE chair, Dorothy Rosenman, worked directly with groups in affected areas and used her and her husband's considerable connections to rally supporters. (Her husband, New York Supreme Court Judge Samuel Irving Rosenman, who also served as an adviser to President Roosevelt, supported formation of the National Housing Agency in February 1942.[32])

The exhibit on display at MoMA when the NCHE made its approach helps make clear why these high-powered, citizen-organizers sought an alliance. Called *T.V.A. Architecture and Design* (April 30–June 7, 1941), the show had been described by one reviewer as "an effective bracer for those who doubt the creative power of democracy."[33] It focused on good design in New Deal public works and had been developed in cooperation with the Tennessee Valley Authority. So far as precedents, however, *Wartime Housing* followed much earlier uses of photography by social reformers to humanize grim statistics. In 1908, for example, members of New York City's Union Settlement and Greenwich House organized an exhibition on population "congestion" and tenement reform that debuted at the American Museum of Natural History before traveling elsewhere.[34] More recent models included federal exhibitions on housing and national defense at the 1939–40 world's fairs and three of MoMA's own exhibitions, in which Bauer had a hand: the *Housing Exhibition of the City of New York* (1934), which focused on supplanting old-law tenement houses with modern housing projects; *Architecture and Government Housing* (1936), which advanced approaches to cooperative and self-sufficient communities; and *Houses and Housing* (1939), which highlighted American-designed solutions to the need for affordable living space.[35] Others, with rare exception, have detailed these efforts within the contexts of MoMA's institutional history and relationship to architecture as an artistic and social medium.[36] Treating these exhibits, as well as the internal struggles associated with them, as institution-specific manifestations of the museum as social instrument sets MoMA's activities during this period within the field's broader history. The way each involved collaborations with local and federal agencies, including the USHA, for example, is typical of how New Deal alliances helped establish the wartime exhibitionary network.

In addition to the precedents offered by earlier social reform exhibitions, the functions of the photographic object within material rhetorics of social instrumentality must also be considered. MoMA's wartime exhibitions, in particular, drew heavily on the photographic object's particular vibrancy as "eye witness." For example, the earliest of MoMA's photo-narrative exhibitions to treat the European conflict featured the work of Thérèse Bonney, who ran a press photo service and had recorded scenes of daily life in Finland, Belgium, and France just as worried anticipation of war in each country gave way to military invasion. The show at MoMA, *War Comes to the People: A Story Written with the Lens* (December 10, 1940–January 5, 1941), complemented a similar exhibit of Bonney's work, *To Whom the Wars Are Done* (November 15–December 15, 1940), at the Library of Congress. MoMA's press release credited Bonney with devising the exhibit's layout and narrative elements, describing the effect as "a running commentary almost like a motion picture soundtrack."[37] The *New York Times* picked up this cue, noting that the presentation of enlarged photographs was "like a movie, except that these shots are all 'stills.'"[38] The synesthetic dyslexia of these descriptions, which scrambles cinematic sound and motion with photographic silence and fixity prefigures, not in implementation but in aspiration, the multisensory, media-mixing experience that *Wartime Housing* would indeed deliver.

MoMA noted that its decision to show *War Comes to the People* rested not only on the "eloquent, timely and very moving statement" of the pictorial record but also because it combined "the literary and photographic arts in a new exhibition technique."[39] That qualification or, more properly, justification, reflects a self-conscious institutional awareness of several debates. It nods to the discussions, just recapped, about whether art and art museums should be aimed toward ideological ends. Also at stake in this and subsequent exhibitions was the matter of museal treatment of the photographic object. That subject had MoMA's Department of Photographs, established in 1940, locked in a skirmish of its own. Those aligned with curators Beaumont Newhall and Nancy Newhall advocated for collection, curation, and display predicated on the primacy of aesthetic considerations; in other words, treatment of photography qua art. The opposition, associated with Edward Steichen, took a more catholic view of the medium. This group embraced photography's functional and communicative uses in the popular and commercial realms, treating all as viable concerns. This included use of photography by museums as a tool of exhibition craft. As a recent history of the department notes, both sides would, in keeping with MoMA's overall institutional stance, direct photographic exhibitions in support of the war effort, but their variant perspectives on the medium resulted quite different installations and emphases.[40]

As a medium for exhibition craft, photography's comparatively low-cost reproducibility made it economically attractive both for large-scale installations and for the production and shipping of scaled-down circulating editions of photo-narrative exhibitions. Also, remediation of the photographic negative's image into different physical forms allowed for alterations in size, shape, and substrate as well as in color, content, and other aspects of the image itself. These qualities ably served the design and rhetorical aims of installation while, at the same time, cultural tolerance for the medium's inherent reproducibility allowed multiple and divergent instantiations of an image to retain, within certain bounds, an aura of credible authenticity in ways that alterations to other artifact types did not allow.

As a genre, the wartime photo-narrative exhibition shared contemporary kinship with the photographic essays of *Life* and other magazines. So these experimentations in exhibition craft fit within museums' ongoing adaptations of mass media communications techniques for educative and popularizing purposes. Genre played a role, too, in photographs' viability as witness-objects within the installation context. Most were products of photojournalism, news gathering, and government-sponsored documentary projects. Some came from the publicity arms of corporations (as seen in Newark's *Three Southern Neighbors*), the armed forces, and government agencies. Documentary and journalistic photography still held status in the popular imagination as being uncomplicated acts and products of eyewitness.[41] Accounts of Bonney's work in *War Comes to the People* noted, "Her photographs are good because they are honest, straight photography."[42]

Archibald MacLeish, just over a year into his job as the Librarian of Congress, likewise underscored the images' value as testimony in the introductory panel he wrote for both the MoMA and LOC installations. "The propagandists for the special causes have all been heard—the apologists also—the appeaser," MacLeish's poetic wall text declared. "In these quiet and unarguing photographs, the people's cause—the one eternal cause which neither force of arms nor fraud of lies can conquer—finds its words."[43] The photographic object stood, in contrast to propagandists, appeasers, and apologists, as the truth teller, as a reliable firsthand witness despite the remediations involved in bringing it to gallery walls. In this context, it is useful to think about Bonney's images as witness-objects. That is to say, Bonney, MacLeish, and other contributors to *War Comes to the People* perceived these artifacts, these photographs, to be capable of bearing testimony to specific external as well as emotional realities. Indeed, photographs and moving images, as recorded traces of human attention, are often taken to function as surrogate "eye" witnesses (despite the forms of mediation involved). Through light, exposure, and chemicals, analog film and photos conjure their subjects—persons, places, things, and events—into convincing, if partial, re-being, allowing the gallerygoer to "see" through the eyes of the photographer-witness who took the shot. Further, when chosen and displayed in ways intended to amplify their emotional impact, witness-objects are perceived as conferring to the gallerygoer the status of being a "'secondary' or 'retrospective' witness."[44] Central to the witness-object's vital materiality is the capacity to stir emotion in human beholders that, if powerful enough, imparts a sense of obligation to share the received testimony, to bear witness to the thing seen. "One of the reasons photography can communicate witness so powerfully," one scholar observed, "is its aura of ontological authenticity, and our willingness to take the photograph as more than a representation, as an actual trace of the experienced world."[45]

The photo as witness-object during this period also had recognized vibrancy in the realm of affect. Roy Stryker, head of the Farm Security Administration's photographic section, which MoMA frequently used as an image source, noted, "Truth is the objective of the documentary attitude.... A good documentary should tell not only what a place or a thing or a person looks like, but it must also tell the audience what it would feel like to be an actual witness to the scene."[46]

The concept of emotional truth recalls museums' ambitions to vivify their subject matter, to animate it in new ways and with more effective "showmanship." They aspired not to distort a subject's truths, as they saw it, but to awaken in the public a more active desire to get at those truths. Still, social instrumentality called for object truths and museums to be in service to action, and wartime exhibitions were no different. The "unarguing" photographs of *War Comes to the People,* for example, served not only to rouse sympathy for afflicted Europeans, as Bonney hoped, but also functioned as a warning to Americans against complacency. Scenes in Belgium and France, some taken just weeks prior to the May 1940 invasions, showed people going about the tasks and pleasures of daily life despite the possibility of war, as indicated by images of smiling men in uniform enjoying recreational activities (figure 3).

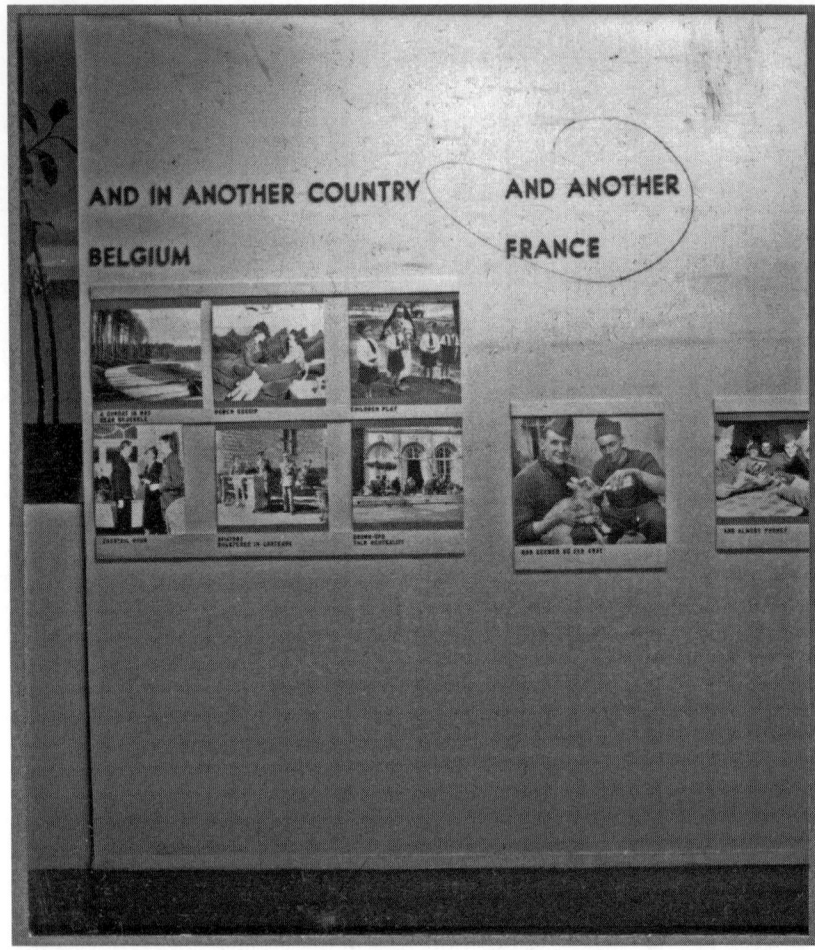

FIGURE 3. When Bonney took these images of civilians and soldiers, neither they nor she knew that a German invasion was but days away. The text transforms the suite into a cautionary message for Americans who, too, might feel that war seems "so far away. And almost phoney." Installation view of the exhibition, *War Comes to the People: A Story Written with the Lens* (December 10, 1940–January 5, 1941). Photographic Archive. The Museum of Modern Art Archives, New York. Digital Image © The Museum of Modern Art / Licensed by SCALA / Art Resource, NY.

Beaumont Newhall, who MoMA's board tasked with overseeing *War Comes to the People*, later regretted his involvement.[47] Given his stance on the museum's photographic debates, it is not difficult to understand why. *War Comes to the People* would be followed by a number of photo-narrative exhibitions that subsumed the photographic object's merits as art in favor of privileging its communicative and affective functionalities as a part within an experiential installation's whole.

The NCHE proposal also met with misgivings from some MoMA staff. In June 1941 Barr informed trustee and Architecture Committee chair Philip L. Goodwin that, while he agreed it might be advisable to do a show that would have "direct bearing on the defense effort," he remained skeptical as to the current proposal's architectural merits. Barr concluded, "I do think we should try to keep in mind the fact that the Museum is an art museum and that shows which have to do purely or principally with technology should be avoided or passed on to the Museum of Science and Industry."[48] Sentiments such as these, along with a recent re-organization that left the Department of Architecture slimly staffed, helps explain why responsibility for the effort shifted over to the museum's newly formed Department of Industrial Design and its inaugural lead curator Harvard Design School–trained architect Eliot Noyes. By late October, Abbott indicated to the NCHE that the museum was willing to move forward, had made space in its gallery schedule, and waited only for word on how to finance the effort.[49]

With planning already underway, both NCHE and MoMA sent out funding appeals to government agencies, philanthropists, and others for what they estimated would be a twenty-thousand-dollar endeavor consisting of three identical travelling exhibitions (one of which would be installed at MoMA before going on the road) and an accompanying thirty-two-page catalogue.[50] The latter, as typical of MoMA's practice at the time, would be a special issue of its members' bulletin. One response to the fundraising appeal came from Winslow Ames, director of the Lyman Allyn Museum in New London, Connecticut. He found the exhibition plan to be "very well stated" but as a "Christian pacifist" could not support the effort, noting "it is a tragedy that public housing, which was usually hard to sell on a humanitarian basis or even on a cost-of-government basis is now being sold as a necessary help in the drive to kill off a lot of people who also need housing to improve their morale enough to help them kill us off."[51] Ames, who had lobbied for public housing in his region for three years, did offer to help with planning. He felt it would be possible to teach the public "without singing a hymn of hate; and it could be good housing propaganda without putting war in a favorable light." His financial support, however, would be going to the American Friends Service Committee.

Internal pessimism about the project still lingered. Janet Henrich, acting curator of architecture, who had been asked to advise the exhibition committee (and clearly felt relieved she had no greater part in the project), lamented to a colleague experienced in public housing that not only had few defense housing projects been completed, making the matter of obtaining suitable images difficult, but even fewer had been built "in interesting form."[52] She also doubted the exhibit would achieve its primary goal of influencing community and policymaker decisions. "It seems to me however," she noted, "a very ticklish question as to how well it can be done to rouse the rabble." Even after reading the prospectus, she confided to her friend, "[I] still can't see that the individual citizen's place in the whole setup has been considered, even; and that would seem to me the only possible excuse for our killing ourselves to do such a show. In other words, I can't believe that the best show in the world put on by us here is going to have any startling effect either on Congress or on individual housing authorities. Well, so much for my carping."[53]

While the committee's vision of how *No More Ghost Towns* would engage the public may have been flawed, its earliest plans make clear the exhibit's desired educational and instrumental effects: "It is planned to keep the presentation extremely simple so that the intelligent layman who is in a position to use his influence toward better emergency housing can quickly grasp the possibilities."[54] Once Noyes took charge, the exhibit's three-part framework evolved into what would become its final form, a multimedia drama related in ten "scenes."[55]

The development of *Wartime Housing* began with a basic description of each scene's didactic focus and a list of photographic content to be sought. In the case of what became scene 3, for example, one would learn "How workers move to new industrial areas, find bad living conditions for themselves and their families, and then move on again."[56] The "photos needed" included, "Rows of workers migrating on foot, in cars.... Shanty towns.... Scenes outside real estate offices with signs showing no vacancies, high prices, etc.... Scenes showing effect of bad housing on families—children in streets.... Interior views of congested and unhealthy conditions."[57] For images that fit the exhibit's aims, staff turned to the Farm Security Administration (FSA), OWI, *Life* magazine, the United States Navy, university collections, the USHA, and others. To emphasize the geographic sweep of the housing problem and to ensure applicability across a range of host communities who might take on a circulating version of the exhibit, the designers sought to provide a general impression, albeit a vivid one, of the housing emergency rather than location-specific details. This focus on audience and didactic purpose raised a difficult question: why debut the exhibit in New York, a city that was not a defense community?

MoMA's Architecture Committee noted that the New York installation would be "not only incomplete in its effect but hardly worthwhile" unless transportation to the museum could be provided to groups from outlying defense communities.[58] They likewise argued that if the twin intent was to sway "Congressmen, government housing officials and the building industry," an exhibition held in Washington, DC, would be "more direct." Meanwhile, the multimedia experience being developed had become too expensive and technology-dependent to send on the road. So Noyes, needing the funds for MoMA's installation, voted to abandon the traveling versions altogether. He was overruled. Disagreement had also surfaced about the narrative tone to be struck. Architecture Committee member Donald E. Hatch complained that the exhibition's "'chin up, carry on, everything's going to be alright' attitude" lacked urgency.[59] "I believe that the show should be as grim as hell," he argued, "I think each guy going through it should come out sweating. I am positive he should have damn near the last drop of emotion rung out of him.... I think we should bring each emotion a twist, make the watcher sick at his stomach with bad housing, sad at the death of some guy, shamed at a break in production."

Carrying forward, the iteratively developing script designated the "mood" to be created by each of the exhibit's sections. Scene 3, for instance, with its dramatization of ill-housed laborers, would strive to impart a "grim, hot, exhausting, dirty, damp, smelly" sensation through visual, auditory and environmental cues.[60] As the material rhetoric of presentation shifted into pathos, some committee members, Catherine Bauer among them, raised objections. She disapproved of the imbalanced emphasis on the war-time context of the housing problem at the expense of clear guidance and architectural exemplars for would-be community planners. "But I do feel more strongly than ever," she cautioned, "while it is obviously necessary to dramatize the immediate social-political-patriotic aspects of war housing need (as is suggested in scenes 1–8 of your outline), the Museum's natural and real response is to encourage better quality in defense housing production. And I seriously hope that a much larger proportion of the exhibit will be devoted to ABC-labeled examples of good architectural design & community planning, and worthwhile technical experiment."[61]

Noyes soon assured Bauer that, following her suggestions, adjustments had been made. "I think we have kept the valuable part of our dramatics," he wrote, "and eliminated the purple patches."[62] Furthermore, four scenes (rather than two) now addressed community planning and emulation-worthy architecture. Still, he reminded her, compelling photographs of the best modernist projects could not be had (just as Henrich had feared); many were still under construction, and the quality of available war agency photographs was poor. As a general rule, MoMA relied heavily on existing photo caches within the exhibitionary network for its wartime exhibits due to budget as well as access restrictions. To properly include the modernist defense housing projects suggested by Bauer and colleagues, MoMA ultimately had to hire photographers. Negotiations such as these about the exhibition's content, form, intended audiences, and most suitable forums for its message continued right through to opening day.

An Exhibition in Ten Scenes

When *Wartime Housing* opened for its three-month run at MoMA in April 1942, it was not the only temporary exhibition on display. It appeared concurrently with *Two Years of War in England: Photographs by William Vandivert* (April 15–June 10) and overlapped with the previously mentioned fundraiser *Art Sale for the Armed Services* (May 6–June 16).[63] If this conjunction of material failed to impress on visitors the museum's commitment to engaging contemporary realities, its program for youth featured the winning results of an "anti-hoarding" competition sponsored with the Women's City Club. City school children had been called on to depict the negative social consequences of stockpiling goods in short supply and high demand.[64] Neither had MoMA ignored its hemispheric unity commitments; drawings of Indigenous Mexican clothing enjoyed a brief run in the Young People's Gallery.[65] *Wartime Housing*, however, offered something these other efforts did not: an experience expressly designed to produce embodied knowing by engaging museumgoers' senses.

The immersion into the *Wartime Housing* experience began with a form of imaginative re-embodiment. At the exhibit entrance Jean Carlu's now famous poster designed by for the Office of Emergency Management declared, "America's Answer! Production." To enter the show, visitors walked into scene 1 and alongside a screen set near ground level onto which a brief rear-projection film showed scenes of housing and factory work culminating with a march of laborers heading, seemingly, into the exhibition. Through this moment of unified, purposive movement, the installation invited museumgoers to "feel like one of the workers."[66] To further solidify visitor-worker unity, a recording of excerpts from President Roosevelt's 1942 State of the Union Address, in which he called for a rapid increase in production in all sectors vital to the war effort, played continuously.

Swept up in what the script described as a "Serious, determined, confident" mood, visitors entered scene 2, where the emotional tenor darkened, literally.[67] Here, standing in gloom, they beheld a spotlit timeline of events related to war production. This transitional passage took museumgoers back in time to 1938, when, they were told, the already acute housing shortage had forced communities to use streetcars for dwellings.[68] From there, they moved forward to the declaration of war in Europe (1939), the passage of the

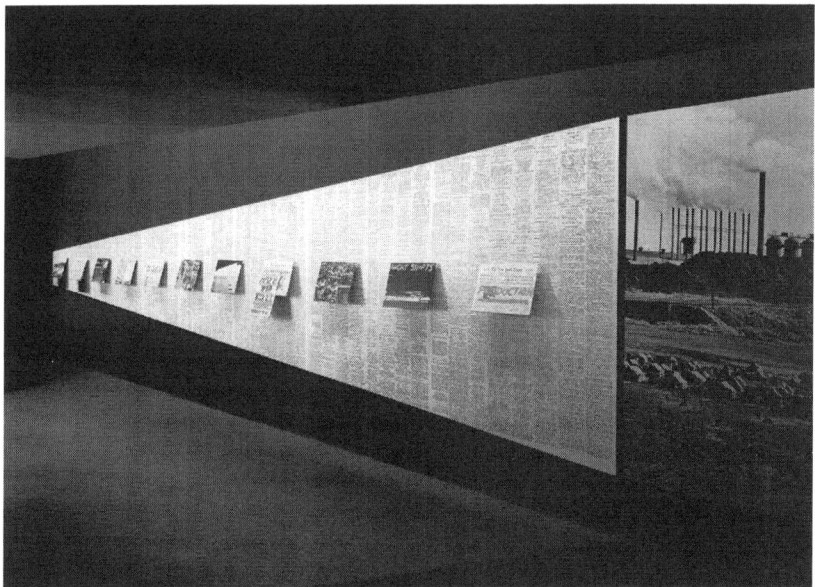

FIGURE 4. This view of scene 2 is taken from the timeline's culmination, looking back toward the point where museumgoers entered the room. The nighttime factory scene (second affixed image from right emblazoned "night shifts") imbued wartime production with a sense of nonstop urgency, while the last image museumgoers saw before entering scene 3 contrasted a bellowing factory's industrial efficiency against the makeshift nature of the workers' tent city in the foreground. Installation view of the exhibition, *Wartime Housing* (April 22–June 21, 1942), Gottscho-Schleisner Collection, Library of Congress, Prints and Photographs Division, LC-G612-T-42206.

Lend-Lease Act (1941), the attack on Pearl Harbor, and on up to present-day delays—all set against a backdrop of help-wanted ads (figure 4).

As one reviewer described it, "The [president's] voice from the loudspeaker pursues them down a corridor where newspaper headlines blazon the depressing progress of the war."[69] The image chosen to signify the present moment on the timeline had, in fact, been taken some time in 1940 for *Life* magazine. The work of Carl Mydans, it showed an exterior view of an immense factory swallowed by night's darkness save for the illuminated glow of it windows, signaling that the laborers within worked around the clock.[70] The last image museumgoers saw as they exited scene 2 depicted rows of tents in the image's foreground dwarfed by the belching factory where their inhabitants worked; nearby text reminded visitors that the "greatest labor migration in U.S. history" was presently underway.

Next, exhibition goers "emerge[d] into a still uglier room with blown-up photographs of men sleeping on benches, in cars." An encompassing photomontage fully consumed the room's walls, with no "breathing space" left between the images of tired women, forlorn children, and unkempt men.[71] The curators intended the varied sizes of the crammed-together photographs to "build up [the] feeling of something dislocated."[72] Scene 3's uncredited glimpses of boomtown communities in and around San Diego (California), Corpus Christi (Texas), Alexandria (Louisiana), and Fort Bragg (North Carolina) had, for the most part, been taken in 1940 by FSA-OWI photographers Robert Lee, Marion Post Wolcott, Jack Delano, Peter Sekaer, and John Vachon. To make the squalor and discomfort of inadequate defense housing palpable as well as visible, the MoMA team had equipped the small, visually cluttered room with a false ceiling set just seven feet from the floor and painted black to amplify the body-encroaching sense of confinement. Rough carpeting, distinct in its texture and feel underfoot from the smoothed, polished floors elsewhere in the museum, changed visitors' tread and, in accord with the script, "muffled" the sound of their movements.[73] Plans included touching up the photographs with fluorescent paint and using "bluish" light from a single, bare bulb to heighten the sense of dis-ease (figure 5a). Installation shots indicate that this tactic may have been implemented, unlike the scheme to add olfactory agents in order to enhance the "dirty, damp, smelly" quality of the simulated environment.

Scene 3's sensory barrage also included an audio track, in the form of a radio drama, complete with a presiding commentator, sound effects, and actors seeming to give voice to the men and women depicted in the room.

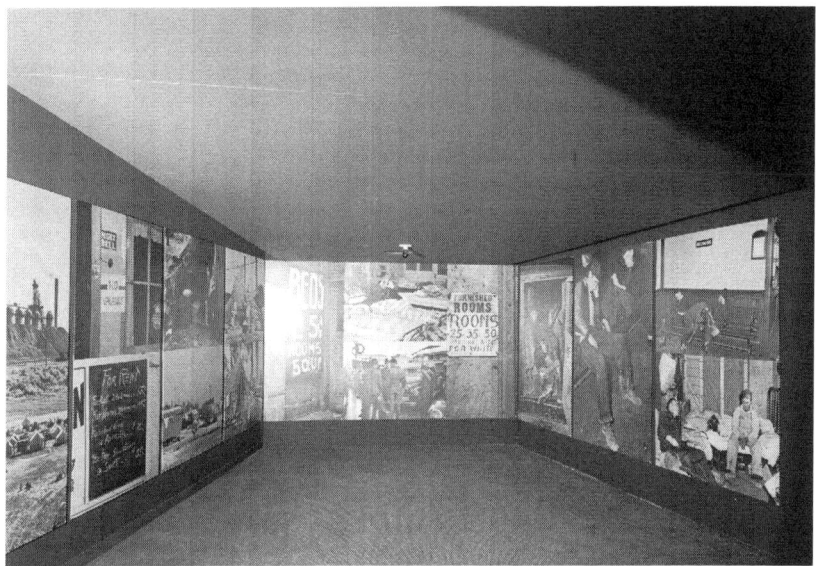

FIGURE 5a. Scene 3, shown here from the perspective of a museumgoer standing on its threshold, not only depicted the wretched living conditions of industrial workers and their families but also simulated these conditions by creating a dark, confined viewing space. Installation view of the exhibition, *Wartime Housing* (April 22–June 21, 1942), Gottscho-Schleisner Collection, Library of Congress, Prints and Photographs Division, LC-G612-T-42207.

A speaker in the ceiling delivered this auditory complement to the experience. "Home is a place where you hang your hat, where you eat, where you sleep," intoned the male commentator matter-of-factly. "It's the place your wife washes your socks and the children do their homework. It's bed, breakfast, parlor, clothes closet, dinner, radiator, rug, washstand, stove, chair, cedarchest, mirrors, kitchen."[74] This catalog of physical comforts called museumgoers' attention to their absence in the room's various photographs. Likewise, the spoken image of home as a place of wife and children situated the images of male-only flophouses and make-do accommodations as socially aberrant. In similar fashion, the image of two unwashed, unattended children in ragged garb peering forth from a tent stood in contrast to the invocation of home as a place to "take a bath" and "do homework," presumably under a parent's watchful eye (figure 5b). By mimicking the popular and prevalent radio drama format, this auditory passage engaged visitors in a familiar form of imaginative spatial cognition and empathetic identification.

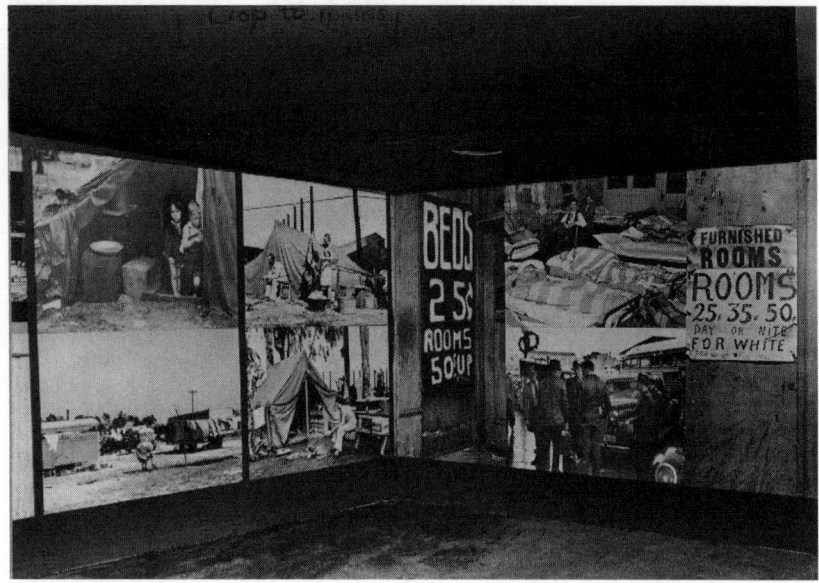

FIGURE 5b. The photographs seen in this detail view of scene 3 underscore the deprivations experienced by families living in tents (left wall) and the racial segregation enforced by landlords (center wall). Installation view of the exhibition, *Wartime Housing* (April 22–June 21, 1942). Photograph by Albert Fenn. Photographic Archive. The Museum of Modern Art Archives, New York. Digital Image © The Museum of Modern Art / Licensed by SCALA / Art Resource, NY.

MoMA, no stranger to experimentation with radio's educative power, had written and produced the program *Art in America* in the mid-1930s. The show, supported by the Carnegie Corporation's interest in exploring mass media as a vehicle for adult education, had taken an interesting turn in the episodes dealing with housing and city planning. Instead of the usual scripted discussion with an expert, these episodes invited the radio audience to listen in on fictive exchanges, such as one between an architect and a client, as a more dramatic means to learn about modern architecture.[75] Functioning as an immersive radio drama, scene 3 of *Wartime Housing* hailed the visceral, affective imagination through active listening that, to paraphrase Susan Douglas, engaged not only the ears but the body, bones, and innards.[76] A short example from the recording that played in the gallery underscores how sound operated in conjunction with the room's material dimensions. Standing in the space, museumgoers would have heard the relentless drip of a leaking faucet growing ever louder. Timed to its cadence, a wearied male voice delivered a terse litany of his surroundings: "The kitchen's in the bedroom and the parlor's in the bedroom and the laundry's in the bedroom and the hallway's in the bedroom . . ." The diatribe ended abruptly, with the "scraping of furniture, the clang of a dropped pot." The concluding silence left room for visitors to imagine that the man, having reached his boiling point, had pushed roughly away from the table where he sat, while his wife, caught off-guard by his outburst, dropped her cooking utensils in shock or fear. Other audio cues, in concert with the visual ones previously mentioned, also hinted at the disruptions to family structure such environments would provoke. So, the scene not only sought to create a visceral connection between museum visitors and suffering workers but also carried an undercurrent of menace, a warning about social breakdown.

Of course, human vocalizations convey more than linguistic content. Tone, volume, pauses, accent, and other qualities inflect delivery, layering additional meaning onto speech acts.[77] The class distinctions conveyed through the wording and the actors' delivery of the *Wartime Housing* script are more sharply perceived when compared to a recording of the remarks made by MoMA president John Hay Whitney, NCHE chair Dorothy Rosenman, and other dignitaries during the radio broadcast of the invitation-only opening gala for the exhibit. The divide between the patrician elocution of MoMA's chosen airwave ambassadors and the accents crafted for the exhibit's fictitious war workers and their family members is sharp and wide. Whitney, Rosenman, and the other speech givers, like the actors of the exhibition's audio track, read from prepared scripts and would have been conscious of "performing" their parts for a listening audience. Still, even if tailored to the occasion, their voices provide a real-life yardstick against which to measure the fabricated vocal personas of the exhibition. Lacking overt regional markers, the voices strove to universalize the defense workers' plight and convey a vague sense of social standing that, while clearly not of the moneyed class, was respectable. The tempos, word choices, and phrase repetitions added a rhythmic flow to the delivery, resulting in a plainspoken poetry of the "everyman."

The trope of the common man, as Roland Marchand observes, populated all manner of corporate communications during the war years. Heartland farmers, regular Janes and Joes, and other incarnations personified white America's nostalgic, small-town psyche.[78] These folksy but wise avatars served as proxies for the voice of the people as articulated by corporations eager to regain public allegiance and thereby preserve the nation's "fifth freedom": commercial enterprise free of New Deal restrictions and, in the peace to come, free of wartime curtailments as well.[79] One also hears—and in the written sound script sees—similarities between *Wartime Housing*'s photomontage with audio and such photo-text productions as Erskine Caldwell and Margaret Bourke-White's *You Have Seen Their Faces* (1937), James Agee and Walker Evans's *Let Us Now Praise Famous Men* (1941), and Archibald MacLeish's extended poem *Land of the Free* (1938).[80] MacLeish, for example, had described his poem as the "soundtrack" for the *Land of the Free*'s photographs, and at one stage, the museum envisioned that James Agee might author *Wartime Housing*'s script.[81] The work went to more modest talents, but the linguistic choices and rhythms of the exhibit's written and spoken words echo with the influence of these well-known photo-text publications.

Scene 4 attempted to produce in visitors a "Feeling of impending disaster bright, hot, frightening," in order to impress on them the national consequences that failure to provide adequate housing would bring. One review noted of this section, "There are pictures of disheartened workers trudging the roads.... A recorded voice intones [Benjamin Franklin's]: 'For want of a nail, the shoe was lost....' From the walls placards answer: 'For want of housing the worker is lost, for want of the worker production is lost.'"[82] The real cost, however, came next in the presentation. The museumgoer walked through a blast of hot air accompanied by sounds of plane engines, dropping bombs, and explosions. Then, as the reviewer recounted, they beheld "two great, blood-red pictures—one of the burning USS *Arizona,* the other of a little girl wringing her hands over her bullet-riddled sister in Poland."[83] The latter image by Julien Bryan captured ten-year-old Kazimiera Mika grieving her sibling Andzia, who, along with other civilian women picking potatoes in fields outside Warsaw, had been strafed by German bombers.[84] One of a series Bryan took in September 1939, it was among the most widely reproduced photographs at the time of the devastation in Europe. The sound effects for this scene suggest the influence of *This Is War!,* a popular radio drama that had debuted some eight weeks before the exhibit and had been created at the prompting of MacLeish, now head of the Office of Facts and Figures. Those who have marked its place in broadcast, home-front, and even hemispheric unity history have noted that its dramatization of facts through crisp writing, vivid scenarios, and battlefield sound effects resulted not only in a captivating sense of "immediacy" but also in it being "hailed as both factual and exceptionally imaginative."[85]

"Imaginative" well describes scene 5, which required museumgoers to pass through a long, dark, cramped corridor where "the hands of a big clock whirl madly and a voice cries over & over: 'The task is long—the time is short.'"[86] In fact, alternating voices of men and women, individually and then in unison, chanted this variation on Roosevelt's State of the Union admonition: "Our task is hard—our task is unprecedented—and the time is short." With the refrain still echoing in their ears, patrons emerged into the spacious, orderly environment of scene 6. Here, as in the remaining galleries, the ceiling height stood at its normal level. This, together with brighter light levels, signaled that visitors had entered a space conducive to greater physical, mental, moral, and social health. The space hummed with "the cheerful noise of hammer and saw . . ."[87]

These sounds focused museumgoers' attention on the topic of demountable or "truckable" housing, prefabricated units that could be assembled quickly on site and, if desired, disassembled and removed with equal alacrity. To complement the message of efficient mass production, the photographs depicting successive steps in the fabrication and installation processes were aligned with regimental precision. This was not the answer to the housing problem that the NCHE favored. It championed permanent, holistically planned communities offering long-term low-income housing and social services. Inclusion of the demountable approach likely represented the interests of another exhibition partner, the three-month-old National Housing Authority and its administrator, John Blandford Jr., who as former Tennessee Valley Authority general manager had experience with such units. As defense housing projects consolidated under the National Housing Authority, policy emphasis moved away from planning communities capable of thriving after the war to quick-fix solutions such as highlighted in scene 6.

Scenes 7 and 8, by means of rational rather than emotional appeals, continued to nudge viewers away from a subject position that identified with the war industry's workers to that of a community planner. Scene 7, through its images and repeating soundtrack, guided viewers through a series of considerations about the nature of the industry, workers, and community that each locale would need to examine in order to lay the foundations for an effective housing plan. Voices representing men and women of the community pondered, "I don't know if the light plant's going to be able to handle the load. What about the schools?" The fictional incomers had a say, too: "How are the rents? Are there any parks? ... With the money I'm making I'd like to buy a house."[88]

Scene 8 reminded museumgoers that good planning in the present would secure a postwar future free of the slums and industrial ghost towns that resulted after World War I. The exhibition script made no mention of an associated mood for these and the remaining two scenes; this absence marked a turn to modern, cool-headed rationality and emphasis on intellectual, rather than visceral, comprehension of the task at hand. Scene 9 provided examples of "bad" and "good" architecture. As the reviewer for *Time* magazine wrote, "The show winds up with photographs of the US trying to make up for lost time, already, in some places, building wartime housing in the pattern of the world of tomorrow—well-planned communities of airy houses, parks, playgrounds, schools."[89] The examples of good design also

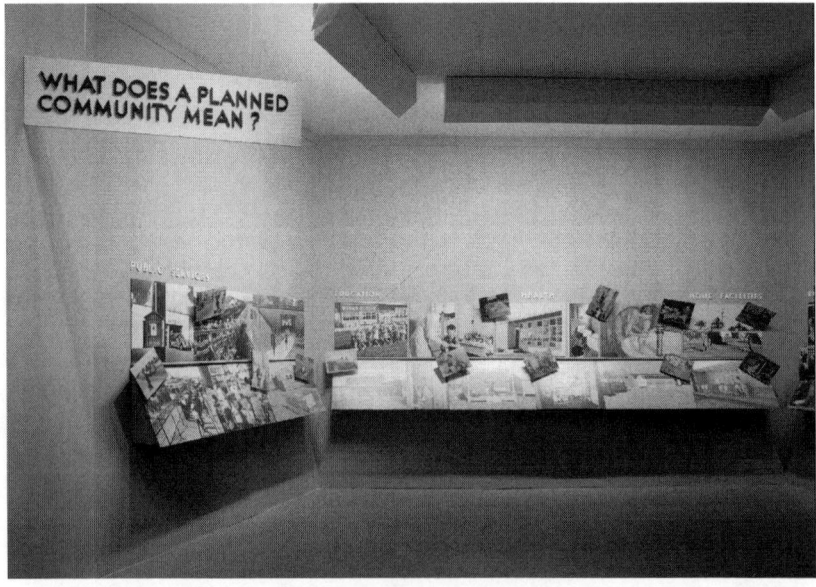

FIGURE 6. The display panels in scene 9 (some of which are shown here) featured elements of cooperative community housing that the exhibitions' more progressive planners wanted to see emphasized. These included integrated facilities for education, health, and recreation. Smaller depictions of substandard accommodations were superimposed at cockeyed angles over the images of the well-ordered community to remind museumgoers of the consequences of poor planning. Installation view of the exhibition, *Wartime Housing* (April 22–June 21, 1942), Gottscho-Schleisner Collection, Library of Congress, Prints and Photographs Division, LC-G612-T-42211.

featured health and community centers as well as modern appliances in both private and shared-access areas. Aligned in well-ordered rows, these photos, in both content and arrangement, offered a rational view of the clean, orderly society that good planning promised to achieve (figure 6).

Striking a dissonant chord were smaller photographs superimposed at odd and precarious angles over the tidy vista. These vertiginous physical misalignments underscored the mismatch between the unsupervised children, tin washtubs, and unsanitary domestic spaces of untended growth and those of the properly planned community.

Wartime Housing's tenth and final scene served as a "clinic" where museumgoers were given a "visual review of the organization needed for a town" (figure 7).[90] This chart situated viewers as "YOU the citizen" in relation to the various municipal and federal authorities with which

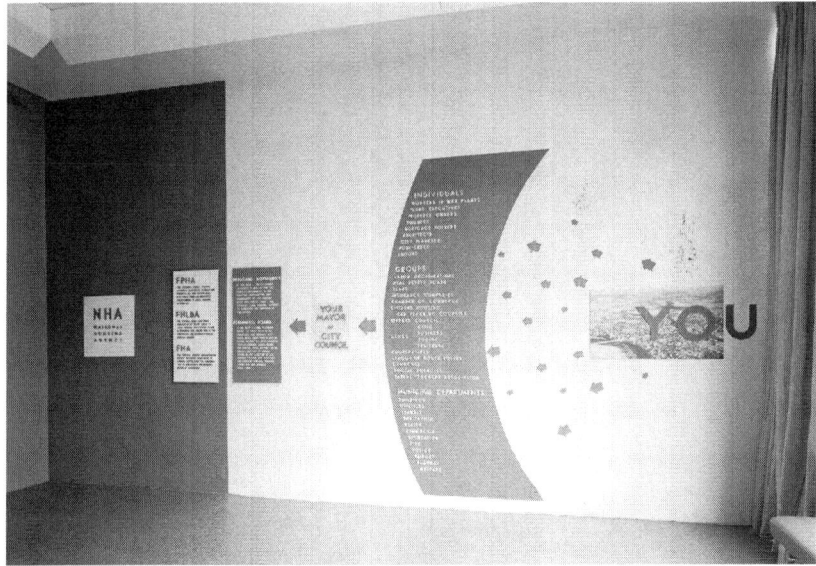

FIGURE 7. Scene 10 mapped out the ways in which museumgoers could become involved in community planning efforts. A more detailed version of the graphic was circulated through the museum's member bulletin. Installation view of the exhibition, *Wartime Housing* (April 22–June 21, 1942), Gottscho-Schleisner Collection, Library of Congress, Prints and Photographs Division, LC-G612-T-42215.

they would likely interact if they took up their civic and patriotic duty as community planners. Also reprinted in the exhibition booklet, the chart equipped the exiting museumgoer-citizen with pragmatic ways to become involved in helping plan a better housing and civic future.

One aspect of wartime housing—familiar to any white community or planner at the time and to Black workers and families seeking accommodations—received only ambiguous, nonverbal attention. War housing for Black Americans was, by 1942, an issue that none involved in community planning could claim ignorance of with honesty. Two months before the exhibit opened, a protracted political struggle over the rights of Black workers in Detroit to occupy the Sojourner Truth housing project that had been constructed on their behalf erupted in violence when an angry white mob overturned moving vans as the tenants attempted to take up residence.[91] Race as well as class prejudice against in-migrants had sparked violent confrontations in a number of other cities, too.

Based on exhibition content alone, the museum and committee's stance on the topic is vague. One image among those in scene 1 that ushered museumgoers into the show depicted a multiracial workforce flowing out from the job and heading to the places now called home. In scene 3, a photograph by Peter Sekaer for the USHA captured a sign advertising "furnished rooms day or nite for white" (see figure 5b). Without record of curatorial intent, any meaning to be made now rests, as it did then, squarely with each viewer of the photomontage. Did the sign provide assurance that in even the worst conditions some social boundaries remained firmly in place? Or did it function as a subtle indictment of the prejudices barring Black workers from housing, suitable or not? Listed among the images used to explicate the negative outcomes of poor planning and bad architectural design on the social life of a community is another by Sekaer. The list maker's shorthand identifies it simply as "colored dice game." Sekaer, who photographed Black communities in New Orleans and elsewhere during the 1930s and '40s, had been attentive to life lived under segregation and Jim Crow, capturing portraits of its inequities and of human resilience.[92] As with all the images in *Wartime Housing*, however, the work appeared untitled, uncredited, and within the larger congregational agency of scenes 8 and 9, which asked and answered, "What Does a Planned Community Mean?" Here, to demonstrate how planning fostered healthy recreation, the "bad" example of the dice game stood in contrast to young Black men enjoying themselves on an outdoor basketball court bordered by tidy houses. Other scenes of play and leisure on the same display panel likewise contrasted various planned recreational spaces against undesirable counterparts. The people in these other spaces read as white, save for one of the "bad" examples. It shows white boys and girls playing in a city street, seemingly under the watch of a nearby man. A slightly older group of boys head away from the camera. One, a Black youth, turns back toward the photographer. This scene's properly planned opposite is one of young boys, all white, playing ball under adult supervision inside a gymnasium. Was the cumulative message of the recreation section that well-planned communities were segregated communities? Or that *all* communities deserved to be well-planned? The racism plaguing wartime housing is there to see or to ignore, there to be read as hesitantly progressive or as squarely segregationist, all according to the white viewer's inclination.

Attempting to ascribe "race" to persons depicted in these photographs is a fraught activity. It reifies the very notion that human beings can be categorized based on physical characteristics, which is, of course, the bedrock of racism and of the socially constructed category of race. The goal here is to understand how racialized readings of these images contributed to notions of Home Front belonging and visions of postwar America. Parsing the designers' intentions is difficult, too. Within the sections highlighting exemplars of modernist architecture, for example, how should the extra-aesthetic dimensions of the Pennypack Woods housing project (1942) by Howe, Stonorov, and Kahn be read? As an initiative of the Federal Works Agency's Mutual Ownership Defense Housing Division, it stood as an example of cooperative programs designed to help renters transition into home ownership when the country itself transitioned from war to peace—precisely the type of solutions the reform-minded members of the exhibition committee wished to advance. Yet Pennypack Woods accepted applications only from white war workers and their families.

What bearing, if any, did plans to circulate the exhibit play in decisions such as these? What discussions did or did not happen, and what was tacitly understood among the white planners with regard to the racial dimensions of housing? In at least one instance, MoMA's own racial boundaries needed clarification. In early March 1942, Mrs. Rosenman inquired about the prospects of inviting Black community leaders to the exhibition's

April opening event. She asked, "Are negroes welcome at the museum? Should we include two or three prominent negroes for the function on the opening night? If there is a dinner should they be included?; Should they be included for the reception? Will you let us know about this as soon as possible?"[93] The museum's reply is unknown. The mere fact that Rosenman knew to probe the fine points of MoMA's unwritten racial protocols underscores the limited sense of "the public" still prevalent among museums. There is bitter irony, too, in the fact that while *Wartime Housing* advanced its vision of socially minded modern housing, Executive Order 9102 enforced a different sort of "communal" living for Japanese-Americans being forcibly housed in hastily erected barracks-like dwellings at Manzanar.

Home-Front Witness

Of *Wartime Housing*'s overall effect, *New York Times* art critic Edward Alden Jewell said, "The exhibition was imaginatively conceived and has been carried out with great effectiveness. Sometimes it may remind one of the tactics of 'high-pressure salesmanship,' but most of the time a visitor is likely to be too awed or scared or—in the final scenes—cheered, to think about anything except the pith of the drama itself."[94] Visitor reactions are harder to come by. One, at least, took time to deposit a card in the exhibition's "question box." He pronounced *Wartime Housing* "magnificent," a "welcome harbinger of museum service to the community in our struggle toward victory," further lauding it as "an altogether unique experience" and "the most effective presentation of a social problem in the museum setting."[95] A delighted Noyes remarked, "It is really gratifying to get expressions of this sort as a check of the effectiveness of the show, and of course it gives us a glow of satisfaction."[96] Even more difficult to judge is whether the exhibition helped advance the various, sometimes conflicting, aims of the collaborating parties. Despite solid newspaper coverage, broadcasted opening ceremonies, promotional placards in subway cars, the hosting of relevant groups, and the promotional efforts of the NCHE, attendance at MoMA was not as strong as hoped. This lent credence to earlier concerns that the topic would be of lesser interest to those who did not reside in a defense community and that a showing in Manhattan would have negligible civic impact.

The recommendation to travel the exhibition to Washington, DC, never materialized, but two scaled-down, circulating versions of *Wartime Housing* did travel for the remainder of the year and on into 1943. These were rented by communities in eight states, a number of which were war industry boomtowns.[97] These incarnations, stripped of all the carefully planned sensory cues, took form as more conventional panel-based presentations of images with captions drawn from the soundtrack scripts. The larger size, at 250 linear feet, most closely matched the flow of the MoMA installation. A one-hundred-foot version accommodated tighter spaces. Press coverage of the exhibit's run in Hagerstown, Maryland, noted, "The city can no longer shut its eyes to the 'boomtown' flush that is being assumed."[98] Area citizenry already studying the issues could now turn to the Washington County Museum, which in offering the show was "proudly proclaiming its 'social consciousness.'"[99] In Denver, the art museum, local housing authority, planning commission, and public school system banded together to sponsor the exhibit's run. In Oregon, the Portland Art Museum added area-specific materials to the exhibition and arranged two public discussions with housing experts. The Baltimore Museum of Art also customized *Wartime Housing;* working with the city health department it gathered photographs documenting the "rats, poor sanitation, faulty electrical wiring," and other hazards endured by those living in makeshift quarters in cellars and garages.[100] Reporting on the exhibit's run at the Houston Public Library, joint sponsors from the city's community planning association and University of Texas, Austin, told MoMA that its exhibit, film, and program series had been "a great success."[101] Not all recipients were pleased, however, particularly fellow art museums. Neither the large nor the small version, rented at $150 and $50, respectively, for a three-week run, lived up to what they had heard of the MoMA installation. Several offered advice for improvement based on their own adaptations.

In describing the import of *Wartime Housing,* Noyes and MoMA asserted that the exhibition would impress on individuals and groups this central message: "The people of a community can do much in planning the future growth of their town; if they fail to do so, they fail in their responsibility as American citizens."[102] This claim calls to mind Walter Nash's argument that affective rhetoric seeks "the entrapment of the audience, the enforced complicity in a ritual act."[103] Indeed, several scholars have theorized the museum as a space of civic ritual in which ideology is inscribed in the very architecture of the building and presentation of its contents.[104] Among those exploring rhetoric's materiality, Carole Blair usefully suggests that attending to the physical, affective elements of environmentally situated artifacts requires consideration of enactments as well as representations.[105] Or, as others have phrased it, in addition to asking what purposive material assemblages mean to their creators and audiences, we must explore how they act on the sensing body and, thus, play a part in the production of subjects.[106]

The absence of audience data makes it impossible to determine whether the affective dimensions of the exhibition's material rhetoric succeeded in achieving its co-collaborators' aims: the production of community planning citizen advocates for modernist-designed defense housing that achieved long-term social goods as well as immediate war and human needs. In New York City, where it "played" to the wrong audience and garnered unimpressive attendance, the results likely proved negligible. In considering the contrasting appeals that *Wartime Housing* made to the public's instinctual and intellectual faculties, the tensions inherent in its complex and conflicted aims become apparent. By draping a progressive agenda for social reform in the cloak of patriotism, the exhibition sought, in essence, to transfer the strong affective valence of one cause (winning the war) to another (long-range planning of low-income housing options). Despite the convenience and, perhaps, even the necessity of leveraging museumgoers' sense of national duty in order to motivate action on social issues, the strategy attempted in *Wartime Housing* grew more difficult to implement—and was less often attempted—as the war progressed.

Although the impetus to engage contemporary events continued at MoMA, subsequent wartime exhibitions, each with its own set of internal and external collaborative tensions to be negotiated, more often conduced to stability in the civic realm rather than change. These efforts often retained and even advanced exhibition tactics associated with the material rhetoric of social instrumentality but for less progressive ends. A prime example of this is *Road to Victory: A Procession of Photographs of the Nation at War* (May 21–October 4, 1942), the best-known and most-studied example of MoMA's wartime exhibitions and, in its own day, the most successful in terms of public attendance and acclaim. Scholarship on *Road to Victory* has usefully situated it within the sweep of pioneering developments in exhibition craft at MoMA and within broader efforts by cultural intelligentsia to devise multimedia communications that fostered democratic collectivity in opposition to the mass mind of fascism.[107] Considering that planning for both *Road to Victory* and *Wartime Housing* occurred at roughly the same time, differences between these two exhibitions shed light on how social instrumentality as a diffuse idea during the 1930s struggled to find its footing amid the many opportunities for public utility that home-front life presented to museums. Divergence between the two exhibits points, of course, to their different aims as well as to the different sets of collaborators working on them. That said, it is how each defined their educative purpose and structured the material appeal to thought, feeling, and action that underscores the field's drift away from instrumentality as a means of informing civic action toward engagement with current events as a civic good in itself.

While pathos hung thick and heavy within *Wartime Housing*'s visceral appeals to museumgoers' empathy for poorly housed workers, the overall balance it struck also moved the visitor toward taking reasoned action on a specific social issue. Put another way, the drama of the educational experience served a clear, if imperfectly designed and executed, point: to help community members and planners in the work of solving a national problem at the local level. By comparison, *Road to Victory* focused on bolstering national morale and, while it engaged with the anxieties of war in a fashion that museumgoers of the time found uplifting, powerful, and emotionally resonant, it did not possess a true educational function. Rather, its primary goal was to situate the individual within the larger whole of the Home Front imaginary. The exhibition's full title, for example, *Road to Victory: A Procession of Photographs of the Nation at War*, speaks to the museumgoers' position and identity within the ideological context established by the display. The designers meant the title to emphasize the orderly succession in which the images unfolded and, as the museum claimed, "The force of the exhibition lies above all in the sequence of the pictures."[108] The context also conjured the military parade, the procession of soldiers, sailors, airmen, and war machinery marching and rumbling by an assembled public as enacted in communities across the United States during the war. *Road to Victory* inverted this ritual, so that the visiting public marched along the exhibit's demarcated route with the assembled photographs of fellow Americans engaged in their peace and wartime pursuits "looking" on. In this parade, the museumgoer occupied the place traditionally accorded to soldiers and weapons, and so the exhibit recast the individual museumgoer-citizen as the nation's might and bulwark. Monroe Wheeler, MoMA's director of exhibitions and OCIAA volunteer, confirmed this as the museum's intent. "Our purpose in preparing this exhibition," Wheeler said, "was to enable every American to see himself as a vital and indispensable element of victory."[109] Further, as MoMA stated in the fall 1942 issue of its members' bulletin, which was devoted to all that the museum had done in support of national defense since 1940, *Road to Victory* served as "Propaganda for Freedom."[110]

In its pursuit of pathos and exhibition craft as art, *Road to Victory* also veered from ethos in ways that would have confirmed the worst fears of those opposed to showmanship and storytelling in museums. Just as *Wartime Housing* oriented its visitors with a selective timeline of events that placed the defense housing crisis in recent historical context, so too did *Road to Victory* situate its present moment of home-front unity within a longer—much, much longer—chronology. Designed to function as a picture book of the nation, *Road to Victory*'s story began in a dateless, mythic before-time of Manifest Destiny with wall text by poet-author Carl Sandburg that read, "In the beginning was virgin land and America was promises—and the buffalo by thousands pawed the Great Plains—and the Red Man gave over to an endless tide of white men in endless numbers with a land hunger and no end to the land they wanted . . ." Journeying forward, museumgoers next encountered images of the fruited plain, of amber waves of grain ready for harvest, of peace and plenty. This agrarian vision gave way to scenes of Main Street, USA, where people worked, gardened, ate, lived, and lifted their voices in song. Next came murals of New Deal projects, industrial endeavor, and defense preparations. Others have read this transition as the mastery of nature by culture and technology.[111] The real taming, however, is that of history. The exhibit chronology obscures the widespread and deep economic collapse that fostered disillusionment in government, commerce, and other institutions comprising the nation's infrastructure.

This home-front homily came at a time when few Americans believed war would bring prosperity. The month that *Road to Victory* opened, MacLeish reported to President Roosevelt results of a poll that showed that "Seven out of ten [Americans] expect to be personally worse off after the war. Six out of ten expect lower wages. Three quarters expect there will be fewer jobs. This feeling that even the winning of the war may bring economic disaster presents a storm warning."[112] Fear of a return to the economic conditions of the 1930s eased with time but never fully abated during the war.[113] So, in terms of tapping into this broader cultural psyche, both exhibitions held out hope for the postwar future. *Wartime Housing*, for all its showmanship, sought to direct thought, feeling, and action toward planning. In this, it was a more progressive form of social instrumentality despite its conventionally conservative message that both Home Front and future stability depended on maintaining the domestic, familial shelter as a well-ordered physical and moral space.

The instrumentality of *Road to Victory* remained on an affective plane, directing museumgoers to a dispositional Home Front belonging predicated on common roots and shared sacrifice as a national family. Perhaps the strongest testimony to *Road to Victory*'s place in knitting together the home-front imaginary was its integration in Americanization classes conducted by the city's Committee on Refugee Education. MoMA's secretary informed Nelson Rockefeller of this development, prejudicially noting, "The groups are of varying levels of intelligence and cultural background, but the Committee believes that the exhibition is of equal value and importance to them all."[114] Led by a museum docent or their teacher, some groups had the labels read to them as they studied the images and text. Others, with a better command of English, took turns reading the wall text aloud to each other. "This procedure makes for a little confusion in the gallery at times, but that is easily forgivable in view of the important part the exhibition seems to be playing in the Americanization of these people," the letter concluded.

This example also underscores the ways in which *Road to Victory*, *Wartime Housing*, and similar museums displays were productive of a witness dynamic. As embodied, affective experiences structured to amplify the valence of photographs as witness-objects, installations such as these produced the sense of connection and obligation that receiving witness instills in its recipients. George Roeder described World War II's home-front culture as having offered citizens "the dual role of spectator and participant."[115] Exhibitions such as *Wartime Housing* and *Road to Victory* that incorporated the material rhetoric of social instrumentality (but not always its progressive aims) teased out these roles in particular ways. The former turned spectatorship into a visceral act of witness in order to compel civic participation; the latter made ambulatory spectatorship its own form of affective participation in Home Front belonging as the individual and avatars of the nation witnessed each other marching through hard work and sacrifice to victory. In providing a public stage for witness at the individual level, museums converted the solo act into a communal activity. These moments of collective witness among museumgoers had an institutional component as well. In constructing wartime exhibitions to meet civic, institutional, and field expectations of public usefulness, museums not only created witnessable events but also testified to their own Home Front belonging and relevance to the body politic.

Chapter Five

GATEWAYS TO GLOBAL CITIZENSHIP IN A POSTWAR WORLD

> We all believed in those days that indeed, we on our level, our intellectual and cultural level, were contributing as the United Nations did on its political and military level, to the elimination of war forever.
> —Grace McCann Morley, founder of UNESCO's Museums Division and founding director of the San Francisco Museum of Modern Art, 1982

From the war's very outset, museum professionals, particularly those interested in social instrumentality, had cast their thoughts ahead to the roles their institutions and the field as a whole might play in reuniting a world torn apart by conflict. In *The Museum as a Social Instrument* (1942), for example, Theodore Low had argued, "The museum's task lies in preparation for the peace to come. It is then, in a world which we hope will be more ready to understand the problems of others, from nations down to individuals and which will be searching for ways to make 'peace' a word having real and lasting meaning, that the museum can assume a leadership befitting its position."[1] This preparation, in Low's and others' view, included taking up the challenge, issued in the 1930s, to take a more active part in contemporary life and to devote greater resources to adult as well as child education. Hemispheric unity and home-front initiatives both offered museums highly visible, relevant means to demonstrate their commitments to these objectives, with the hope that the public and purse string holders alike would recognize, remember, and reward this work come peacetime.

Before the United States even entered the war, the Department of State and its external advisers had already begun discussions about possible postwar roles and conduits for cultural diplomacy.[2] Would independent cultural organizations, including museums, lead the charge in pursuit of an ecumenical internationalism, free of national policy agendas but, perhaps, aided by federal funds? Or would the government include cultural goods among its scientific, technical, and other nation rebuilding exports as a means to ensure that the ideological as well as physical infrastructures in war-torn countries bore the imprint of American influence? Indeed, throughout the entirety of war the various participants in the exhibitionary network kept sight of their possible peacetime work. By March 1943, these anticipations of the peace to come took on the power of a cultural imaginary when Wendell L. Willkie's book *One World* captured the nation's attention. The book, which chronicled the author's forty-nine-day trip by plane to various points around the globe in the summer of 1942, emphasized the urgency of supporting the newly formed United Nations as well as the need to avoid the paths of isolationism or imperialism once the war concluded. Nationalists, or unilateralists, meanwhile, geared for the two-world contest of superpower-backed ideologies that would ultimately gain political and cultural traction as the Cold War.[3] Regardless of their leanings, Americans involved in these discussions envisioned the United States assuming a leadership position in shaping the world to come.[4]

Museums, like the public at large, found inspiration in the book, which sold more than 1.2 million copies in the five months after its release.[5] The domestically focused cultural diplomacy work of museums, first in hemispheric unity and then in knitting bonds of Allied friendship, set in place useful foundations for their roles in materializing the "One World" imaginary at home. A key distinction, however, lay in the new imaginary's greater elasticity in terms of representing cohesion while also accommodating national and cultural differences as points for celebration rather than minimization, as had been the case with the Good Neighborhood. Museums that took up the task of preparing their publics for participation in a global postwar society frequently situated themselves as gateways to a new cosmopolitan citizenship. US museum professionals played an active part, too, in the formation of international professional bodies seeking to harness educational and cultural resources for peacekeeping aims, with Americans taking up leadership of the Museums Division of the United Nations Educational, Scientific and Cultural Organization (UNESCO) and the International Council of Museums (ICOM).

For the more progressive practitioners in museums, the internationalist One World spirit of inherent human sameness and respect for cultural diversity seemed an apt match to prewar visions of what museums might accomplish in terms of civic good on complex social issues. One art museum educator (while calling for better funding and training to allow for greater strides at home) even saw an opportunity for the model of the museum as a social instrument to be sent abroad. "The observation has been made by European experts in the field," he wrote, "that the emphasis in social responsibility which has been so strong a factor in American museum policy, is a peculiarly native development and as such has been an export item, one which, it is reasonable to add, may be delivered in greater amounts to Europe when continental museums are once again able to resume full operation."[6] Yet, even as the idea of the museum as social instrument continued to percolate in the professional literature and in practice, it did not emerge as a well-defined movement during the war. Likewise, the material rhetoric of exhibition craft suited to social instrumentality did not coalesce as a specific set of widespread practices. As museums began, yet again, to re-examine their missions and actions as public institutions in light of the coming peace, the vision, definition, and implementation of social instrumentality remained as it began: diffuse.

Several factors affecting the field contributed to this, including realignments of staff at the war's start and end; conflicts between the resourcing demands of temporary exhibitions and those of collections-focused permanent galleries; and the complexities of navigating the postwar political scene. As conceived by the likes of Low, Arthur Parker, Beatrice Winser, Laura Bragg, and others, the museum as social instrument meant, first and foremost, providing education that connected museum holdings, knowledge, and resources to the concerns of contemporary life. Exhibition craft in pursuit of this ambitious yet fuzzy goal had always ranged from rarer projects such as *Wartime Housing*, which sought through material rhetoric, multisensory appeals, and storytelling to inspire action based on an intellectual, emotional, and physical knowing of the issues, to the more numerous displays whose chief innovation, while not small, rested in the fact that they addressed current events at all. The arrival of One World consciousness not only saw the continuation of this pattern, it ushered in a universalist strain of object-based epistemology that passed as social instrumentality while neutering its more progressive aspects.

From Grasping the World to One World

Museum exhibitions that oriented visitors to the war's shifting coordinates and widening terrain had become common by 1943. With millions of Americans deployed overseas, many on the home front now had newly personal stakes in getting to know the world beyond US borders. Museums, libraries, mass media, and other outlets met this burgeoning interest. Orders for National Geographic maps had increased 600 percent since the start of the war, and when giving his radio addresses, President Roosevelt often advised listeners to consult a world map.[7] All manner of publications made note of this rising interest in geography. "In these map-conscious days we have all become more conversant with many remote areas of the world," wrote one art historian. "Especially has this been true of the vast south Pacific region, where such names as Guadalcanal, Rabaul, Buna, and New Caledonia are now front-page, household words."[8] He recommended that educators either visit Miguel Covarrubias's "Pageant of the Pacific," a set of mural maps from the Golden Gate Exposition then on display at the American Museum of Natural History (AMNH) in New York, or buy reproductions for instructional use. Although he deemed them flawed as anthropological and geographical documents, he thought the maps' popular appeal might do much to "dispel the general lack of knowledge of the Pacific region." For its part, the AMNH reported, "The war has stimulated people's interest in the whole world of nature, including the various peoples inhabiting the earth. This renewed interest is indicated at the Museum by great increases in membership, in visitor attendance, and in the number of subscribers to the Museum's popular publications. Anyone mingling with the great crowds on Saturdays, Sundays, and holidays is struck with the eagerness and intelligence which our visitors display in their choice of subject and their attention to it."[9]

As grasping the world became a national preoccupation, many museums mounted quick-changing exhibits that followed headline events. For example, *The Living Map* series of the Illinois State Museum highlighted a new locale every fortnight. The effort also reinforced the institution's chosen sobriquet: the living museum. The installation consisted of a large wall map with a movable red arrow that pointed to the current area of interest, be it Australia, Japan, Algeria, Greece, or Java. A companion display of cultural artifacts and natural specimens set before the map provided a sense of the spotlighted region's unique features.[10] In similar fashion, the Newark Museum presented *Theatres of War,* an exhibition series that ran from 1942 through 1944, and the Field Museum offered *War Theatres,* which it promised would "keep pace with current front page news" from battle areas.[11] Such undertakings were easiest for museums with robust art, anthropology, and natural history collections—not to mention well-traveled local lenders. On one occasion, at least, community institutions banded their collective strengths together. The Albright Art Gallery,

Buffalo Historical Society, Buffalo Zoological Gardens, Buffalo Museum of Science, and Buffalo Public and Grosvenor Libraries coordinated the yearlong series *The World You Must Know When the Boys Come Home* (March 1943–April 1944) so that city residents might understand distant cultures from a variety of disciplinary perspectives.[12]

Museums also instructed military personnel, from strategists to grunts. Researchers at the Smithsonian and the AMNH produced materials on navigation, survival, Indigenous customs, and, for budding naturalists in the ranks, tips on specimen collection. The New York Zoological Society (classified as a living museum by AAM standards) invested the energies of its tropical research staff in developing shark repellants and methods to make seawater drinkable. The society's *Life in the Jungle* exhibit drew some 232,000 persons, including service personnel who reportedly took notes on how to find water and food should the need arise.[13] Training expressly for military personal occurred not only at museum sites, as in the case of celestial navigation courses at the Hayden Planetarium, but also on bases through in-person and exhibit-based instruction. The military also sought museum guidance on how fighting forces, particularly in the Pacific, might distinguish allies from enemies—on sight. The AMNH reported having produced 162 portable exhibitions on "racial identification" for the army. In the Mile High City, the Denver Art Museum developed the exhibit series *Peoples of Our Fighting Fronts* to help acquaint military trainees with the Indigenous groups they might encounter overseas.[14] Even when such undertakings explicitly endeavored to promote cross-cultural respect, as was the case in Denver, the reductionism required to condense human complexity down to a recognizable "type" frequently undermined curators' better intentions.[15] Indeed, even when up to date in refuting scientific racism, this body of work still naturalized race as a legitimate form of human categorization. Hierarchical equations of whiteness with civilization, modernity, and progress (as defined by Euro-Western standards) persisted as well. These shortcomings would carry forward into exhibitions designed to cultivate a One World ethos of seeing human sameness and diversity as two equally valued sides of the same coin.

Among the more progressive One World exhibitions in its intent, *The Races of Mankind* (January–February 1944) at the Cranbrook Institute of Science in Bloomfield, Michigan, aimed to redress the interracial violence that had erupted around Detroit in 1943 as much as it sought to mitigate divides that led to war. Based on the public-facing work of anthropologist Ruth Benedict, the photo-narrative style exhibit included sections devoted to such topics as "All Mankind Is One Family," "No Race Is Mentally Superior," and "Negroes Are an Integral Part of Our Culture."[16] In some sections, mannequin-like photo cutouts of children and adults appeared in settings with objects to add a sense of three-dimensional realism. However, as Tracy Teslow notes, the exhibit remained blind to the ways in which its use of science to deconstruct racism remained invested in race as an observable reality and viable taxonomy.[17] Its visual elements, too, privileged whiteness as the template for national belonging and cultural attainment. An ambitious undertaking for its time, the project sought to bring a fractured community together. Social services executive Beulah Whitby spoke at the exhibit opening; a leader within Detroit's Black community, Whitby had been appointed to the Interracial Committee that the city formed in the wake of 1943's deadly clashes. The Cranbrook installation as well as reproductions of it circulated first through public schools and library branches in Detroit and then to sites including Fisk University and the Newark Museum.

Unsurprisingly, community groups, not museums, led the way in aligning racial equity work with the rising tide of cultural internationalism and, occasionally, they sought out museums to advance their agendas. The Pan-American Women's Association, for example, tapped into the AMNH's institutional expertise when it held its conference there in 1943 on the theme of "Inter-Racial Understanding—a Key to Inter-American Unity."[18] Staff of the AMNH numbered among the speakers, and the AMNH helped sponsor the event as part of its efforts to more broadly communicate its contributions to the scientific understanding of race. Indeed, as pointed out by others, the conference's timing coincided with the AMNH's recently released annual report, which called attention to how the institution's research undermined Nazi theories of a master race.[19] Newspaper accounts in the days of the conference quoted the report in such headlines as "Races Are Not 'Superior' or 'Inferior,' but Only 'Different,' Scientists Emphasize."[20] They quoted, too, the report's added caveat that this proved true "save for a comparatively few primitive tribes."[21] If the Pan-American Women's Association sought to leverage museum expertise, the National Association of Negro Business and Professional Women's Clubs (NANBPWC) sought to challenge and expand it. The group chose MoMA for its major convening, which included an international roundtable that drew together discussants from Brazil, China, Mexico, Liberia, India, and other nations to address "The Role of Women in Shaping the Peace and Reconstruction."[22] The NANBPWC, which counted among its activities support for Black professionals in the arts, stated that it chose MoMA for two reasons: "First because there is a need to find a place where Negro artists can exhibit their works permanently, and second—because there is a need for understanding and integration."[23] This example, in particular, is a small but suggestive glimmer into early work by civic groups to claim space in the white museum.

In the months following the NANBPWC gathering, racial equity received little more than lip service in MoMA's exhibition *Airways to Peace: An Exhibition of Geography for the Future* (July 2–October 31, 1943). Based on Willkie's book, the installation's One World message inverted that of the Science Museum of the St. Paul Institute's earlier *Can America Be Bombed?*. Both efforts focused on how advances in aviation seemed to draw distant points on the globe closer by virtue of shortening transit times from one to the other. But whereas the St. Paul exhibition focused on the increased military threat posed by plane-borne proximity, MoMA's rehabilitative effort, in addition to educating museumgoers about historical developments in mapping and flight, war uses of planes, and details of atmospheric composition, struck a culminating note of hopeful possibility for the air age to come. Praised by *Time* magazine as "A brilliant educational exhibition," the show, by the *New York Times*' reckoning, was a "timely reminder of the change, growth, and ever-new responsibilities entailed in the progress of civilization."[24] The issue of *The Bulletin of the Museum of Modern Art* that reprinted these and other accolades from the press, also underscored, in an article by Monroe Wheeler, the internationalist spirit at the exhibition's core. "Not only in idealistic theory but in actual fact the world today is one unit: air neighbors are near neighbors," wrote Wheeler, who in 1940 had become the first person to hold the post of director of exhibitions for MoMA.[25] Further, he said, "Whether we like it or not, each nation is a portion of the world-nation. Over our heads the airways have woven a web of intimacy, a new scene of mutual advantages, a world-brotherhood."

The show, which also traveled widely in circulating editions, featured section labels written by Willkie himself. Other scholars, who have treated *Airways to Peace* in detail, note how its design repeatedly situated the museumgoer—and by extension the United States and her citizens—as being the vital center and origin point of a reconfigured postwar world.[26] This emphasis effectively nullified the unitive internationalism gestured to in Willkie's exhibition copy. Unsupported by the bulk of the exhibit's visual and spatial rhetoric, the closing exhortation, which included the line "We must learn that narrow nationalism and racial and religious intolerance are suicidal," appeared alongside a happy, homogeneous riot of youngsters perched on an impossibly Escheresque set of monkey bars (figure 8). Their upturned smiling faces created the illusion that the air-age museumgoer viewed them from above, perhaps from the futuristic transport, a Northrop all-wing prototype, that hung from wires in front of the scene.[27] Off to the side, and easy to miss at first glance, a crying child, at smaller scale than the rest, floated alone in his own photo bubble. Described in the exhibition checklist only as "Little Jap boy," his position seems to suggest that the racial "other" of the Axis sat outside the reach of reconciliation.

As Allied victories mounted, museums increasingly turned their attention to the resumption of operations free of the war's curtailments. Plans to expand or upgrade facilities, to reinstall collections being retrieved from storage, and to realign staffing as deployed personnel returned home began to occupy museum leadership. The field also continued its

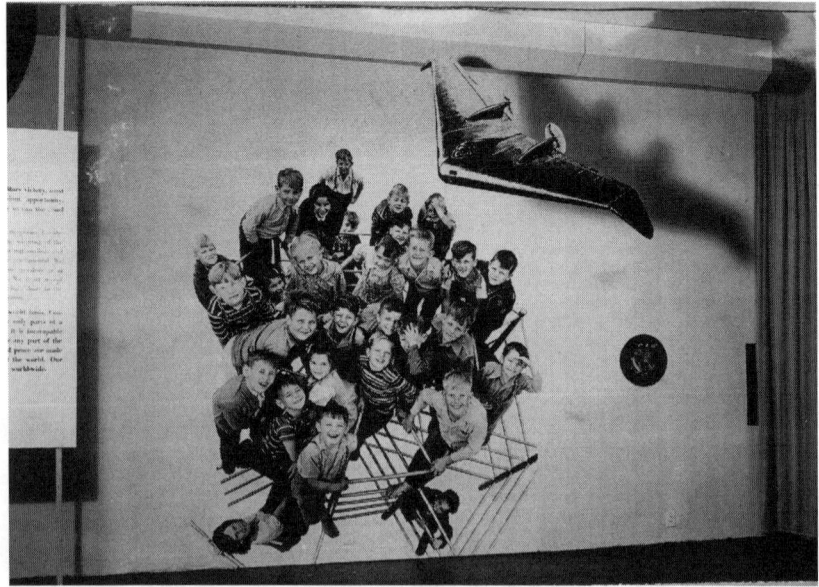

FIGURE 8. The culminating image for *Airways to Peace* situated the museumgoer as gazing "down" at the smiling generation of a peaceful tomorrow as imaginatively viewed from the cutout of a Northrop Flying Wing prototype hanging before the photographic backdrop. Off to the side, like an odd punctuation mark, a young Japanese boy in fancy military dress cries alone. Installation view of the exhibition, *Airways to Peace* (July 2, 1943–October 31, 1943). Photographic Archive. The Museum of Modern Art Archives, New York. Digital Image © The Museum of Modern Art / Licensed by SCALA / Art Resource, NY.

exchanges on adult education, attention to social issues, and the merits of storytelling approaches to exhibit craft—topics of the late 1930s that, having been grafted onto wartime work, now had to be considered anew. The service climate encouraged by the war had made some inroads in these areas possible, as had the fact that museum educators often enjoyed greater leeway under managerial realignments necessitated by wartime absences. New arguments in favor of social instrumentality came with the public's rising sense of obligation to returning soldiers. Communities began calling on museums, particularly those with arts programs, to provide resources for injured and war-harmed veterans' rehabilitation. Great enough was the need to coordinate effectively with hospitals, the Red Cross, scout troops, and others involved in such services that the Museums Council of New York and the New England Inter-Museum Committee each published guides for their regions.[28] While art-making programs predominated, the Natural History Museum in San Diego engaged reacclimating sailors in the work of the museum, training them to check and improve catalog entries for the collection as well as gather specimens for the herbarium.[29] For its part, the Detroit Institute of Arts worked with a psychiatrist to devise "A Tour for War Nerves: A Guide to an Hour in the Galleries." With brochure in hand, anyone seeking respite might find it in the fifteen paintings "selected for their qualities of order, harmony, and serenity."[30] More can—and should—be said about the social services that museums provided during and immediately after the war, but this, too, is an aspect of the field's history awaiting further research.[31]

On the matter of socially engaged exhibition craft, art museums, as before, launched the sharpest debates on these matters. These exchanges often cast the struggle as one of extremes, with one side determined to rescue scholarship from crass attempts at popularization and the other choosing the good of the people over the narrow self-interests of the governing elite. MoMA's Alfred H. Barr attempted to describe the dilemma, as it manifested at his often internally quarrelsome institution, more evenhandedly. Even when justified, the "intensive pressure to popularize" placed staff under a frenzy of exhibition and catalog deadlines, which, Barr noted, inevitably impinged on the "integrity and intellectual quality" of the supporting research.[32] The demands of postwar society, he imagined, would not improve the situation. So, instead of setting research and popular education in opposition, he proposed that collections-based scholarship might be directed toward enhancing public knowledge through more labels but fewer special exhibitions *and* through more frequent use of media the public already embraced, from articles in the popular press to film and radio broadcasts.

Others argued for the benefits of multimedia in the galleries, too. Envisioning the future of natural history museums, one commenter lamented that his sector of the field still had not adequately revealed "the fascinating stories" that lay behind the objects on display.[33] Museums, he argued using familiar terms, "must tell a story, and tell it effectively, through the use of the best available modern aids to exhibition and showmanship."[34] The aids he recommended included purposeful use of darkened spaces and synchronized light, motion, and sound used to dramatic effect. "The creation of an exhibition hall is every bit as complicated as the creation of a good motion picture," he counseled.[35] It needed, therefore, to be a cooperative venture rather than one led primarily by the "veto power" of the curator.[36] Arguments for media were made on the merits of their educational outcomes as well. One art institute reported that installing visitor-operated record players had encouraged patrons to spend more time looking at the artworks than when they were led by a docent. The recorded talks had added social benefits as well. They "tend[ed] to break down the reserve found in galleries, visitors laughing and talking as they would in their own homes instead of whispering as had been the usual reaction before the records were installed."[37] Staff, who wrote and recorded the scripts, also found that the flexibility to add complementary background music, stage the explanation as discussion between two parties, and even act out a dramatization of the painting's subject, history, or maker provided "a great deal more atmosphere" than a docent could muster.

Voices opposing multimedia distractions, narrative frameworks, installations lacking in collections objects, and other trends associated with popularization of the didactic experience frequently took aim at the vehicle primarily responsible for their manifestation: the temporary or "theme" exhibition.[38] These had proliferated for a variety of reasons. One challenge facing museums that wanted to take on contemporary issues was whether or not existing collections and in-house expertise could support the making of meaningful connections. Some creative approaches to the dilemma prefigured rapid-response installations and community-sourced exhibits. Many institutions also relied on ready-made loan exhibits to address wartime topics. These had proliferated not only due to the material affordances of the photo-narrative model but also because all sectors of the exhibitionary network had a hand in their availability.

Corporate efforts made traveling exhibitions of war art another option, even as many museums organized showings of their own featuring artworks made by local soldiers, children, and veterans. These retained the customary object focus that photo-narrative displays lacked *and* provided the sense of contemporary relevance that performative patriotism and social instrumentality alike demanded. Examples include *Life* magazine's *War Art* (1943) and *Art in War: The Abbott Collection of Paintings of Naval Aviation* (1943), which featured explanatory labels written by the US Navy's Bureau of Aeronautics.[39] Both *Life* and Abbott Laboratories, working in collaboration with different military branches, had commissioned artists to record the war. Each also coordinated with the National Gallery of Art to tour the resulting collections, both of which had been gifted to the government. By 1946 *Life* formalized its efforts in this arena by setting Thomas Dabney Mabry Jr., who had worked at MoMA, the National Gallery of Art, and the Office of Facts and Figures, as director of its new photographic exhibitions department.[40] The Metropolitan Museum of Art, the AMNH, and the California Academy of Sciences counted among the museums, universities, libraries, and other institutions that took on such offerings as *The Incas, Photographing Science,* and *Fine Arts Under Fire*.[41]

At the local level, museums and corporations sometimes worked together to highlight community contributions to the war effort. *Airacobra* (1943), an exhibition by the Albright Art Gallery in conjunction with the Bell Aircraft Corporation, touted Buffalo's role in making the "cannon-on-wings" by tracing a single plane's journey from drawing board to active duty.[42] Similar efforts include the Newark Museum's *War and Peace: The Industrial Front in the Newark Area* (1945). Its nighttime programs allowed visitors to scan the city's skies with remotely controlled army searchlights.[43] A few businesses instituted more permanent displays of their own. Textron set up its War Products Museum on the forty-second floor of the Empire State Building, where visitors who purchased a dollar's worth of war stamps could gain entry to exhibits detailing past and present uses of textiles in combat.[44] Government entities remained active in the exhibitionary network as well. In addition to collaborations with businesses and museums, they produced their own photo-narrative exhibitions. The widely distributed *Wings Over America* (1943), from the Army Air Forces Training Command, outlined the stages involved in pilot training. Used for active as well as passive looking, in Newark at least, the exhibition was incorporated into drawing exercises for children's classes, with occasional

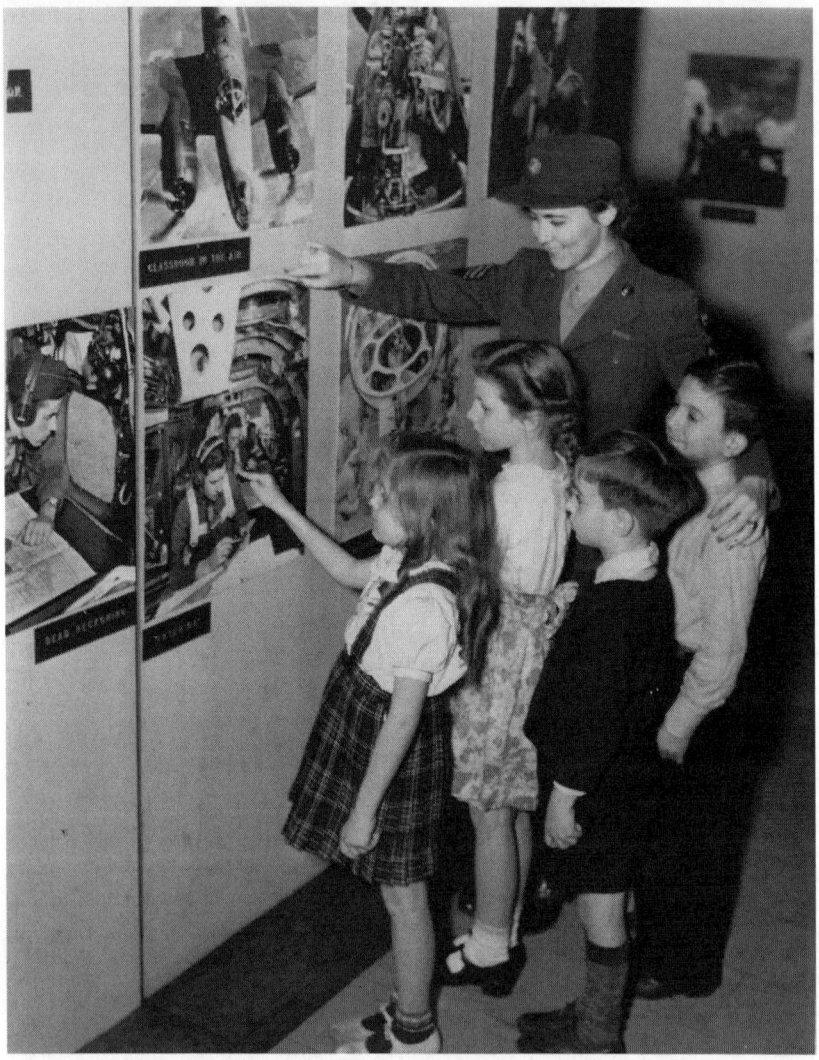

FIGURE 9. While touring a group of children through *Wings Over America* at the Newark Museum, AIR-WAC technical sergeant Caroline Nelson of South Carolina responds to their question about "how airmen sleep in the interior of a heavy bomber." *Wings Over America* Exhibition Photographs, 1942–1943, Box 36, Folder 10417: October 1943 *Wings Over America*. Archives of the Newark Museum.

tours given by service members (figure 9). By this point in the war, Winser continued as museum director, taking no salary, having resigned her other appointment as head of the library in 1942 over administrative tussles with the board of trustees.[45]

Like so many other museums, the Art Institute of Chicago (AIC) museum took on its fair share of these circulating shows, including MoMA's *Road to Victory*, *Life* magazine's *War Art*, and Abbott Laboratories' *Art in War*. So, when Daniel Catton Rich, the AIC's director of fine arts, enumerated what he saw as the pitfalls of temporary exhibits, he spoke from experience. He blamed their proliferation on the ceaseless quest for publicity and unsubstantiated claims that special exhibits would "'enliven' the museum, 'keep it up to date,' 'stimulate interest,' 'present something new,' 'get the public in, and so on.'"[46] In addition to the very real pressures that a merry-go-round cycle of production placed on war-depleted staff, Rich's displeasures included the display of "non-art described as art" now that cultural agencies, war concerns, charities, and others had "seized upon" the exhibition as a vehicle for reaching the public. He also placed photo-narrative exhibitions in his crosshairs, castigating MoMA's work, including *Road to Victory*, as possessing the air of having been "steam rollered into flatness."[47] "In the long run," Rich concluded, "the American art museum, no matter how great a social instrument it becomes, will continue to remind us more of the Louvre than last week's copy of *Life*."[48]

Rich's own curatorial response to these shortcomings—and the AIC's contribution to the One World imaginary—embraced object-based epistemology as an ideal mode of supporting the spirit of humanistic internationalism. Roughly eighteen months in the making, *Art of the United Nations* (November 16, 1944–January 1, 1945) drew together thirty-seven diverse objects, each one "a symbol" of the UN member country in which it had been created.[49] Throughout the exhibit's run, the museum restaurant featured lunchtime dishes from recipes given to it by chefs from Ethiopia, China, Russia, Mexico, Britain, and other UN members.[50] Consular representatives from all the included nations attended the opening reception, as did delegates of the Convention on International Civil Aviation, then meeting in Chicago to establish standards for peaceful access to airspace. About the exhibition, Rich and AIC publicity endeavored to make one point abundantly clear: no matter the title or current context, the effort was about art and its appreciation—nothing else. "*Art of the United Nations* is not a political exhibition," Rich wrote for the catalog's opening pages.

"It suggests nothing beyond the fact that every people make art, and that when art is good other people like to see it. Neither is it a war exhibition. No object, even those by contemporaries, treats of the present struggle. It is not educational in the sense that you are invited to read this art in terms of history, philosophy, religion or geographic boundaries."[51] Lest this declaration prove an insufficient statement of the exhibition's purpose, Rich concluded, "Such an exhibition can widen our aesthetic horizons and increase our pleasure in art. If it accomplishes these things, the Art Institute will consider it a success."[52]

Despite such strenuous protestations, the logic of the installation—as well as the cultural and political context of its creation and reception—made it a contributor to museums' part in building the One World imaginary. It had been designed by György Kepes, whose book *Language of Vision* came out concurrent with the exhibit. The volume, which went on to influence graphic design, arts education, and other fields, advanced ideas based on gestalt theories. Echoing sentiments advanced by earlier proponents of visual education, Kepes wrote, "Visual communication is universal and international: it knows no limits of tongue, vocabulary, or grammar, and it can be perceived by the illiterate as well as by the literate."[53] In terms of exhibition craft, this—along with cultural internationalism's desire to break down boundaries to human connection—provided further impetus to once again let objects speak for themselves, with strategic help from nonverbal means of display to amplify the single object's voice and the arrangement's chorus. With *Art of the United Nations,* Kepes's task was to harmonize the whole, which ranged from ceramics, textiles, and paintings to sculpture, metalwork, and illuminated manuscripts spanning some forty-one centuries, while also emphasizing the distinctiveness of each AIC-chosen national symbol. The installation accomplished this through carefully planned shifts in lighting, application of different color schemes, use of see-through and waist-high partitions, and landscaping effects. The latter included a grid-like box garden of blooms, segregated by color, in shades complementing those in Georges Seurat's *A Sunday on La Grande Jatte*, which hung nearby. In another gallery, a Coatlicue figurine on loan from Mexico sat atop a hillock of stone, gravel, and cacti.

The exhibition's design, considered novel at the time, rested in what Michael Golec has termed the *Language of Vision*'s central thesis: "Our vision of the world is alterable."[54] Here, theory aligned with internationalism's call for old world views to be realigned. Kepes and likeminded creators held that effective visual design did more than communicate ideas; it strengthened the beholder's cognitive skills, understood as a process of integrating discrete, disparate fragments into meaning, of creating harmony from disharmony. This empowered the individual not only to see their world anew but also to enter into a generative cycle of world remaking and re-envisioning that would conduce toward a more ideally integrated society. As one scholar put it, Kepes advanced "a manifesto for social change through positive visualization."[55] The exhibit's reliance on nonverbal design as didactic signposts to presumedly inherent object meanings did not, however, sidestep the individual, institutional, or societal prejudices shaping the era's museum work. In *Art of the United Nations* the biases shaping the selection and presentation of its designated French and Mexican objects also informed the respective catalog entries. The Seurat, like the cultivated garden before it, is aligned with "the best of French traditions: order, restraint, logic, balance, thought, emotions," whereas the Aztec figure offered "a magnificent beauty in its vigor and in its savage force."[56]

Material rhetoric of this vein, prevalent always in art museums, held that artifacts, as tangible human expressions, possessed inseverable relationships not only to their makers but also to the deeper spark common to all humanity. In other words, certain art, modes of dress, folk craft, and other hand-produced items embodied the intangible essence that made "recognition in common" possible through the human-thing encounter. So, while provoking affective connections remained a central concern of One World–minded exhibits, reliance on overt narrative scaffolding for information delivery and prompts to action very often fell away. If the object-based epistemology of the Victorian era espoused "unmediated" encounter as the route to scientific and aesthetic truths, universalist object-based epistemology preached it as the path to affective truth.

If *Art of the United Nations* represented a concerted backlash against objects as narrative devices, heavy-handed social instrumentality, and other promiscuities in museum exhibition craft that wartime had encouraged within art museum galleries, then *What the Boys Send Home* (April 8–May 8, 1945) at the Wadsworth Atheneum in Hartford, Connecticut, represented the ways in which institutional disruption could encourage experimentation even alongside a universalist approach to object-based epistemology. Like many mainstream museums, the Wadsworth Atheneum (today called the Wadsworth Atheneum Museum of Art) struggled to maintain operations during the 1930s and into the war years. It suffered, too, a protracted and fractious internal battle for control of the museum's aesthetic and financial direction that often pitted director A. Everett Austin Jr. against the board of trustees.[57] Many of the activities for which Austin is lauded today—avant-garde theatrical programs and modern art purchases and exhibitions—had, along with poor fiscal management and declining membership, caused the rupture.

Austin's grievances included what he saw as society's—and the trustees's—"abandonment of spiritual responsibilities, the insistence on the values of mere entertainment, the pedestalling of mediocrity, the cult of compromise," and "the mesmerism exerted by numbers."[58] Austin had asked his opposition, "Do you think that attendance is important? If so, how far do you wish to go towards the achievement of that end? Or do you believe as I do that a lack of attendance should in no way discourage us or deter us from our activities?" Austin soon went on leave, which the board extended so he could quietly find a new post. In 1943, they appointed long-time Atheneum general curator Florence Paull Berger as acting director (a post she held through 1946).[59] Berger, in turn, brought on Gladys Lynwall Pratt as her new assistant. The special charge given to Denver-born Pratt, who was then in her late forties and had worked for seventeen years as an associate in the AMNH's Department of Public Education, was to stimulate public interest in the museum and to build membership.[60]

"Mrs. Pratt's Ambition: Open Atheneum to All," read the newspaper article declaring the museum's new arrival.[61] As to how she would pursue that goal, the reporter noted, "Mrs. Pratt tries to keep the exhibits and entertainments close to the normal person's daily life. 'You must humanize,' she says earnestly, 'I don't believe in exhibiting anything that is so removed from the human element that it is beyond the scope of most persons.'" Pratt conceived of *What the Boys Send Home* as the first in a series of exhibitions designed to tap into the existing interests and club activities of the community. Through various forms of outreach, she called on area residents to loan "native crafts, pictures and other objects of general interest" that they had received from service personnel. Pratt observed, "There are few people today who are not closely connected with the far-flung theaters of war."[62] As to the parameters for loaned objects,

"She requests that no explosives or such things as embellished pillows be included and emphasizes that the crude object may have more inherent value and interest than the one that apes the elegancies of civilization."[63] Drawing on her AMNH background documenting folkways, Pratt sought to separate objects emblematic of craft traditions from tourist goods. The statement also reveals the prejudicial contours of her internationalism as well as that of the United States more generally.

Some fifty people loaned more than five hundred items to the effort.[64] The three hundred or so artifacts chosen for display included embroideries, silver, dolls dressed in ethnic garb, jewelry, slippers, postcards, grass skirts, Chinese robes, crafts from New Guinea, a Japanese soldier's diary, and a commando's knife.[65] There is no indication of an interpretive scheme beyond that of cited arrangements by geography (e.g., items from Greenland) or type (e.g., a case of slippers from different nations). Organization by country or region conveyed particularity of place and culture, consistent with the One World emphasis on respect for cultural diversity, whereas assembly by type spoke to the universality of human needs and customs, thus highlighting inherent human sameness. *What the Boys Send Home* also illuminates how, even in such basic display configuration, a witnessing dynamic could exert itself on multiple levels. First, the artifacts as witness-objects functioned singly or in combination as surrogates for the soldiers who had sent them, the defeated enemies who had owned them, and the persons who had made them. The artifacts selected for exhibition bore additional witness to the senders' and lenders' wartime experiences, validating these as having community significance—even as the exhibit's spare interpretive framework rendered each artifact's personal testimony latent.

The human origins and transits of the assembled artifacts spoke in aggregate to the extent of America's military reach and, as museum workers such as Pratt hoped, to the nation's expanded intellectual horizons. To apprehend the objects as artifactual stand-ins for others in the international community required a unitive act of forgetting, a relinquishing of the military contexts of procurement in order to see each token as part of a peaceful world waiting to be grasped. The personal became global as Home Front belonging transitioned to One World citizenship. That Pratt intended such associations for this community-sourced exhibit is made clear by the membership campaign she devised to go along with it called "Your Share in the Postwar World." The appeal situated the museum as uniquely qualified to meet the needs not only of returning soldiers, "whose horizons have been broadened during long years in foreign places," but of all those newly interested in global affairs.[66] "This invitation to become a member is your privilege, to share in the postwar activities for a lasting peace. We live in 'one world' and by stressing the humanities, we are broadening our vision and giving something to posterity which is imperishable."

In presenting the museum as a gateway to One World citizenship, Pratt and the Wadsworth Atheneum, like many of their peers across the country, sought, once more, to consider their public worth in the face of social uncertainty. While opinion surveys showed that the US public viewed its postwar future more optimistically than it had in the conflict's early years, many still worried that peace would turn the military economic boom to bust.[67] This, along with the return of millions of veterans seeking employment, pointed, some feared, to a new, possibly more severe, financial depression with attendant political and social disruptions. Such institutionalized witnessing opportunities provided by museums during World War II did more than contribute to broader efforts to cohere various forms of national and international belonging. They also functioned to codify the museumgoing public's experiences as meaningful, and potentially fulfilled a need to see reality restated, as one scholar of memory put it, "in ideal rather than complex or ambiguous terms."[68] Exhibitions that engaged war-related issues, whether they also leveraged a witness dynamic or not, enabled originating and host museums to demonstrate their civic belonging and relevance. By August 1945, following the atomic devastation of Hiroshima and Nagasaki, conjecture about what the war's end would bring had started to become reality. The next year saw Berger returned to her position as general curator when the Atheneum filled the director's spot with a man.[69] Pratt, having departed the museum to marry at the age of forty-nine, later moved to Key West, Florida, and became involved with the historical society and arts there.[70]

Recognition in Common

As the first year to dawn under the under the shadow of nuclear annihilation, 1946 also brought British prime minister Winston Churchill to US shores, where he famously warned of the "iron curtain" descending across

Europe as Soviet and communist influence advanced beyond Russian borders.[71] His itinerary also included a visit to Colonial Williamsburg, where John D. Rockefeller Jr. had funded education and recreation programs for military personnel throughout the war so that they might be fortified by what the site's restorers saw as its testament to the nation's founding ideals.[72] The living history museum had also hosted the AAM's 1942 conference, its last during the war, so news that the annual event would resume in May of '46 provided the field cause for celebration. A record-setting roster of some five hundred attendees, including colleagues from Latin America, Europe, and Canada, assembled in Washington, DC.[73] Whereas the meeting themes of 1941 ("Defense and Hemisphere Solidarity") and 1942 ("Wartime Duties of Museums") had focused on museums' roles and responsibilities in relation to significant current events, the sessions of 1946 looked inward. The "Timely Museum Problems" on the docket concerned personnel, collections, and facilities—matters given looser reign or kept on a make-do basis during the war.[74] The planning of museum buildings, as well as defining the education and training required for various types of museum work, commanded not only the general sessions but many of the subspecialty sections as well. As Samuel J. Redman has argued, an era of systematizing museum methods for dealing with human, built, and collection infrastructures had begun.[75]

Despite there being no grand conference theme pointing the field outward, internationalism made its presence known in multiple ways. A special delegate from France highlighted opportunities for renewed cultural collaboration. An event at the Pan-American Union gathered members to preview watercolors being sent south by the vestiges of the government's hemispheric unity programs now managed by the Inter-American Office at the National Gallery of Art. The AAM announced it had accepted the invitation by Canadian colleagues to hold the 1947 conference in the city of Quebec. This all followed the opening address by Archibald MacLeish titled "Museums and World Peace." MacLeish, now a member of the US delegation appointed by the Department of State to guide UNESCO's formation, had played a determining role in authoring the organization's constitution, which he invoked in calling museums to do their part in birthing the world anew. Reminding attendees to hear his words not as "rhetorical idealism" but as urgently direct, MacLeish said, "The work to be done is the work of building *in men's minds* the image of the world which now exists in fact *outside* their minds—the whole and single world of which all men are citizens together. The constitution of Unesco puts part of the labor in these terms: 'Since wars begin in the minds of men it is in the minds of men that the defenses of peace must be constructed.'"[76]

MacLeish, pointing to the ruptures and distrust already present in peace efforts being undertaken through statecraft, called on museums and other cultural institutions to direct their collections and educational resources to a common task: the cultivation of "a recognition in common."[77] In every disciplinary field, from art to science, history to natural history, "The labor to be performed is a labor of recognition—of vision and imagination and recognition," he said.[78] In terms of social instrumentality, the outcome of such labor would be "an agreement that we are, and must conduct ourselves as though we were, one kind, one people, dwellers on one earth." MacLeish acknowledged that there still existed "a vigorous and well armed opposition" to museums being more active agents of adult education but called it "a little hypocritical" to withhold the scholarship, histories, geographical circuits, and other factors that brought objects into a collection and rendered them meaning rich to specialists. MacLeish described museums as unique in their communicative powers in that they not only reached the intellect but also expressed and made "palpable" a deeper form of human knowing.[79]

MacLeish, acknowledging that he commented as an outsider to the museum profession (but not to exhibition craft as earlier noted), offered no specifics on implementation, but others in the AAM's ranks, some working alongside him, had already begun to think about the issues. UNESCO, ICOM, and the State Department's Office of International Information and Educational Exchange provided the chief institutional frameworks through which US museum professionals channeled their internationalist impulses abroad.[80] Grace McCann Morley, founding director of the San Francisco Museum of Art, took the helm of UNESCO's Museums Division, and Chauncey Jerome Hamlin, president of the Buffalo Society of Natural Sciences and former AAM president (1923–29), assumed leadership of ICOM.[81] Morley drew on international experience and connections cultivated through her involvement in the Golden Gate Exposition and various Pan-American initiatives, which included advising and exhibition organizing for the OCIAA and Department of State. It was the latter who appointed Morley as consultant to the UNESCO

Secretariat in 1946. Morley, who spoke French as well as Spanish, served on the Libraries and Museums Sub-Commission and, by her account, it was she who suggested the formation of a separate museums division.[82] In 1947, she took a roughly two-year leave of absence from the San Francisco Museum of Art to serve as that new division's head.[83] Morley also secured UNESCO's financial support for the formation of ICOM, which she described as one of UNESCO's earliest and most valuable nongovernmental collaborators on museum-related projects.[84]

Hamlin had been instrumental in getting the AAM on surer financial footing in the 1920s and had marshaled funds, including his own, for the founding of the Buffalo Museum of Science in 1929. A prolific and amiably chatty letter writer, he had built an international network of museum, foundation, and government contacts throughout his long and varied career. In 1945, he took up a letter writing campaign enlisting colleagues in forming an international museum confederation to replace the League of Nations' war-stalled International Museums Office.[85] So when in 1946 the State Department invited the AAM to appoint a member to the national advisory committee to UNESCO, they named Hamlin.[86] Supported by new allies, including Morley, ICOM organized that year in London. By year's end, the council had headquarters in Paris, where UNESCO had granted it office space, and had confirmed Hamlin as its first president (a position he held through 1953).[87]

Priorities of the Museums Division and ICOM included providing support to war-damaged institutions, encouraging professionalization of the field through training and staff exchanges, and advocating for object loans, gifts, and acquisitions to assure the availability of a universal collection, a One World gateway, in as many locations as possible. Early on, both groups also sought, as one division staffer, Raymonde Frin, recalled, "to envisage the prospects of museums in a world springing back to life, to call attention to the changes taking place in the conception of museums and their objectives," particularly in terms of education through programs and exhibitions.[88] Here, through their early publications and meetings, the two organizations emphasized museums as sites of popular education for all ages and as indispensable resources for achieving the social and cultural changes necessary to making international accord a lasting reality. This came at a time when such education work remained, according to Frin, inaugural editor of the division's magazine *Museum*, "still little practiced and often unfamiliar" the world round. As Morley later recalled of the animating ambitions and idealism shared among the period's museum internationalists, "We all believed in those days that indeed, we on our level, our intellectual and cultural level, were contributing as the United Nations did on its political and military level, to the elimination of war forever. There was then a hope and a confidence that in retrospect one recalls as a sort of guiding light and article of faith, that meant a tremendous amount to all of us."[89]

On the Brink, Again

One World idealism as carried out by US museums in the 1940s remained circumscribed by deep structural flaws that the field has only more recently begun to recognize and address. The commitment to museums as a civilizing force, imperial habits of acquisition and display, the predominant whiteness of the field, and the patriarchal whiteness of the disciplinary canons it constructed and celebrated numbered among the persistent headwinds not only facing the internationalist agenda but shaping it as well. Also, as W. E. B. Du Bois had noted in his critique of the United Nations, nationalism, imperialism, and racism all had powerful seats at the table, leaving much of the supposed global community disenfranchised.[90] Likewise, efforts by stateside museums to advance One World belonging tested the institutional will to address the separate, unequal worlds created and perpetuated by entrenched racism at home.

Committed internationalists knew, and hoped, that the twinned messages of inherent human sameness and respect for cultural diversity would haul domestic racism into the spotlight in ways that the government's anodyne war unity campaigns had not. Exposing racial injustice, however, carried more risk of alienating museums' white constituencies than did messages of universal toleration. The frictions surrounding development of the Museum of Modern Art's *Manzanar: Photographs by Ansel Adams of Loyal Japanese-American Relocation Center* (November 10–December 24, 1944) provide one example. The exhibit, as scholar Jasmine Alinder recounts, came to fruition after much internal debate, long delays, and significant modifications, which included the abandonment of its working title, *Born Free and Equal: Appeal for Justice*. Highlighting the title's rhetorical shift—from justice seeking to an affirmation of legitimacy by litmus test—serves here as shorthand for the compromises reached through a more complex process of negotiating the institutional boundaries of antiracism, which others have detailed. These authors also explore the problematic nature of the photographs themselves and their later circulation, with Adams's permission, by the OWI in Japan to countermessage claims of America's "monstrous" behavior toward internees.[91] Taking a bolder stance on race in the context of internationalism required, as one librarian whose institution had exhibited the Cranbrook Institute's *The Races of Mankind* put it, the ability to accommodate "ardent interest" from "enthusiasts and irate objectors" alike, from patrons praising the effort to others hurling racial slurs in defense of their white pride because "everyone is working very hard to put the [racist term for Black person] and Chinese on the same basis as me."[92] In recommending the exhibition to other institutions seeking "concrete" public value, the article's author noted, "It is equally a stimulus to those in complete agreement, and an agent provocateur to those who remain unconvinced."[93]

Postwar, domestic efforts to promote accord with former allied nations became fraught as well. As divergent political ideologies and national interests asserted their places in the UN and UNESCO, critics increasingly castigated "one world propaganda" that elevated "single-state" allegiance at the expense of domestic pride in US institutions and traditions.[94] Although educational efforts aligned with cultural internationalism now carried greater risk of being tarred as anti-American, for many the commitment to peace had intensified after US testing in 1946 of nuclear weaponry in the Bikini Atoll. Some, looking to museums, began calling for the defensive formation of "arsenals for the data of civilization" so that survivors of a nuclear conflagration might have hope of rebuilding from the ashes.[95] Hamlin, ICOM's president, quoted this line and acknowledged his own concerns in the article "Arsenals of Knowledge: In an Era of Atomic Peace." He suggested a path forward that, much like nuclear arms race ideology, proposed museums as having both offensive and defensive functions. "On two counts, then, museums of the world will bear an increasing responsibility in the post-war world," Hamlin wrote. "First, by nurturing international understanding and cooperation among the people of the world and second, by establishing a guard against atomic malcontrol and the disappearance of knowledge from the world."[96] In addition to reasserting museums' first value as active instruments of the peace offensive, Hamlin directed readers back to an earlier article he had written about the role of museums' exhibitions and education programs in working cooperatively with ICOM, UNESCO, and other such bodies to create the conditions necessary for a "permanent peace."[97]

Among those undertaking this work on the domestic front, the Brooklyn Museum organized one of the more comprehensive efforts to address flagging public faith in the United Nations. The museum, which had run programs in 1942–43 spotlighting UN signatories, timed two new exhibitions, *Know Your United Nations* and *Clothing One World* (September 16–November 23, 1947), to coincide with the second meeting of the UN General Assembly. The first exhibit, designed by the UN department of visual education, took a primarily photo-narrative form and circulated in different languages through several countries after its Brooklyn debut. Informationally, *Know Your United Nations* set out the organization's history and accomplishments, which it presented to museumgoers as "Our Road to Peace." A contrasting account of war's recent human devastations signaled the alternative path. Affectively, the exhibition as installed at the Brooklyn Museum offered fifty-five photomontages, one for each member nation, that literally put faces to numbers by pairing distinctive locals and locales deemed representative of a nation with its population count. The exhibit also invited visitors to see themselves as members of the global collective by means of a mirror set into a photographic medley of smiling faces (figure 10). "*You* are the United Nations," read the nearby affirmation. With regard to action, the exhibit concluded with practical ways individuals could stay informed and involved at the local level.

The curator of the Brooklyn Museum's Industrial Division, Michele Murphy, had organized the companion exhibit, *Clothing One World,* from the museum's costume and anthropological collections. She grouped the chosen items according to similarity of form and use, rather than by chronology or country of origin. Footwear, head coverings, torso-draping garments, and more appeared on wire mesh forms. In order to support the exhibition's contention "We are all the same underneath," the wire frameworks lacked individuating details and gestured to only as much of the human figure as was needed to animate the specific item of clothing for which it had been designed.[98] The centrality of universalist object-epistemology to the enterprise is reflected in the following curatorial remark: "And of all the mute 'dialects' spoken by the universal language

Gateways to Global Citizenship in a Postwar World 153

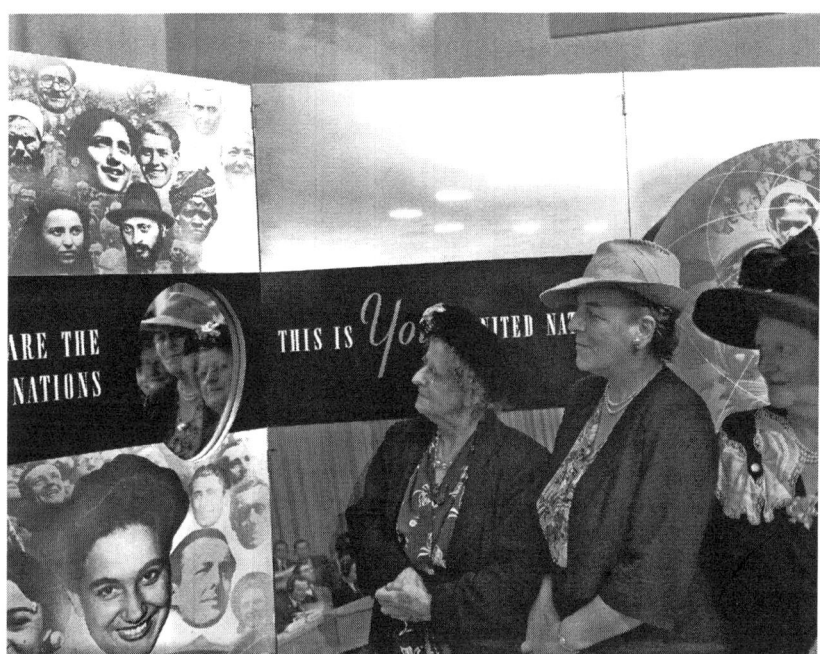

FIGURE 10. A trio of museumgoers takes up the invitation to see themselves as members of the United Nations' global family of One World citizens. Installation view of *Know Your United Nations* at the Brooklyn Museum (September 16–November 23, 1947), UN Photo/ Kari Berggrav. Courtesy of the United Nations Photo Library.

of art, costuming is probably the most 'colloquial'; everyone can understand and enjoy it."[99] The museum's educators played a significant part in the effort as well. Under the direction of the curator of the Educational Division, Hannah Rose, and in collaboration with several community groups, the museum assembled a roughly nine-week-long program of international music, song, dance, and film events. The Board of Education of the City of New York sponsored both exhibitions, integrating them and related materials into classrooms and field trips (figure 11).

Director Charles Nagel Jr. explained the museum's purpose for what had taken it almost two years to achieve: "The United Nations face a problem so enormous that it is difficult to come to grips with it. Most people, even those who want to help, are defeated by its size, and just go away, saying: What can *I* do? We must create a climate in which the U.N. can flourish. . . . Everyone has to care personally about the success of U.N. to make it a

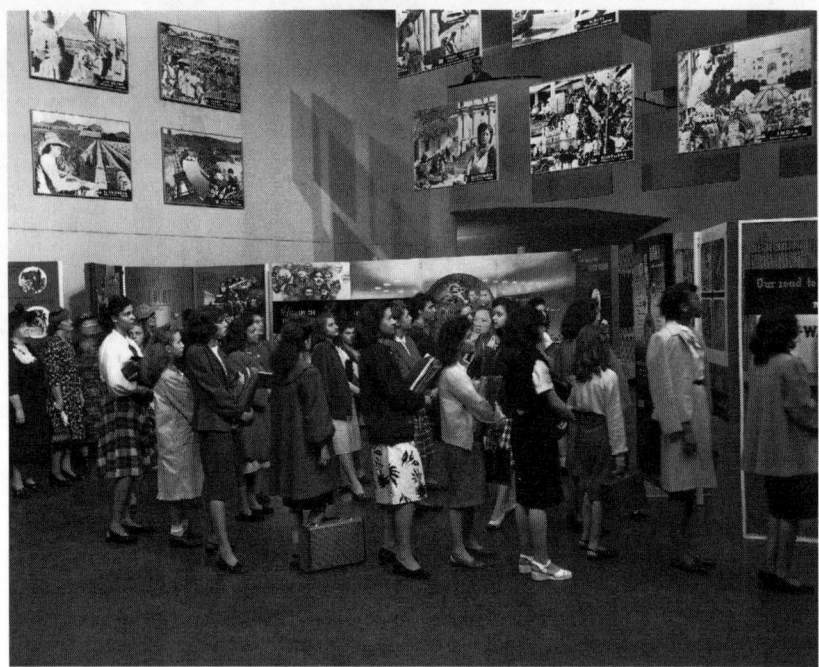

FIGURE 11. Crowds in the main hall of the Brooklyn Museum make their way through the *Know Your United Nations* exhibition, which the board of education sponsored, along with *Clothing One World,* as encouragement for schools to integrate these internationalist efforts into their curriculum. Installation view of *Know Your United Nations* at the Brooklyn Museum (September 16, 1947–November 23, 1947), UN Photo/Kari Berggrav. Courtesy of the United Nations Photo Library.

success."[100] Furthermore, he remarked, "It is easier to establish sympathy through peoples than through their governments. We can do something to build up universal good will, regardless of diplomatic tiffs. This is why we took hold here at the Brooklyn Museum, feeling that the visual approach is as potent as any in putting the question squarely up to the public."

The creation, contents, and circulation of each exhibition deserve deeper scrutiny, but here recorded public responses to *Know Your United Nations* will have the last word. One young Brooklynite, reportedly eager to talk about peace and the UN, regretted, "The people who would benefit by this exhibit are the ones who won't see it."[101] A museum guard of Hibernian heritage worried over Ireland's absence in the UN. Commending the exhibit as "very effective," a shipping clerk observed, "People are interdependent. Eventually exploitation of colonial peoples must stop."

Then, with equal conviction, he commended the "very concrete efforts of the U.N. to improve the lot of backwards peoples." These final words, ever emblematic of imperialism in its multiple forms, speak to the persistent backwardness within US cultural internationalism.

For the less savvy museum, misreading the postwar political terrain could bring recrimination, as seen in the compounding missteps of the New York Museum of Science and Industry (NYMSI), which occupied leased quarters in Rockefeller Center. As previously noted, the museum had exhibited the OWI-supported *Two Allies—One War—One Peace* in 1943. The effort had been sponsored, too, by the National Council of American-Soviet Friendship, a group sympathetic to socialism and, like the OWI, using the fight against fascism as reason to cultivate warmer feelings between the two powers. The museum received favorable press coverage for the exhibit, coming as it did when establishing cultural commonality between the two Allied nations held critical war value. But in 1948, when the NYMSI showed *Thirty Years of the USSR*, a circulating exhibition organized by the Soviet Embassy, the event stirred public outcry. Lithuanian refugees picketed outside the museum bearing signs denouncing "the exhibit of lies" and called for the NYMSI "to grant the same facilities to the peoples of the enslaved countries by the USSR to tell their graphic story in the same space which is allotted to their Soviet oppressors."[102]

If the museum's first misstep was to assume repeated success based on a superficial similarity to a past exhibition, then sheer opportunism caused the fall. Showing signs of misgiving, NYMSI director Robert P. Shaw took the unusual step of seeking out Nelson Rockefeller's advice on whether showing the Soviet Embassy exhibit "would be proper and helpful at this time" and also asked the center's opinion on this "border-line case."[103] Shaw described the show as factual in its summary of Russian industrial, agricultural, governmental, and postwar developments (despite the museum's lack of expertise in these areas) but acknowledged, "[It] isn't too good from an exhibition standpoint." However, he felt it might still draw a crowd—something the struggling institution needed. Neither the center nor the former OCIAA head offered advice, stating only that such decisions should be made by the museum's board of directors.[104] (The center's public relations staff did, however, monitor the exhibition and public reaction closely. Their detailed report, which included information gathered by staffers who had posed as members of the press in order to suss out opening night attendees and responses, helped confirm the center's earlier decision not to extend the museum's soon-to-expire lease.[105]) To be clear, the NYMSI, even before its waning years, had, like other industrial museums, already departed from traditional museum practice in the 1930s with its close reliance on the industries whose scientific work it showcased—an impropriety Laurence Vail Coleman had called out in 1939.[106] So, while more mainstream museums might have handled the Soviet Embassy's invitation with greater rigor, the contrasting reception received by the two differently timed exhibitions about the USSR, each one rooted in government propaganda, speaks to larger issues confronting the field in the immediate postwar period.

With social instrumentality and patriotism as bedfellows, propaganda had indeed entered the museum at its own invitation. It typically took the form of photo-narrative exhibitions produced by or in collaboration with corporate and government actors in the exhibitionary network. Museums' varied motivations for taking such extramuseal exhibits on loan included attracting patrons, garnering publicity in order to stay in the public eye, and keeping galleries lively at a time when many institutions had to scale back on in-house production of temporary shows. Also, in cases where educational staff, already accustomed to using photographic surrogates for instruction, had been given command of gallery spaces, photo-narrative exhibits often made practical sense as a means to keep museum work connected to the present. With their lack of objects—and object-based knowledge in the traditional museal sense—photo-narrative exhibitions also fulfilled the worst predictions of those opposing storytelling approaches in the 1930s. When these productions also stood devoid of research and tools for decision making, they fell afoul of social instrumentality's best aspirations, too.

The availability of offerings wholly or partially conceived by the exhibitionary networks' corporate and government actors further clouded, through similarity of form, the distinctions that proponents of social instrumentality sought to make between their work and propaganda. For those inclined to see the museum as social instrument, exhibitions that used the tools of mass communications in conjunction with the knowledge resources of museums offered the means to inspire thoughtful, informed civic participation. Emotion and affect played a part, too, but alongside consideration of the presented evidence. This constituted the chief distinction that some members of the field saw between propaganda, which leveraged emotions to ply the public from its reasoning senses, and their own purpose-focused education. For many museumists, the shades of difference seemed negligible in the face of what they saw as the larger issue: the use of artifacts and specimens to tell stories. To paraphrase Coleman's earlier caution, to show objects as suggestions rather than examples, to make a tangible thing support an abstraction rather than stand on its own merits, constituted a slippery slope.[107] His objection dealt not with item labels but with the larger exhibitionary framework. Whether narration came with collections materials or, worse, without them, he offered the same caution: "This practice can lead on to indoctrination. It gets away from what museums are for—to give evidence, primarily."[108] Practitioners experimenting with the material rhetoric of social instrumentality during the war years felt that this was a needle they could thread, that narrative presentations of objective evidence (in both senses of the word) could lead not to indoctrination but to educated civic participation.

This, then, provided the animating spirit behind such efforts as the Newark Museum's *Three Southern Neighbors*, MoMA's *Wartime Housing*, and the Cranbrook Institute of Science's *The Races of Mankind*. It might seem straightforward enough to distinguish state-produced propaganda, to take *Thirty Years of the USSR* as an example, from the social instrumentality of an effort such as *The Races of Mankind*, which was considered as public-facing scholarship of its time pointed toward a civic good. Simpler yet might seem the task of separating each of these from the era's traditionalist exhibitions in the arts, sciences, and other disciplines that museum practitioners claimed had no position, no point of view, other than that of the objects' material truths. Consider, however, where, from past or current vantage points, to position the Brooklyn Museum's *Clothing One World*, MoMA's *Road to Victory*, or the Wadsworth Atheneum's *What the Boys Send Home*. In addition, where should nonmuseal works, such as *Know Your United Nations*, which appeared in museums and other contexts, sit? Determining where to locate specific museum exhibitions of the period within the matrix of social instrumentality and propaganda requires—when archival traces exist—careful study of the myriad details of the exhibition's making and reception and of the internal and external factors bearing on those processes. It also requires giving weight to creators' intentions alongside analysis of the cultural work such exhibitions performed. It demands recognition that any determination is relational and that throughout the period examined here practitioners, critics, and publics often reached different determinations about the same exhibition. Ultimately, the point of this aspect of my research is to sweep away narrow assumptions about the nature of museums' diverse undertakings during the war period and to illuminate the challenge that the material rhetoric of social instrumentality, with its emphasis on storytelling, posed to traditions of museum objectivity and neutrality.

Conclusion

MUSEUM STORIES, OLD AND NEW

> How can we situate "radical museology" in the long history of the movement by museums towards more inclusion, civic discourse and public engagement?
>
> —Jennifer Scott, director and chief curator of the Jane Addams Hull-House Museum, 2016

Addressing the international museum community in 1949, Grace McCann Morley, who had recently stepped down as the inaugural head of UNESCO's Museums Division, noted that the war had been a "major disruption" even for institutions operating in safety far from the battlefields.[1] This, she reflected, also made the years of struggle "a period which challenged professional museum people to examine their traditional conceptions and to adapt their thinking to a wide range of possibilities." Such examination, in the United States at least, traced back to the 1930s. Shaken by the social, political, and financial disruptions of the Great Depression, the museum field took stock of its civic viability. Some in the ranks, which included museum educators in greater numbers, looked back to unrealized ambitions of Progressive Era practitioners and found synergies with the adult education movement and the populism of the Works Progress Administration. They worried, too, about the power of mass communications, European fascism, and the ways in which these might erode the capacity for informed individual reasoning deemed essential for a participatory democracy.

Shaped by these forces, opportunities, and concerns, the conception of the museum as a social instrument aspired to active engagement in community life by providing purpose-driven education on contemporary civic issues through exhibitions and other means. Proponents of social instrumentality believed this would both serve and attract a wider portion of the public than most museums typically served. Concurrent with this school of thought came experimentations in exhibition craft, which conceived of objects, installation materials, and the spaces these occupied as constituent parts of an expressive, narrative-driven medium. These changes signaled more than adjustments to form and delivery; they constituted shifts in ideological assumptions about the nature of knowing from things. This material rhetoric of social instrumentality implicitly recognized museumgoers as embodied beings and the knowledge derived from human-thing encounters as being conjointly intellectual, physical, and affective in nature. It recognized, too, the persuasive potentiality of arranging and directing the embodied museal encounter toward what its creators deemed to be civically relevant and useful ends. The war in its various stages became a proof test for social instrumentality, but along with this came problematic entanglements with agendas set by others in the exhibitionary network as well as different approaches to discerning how best to stimulate thought, feeling, and action through exhibition craft.

By borrowing the term "social instrument" from Theodore Low and assigning it weight as a museum paradigm and substance as a form of material rhetoric, the goal is not to declare either as being well-defined, consistently implemented, broadly adopted, or uniformly labeled as such in the period covered here. Rather, it is to give name to the ideas and related practices (here focused on exhibition craft) for which this study has sketched the contours so that further research into its manifestations at the institutional level and through specific individuals can better mark its nature and boundaries. George Hein, for example, has focused on social instrumentality in museum education, as this was, after all, the subject of Low's research and report. In tracing precedents as well as legacies of the museum as social instrument, Hein observes that the phrase and animating ideas behind it underscore that across time there has been "a conscious recognition that museum education should provide both pedagogic and political goals—that is, through method and intention—that strive to improve the social conditions of society."[2] My aim in this work has been to chart that conscious recognition within the educational work of exhibition craft and to create a framework for continued research.

Why, one might ask, approach this subject through a history of US museums' wartime engagements? As noted elsewhere, I am animated by Julie K. Brown's insistence on attentiveness to the particulars of the many short-lived experiments, "aberrant" forms, and "failures" that appear and recur in museum history.[3] Related to this is Jennifer Scott's call to deepen our knowledge of the historical manifestations of the radical in museum practice. "Working consistently with feminist, anti-racist, anti-patriarchal museums, which represent histories of working, poor, disenfranchised communities, and communities of color, I find myself repeatedly placed in a category of 'radical museology' and asked to speak and write about it," reflects Scott.[4] "But is this radical? Is it radical to center non-elite histories and to promote inclusion in museums? What makes the work that people like myself do 'radical'? How can we situate 'radical museology' in the long history of the movement by museums towards more inclusion, civic discourse and public engagement?" Similar questions led Denise Meringolo to seek out the roots of radical public history, asking, "What larger trends in history, education, museum studies, oral history, preservation, and other fields (formal or vernacular in nature) led some groups or individuals to mobilize core public history practices for the purpose of facilitating civic discourse and promoting social justice?"[5]

To be clear, as seen in the specific cases examined here, normative whiteness, racism, class prejudice, and other biases circumscribed the bounds of what was, compared to much of the field, a progressive, even radical vision of museums' public responsibilities in the years preceding and during the war. Also, as a phenomenon arising out of a predominantly white profession, social instrumentality as discussed and implemented by white institutions typically defined the public of its widening embrace in broad, vague strokes. Still, with attentive reading, evidence of Jim Crow and other exclusionary frameworks can be discerned in the holdings of museum archives. Likewise, community-based newspapers and other sources sometimes yield traces of what the publics marginalized by museums thought of prevailing practices. On the institutional side, it is more often in the details of specific undertakings that one can gain a clearer sense of the unwritten norms and rules concerning who, exactly, a specific institution and set of professionals meant by "the public," what attitudes they held toward those museum-defined sets of individuals, and how they determined both the civic need and good to be achieved *for* that public.

Politics provides another boundary marker. Instances in which mainstream museums pursued more politically ambitious social agendas through topical exhibitions and programming appear, based on the materials examined for this research, to be few in number. Borrowing wartime momentum on proximate issues proved a limited means to pursue change, as did the fact that temporary exhibits often betokened equally temporary or sporadic commitments on the part of initiating and host museums to the issue in question, be it public housing, racism, or cultural diversity. For progressive work of a more radical vein during this period, one must look to the individuals and collectives rooted in the very communities historically marginalized by the mainstream white museum field. The 1930s, for example, saw the founding of two Indigenous museums still active today: the Tantaquidgeon Museum of the Mohegan Tribe (1931), eponymously named for the family who formed it, and the Osage Tribal Museum (1938), which is now called the Osage Nation Museum.[6] In Chicago, the political and cultural activism of Margaret Taylor Goss Burroughs and others powered such undertakings as the South Side Community Art Center, founded in 1940 with WPA Federal Arts Project support, and formation of the National Negro Museum and Historical Foundation (NNMHF).[7] The latter never materialized as an institution but contained the germ of the idea later realized in the DuSable Museum of African American History.[8]

The NNMHF's organizers, as both Mabel O. Wilson and Ian Rocksborough-Smith detail, pursued their civil rights activism through multiple affiliations and channels, including Negro History Week, labor unions, and left-leaning political parties.[9] The greater stakes of this work are underscored by the fact that several in the group were subjected to Federal Bureau of Investigation surveillance, which began as early as 1944 for some and carried on through the McCarthy era. The FBI treated the educational work and aims of the NNMHF (and later the DuSable) as suspect by association. So, within files kept on individual activists are documentation of the NNMHF's papers of incorporation, newspaper mentions of it, and such firsthand intelligence as "It was reported that the Foundation would be used as a means of extending Communist activities among Negroes."[10] This February 1945 speculation came from a "Source not identified but evaluated as usually reliable and probably true."

Acknowledging the bounds of social instrumentality as practiced in the US museum mainstream does not discount the efforts of those who sought to reconceive the nature of individual education as it occurred in the galleries to be an impetus to action for a collective good. From hemispheric unity to the peacetime rebuilding of international relations, museums contributed to and fostered dialogue on headline-news topics. Idealism animated much of this work. Looking back, however, it is clear to see the ways in which materializations of wartime imaginaries also performed the cultural work of coalescing and extending state power. The Good Neighborhood brought expansion of US political and economic influence in Latin America, along with access to war-critical raw materials and defensive positions. The Home Front procured the public will necessary to accommodate the disruptions, rationing, sacrifices, and human losses required to wage war.[11] Even One World advocacy of human and international unity ultimately cloaked US economic, cultural, and military imperialism.

Of the imagined national communities advanced during World War II that of the Home Front has proven to be the most enduring, ensconced in public memory as the Good War or, as Michael C. C. Adams's book title ironically phrases it, *The Best War Ever*.[12] The domestic arm of the US Office of War Information, which focused on stimulating and shoring up a sense of common civic purpose, contributed to its construction, as did the cooperative efforts of newspapers, magazines, radio, and film. These narratives of civic behavior typically replaced complexity with idealized simplicity.[13] Strategies of elision and denial also served as psychological tools for individual reconciliation of dissonances between lived reality and promulgated ideals. George Roeder, for one, theorizes that the visual culture of the home front "foster[ed] habits of looking at the world in search of symbols that viewers could retain in their memories as reminders of their commitment to the war effort."[14]

This phenomenon can better be characterized as a compulsion to testify to one's own civic belonging so that it might be actualized by the witness of others. Ways that individuals made their allegiance witnessable by others during the period included wearing factory badges off-shift, hanging service flags in windows, attending war bond rallies, planting victory gardens, and donating everything from metal to cooking grease to salvage drives. Exhibitions that fostered a witness dynamic, such as *Three Southern Neighbors, Wartime Housing, Road to Victory, What the Boys Send Home,* and *Know Your United Nations,* also served as communal spaces where the museum and museumgoers alike could give, receive, and affirm testimony of mutual national belonging. Indeed, the framework of testimony, obligation, and witness also helps to address the question of why, in a culture saturated with wartime messaging, some members of the public sought out such exhibitions, some of them quite well attended. In other words, what satisfactions might these encounters have offered to those who partook in them? Witnessing, as a generative dynamic, is closely linked to events that engender a shared sense of psychological or psychophysiological dislocation. Life on the World War II home front, complete with societal and geographic displacements, racial and ethnic tensions, shortages, shifting gender roles, and other uncertainties, constituted such an event. To quote just one observer writing in 1944, "It is obvious that there are many developments in our culture during the present war which are productive of feelings of marked anxiety, tension, fear, apprehension, and the like."[15] Although World War II is popularly recalled today as having been the "good war" fought on all fronts by "the Greatest Generation," historians have called this feel-good narrative of rather recent coinage into question.[16] It is in these works that restore complexity to the domestic front that an understanding of it as a witnessable event emerges.[17]

The war years in many ways encouraged experimentation with social instrumentality, but what is difficult to discern—without substantive study of changes in individual institutional patterns from the 1930s through 1950s—is the degree to which wartime practices undertaken in the spirit of social instrumentality survived the business of "getting back to normal" as well as the complexities of postwar global politics. Certainly, there is evidence in the formation of ICOM and UNESCO's Museums Division as well as in such exhibitions as MoMA's *The Family of Man* (January 24–May 8, 1955) that the goal to have museums remain engaged in contemporary issues did not disappear altogether—and neither did the exhibitionary network. Indeed, this examination of the domestic war work of US museums closes just as the various actors in the exhibitionary network were each reconfiguring to meet the perceived and emerging realities of a postwar society. While scholarship on the role of museums, exhibition craft, and the exhibitionary network in world affairs from the war's end through the 1950s is reasonably ample, it focuses primarily on the promotion of US culture and power abroad.[18] There is less emphasis on developments in the domestic field during the 1950s. Scholarship on the Black museum movement in the United States is an exception.[19] It typically gives sustained attention to developments across the 1930s through the war years and on through the 1950s—and is an essential starting point, and counterpoint, for the research to be done on the domestic state of the wider museum field during this period.

Topics awaiting investigation include how the actors and activities of the exhibitionary network realigned and participated in the construction of stateside postwar society and how the ideas and practices of social instrumentality, from basic engagements with current events to the promotion of action on social issues, fared after 1946. In addition to scholarship that breaks open new material and topics, reevaluation of existing scholarship is needed, too, as work on *The Family of Man* underscores. Prior attention to the massively popular exhibition, which between its New York debut and ten-year global tour was seen by an estimated 7.75 million people, had focused chiefly on the cultural work it performed as an exemplar of Cold War propaganda. Newer works, however, drill deeper into the facts of its making to draw attention to the beliefs and ambitions of the museum's design team.[20] *The Family of Man*'s cultural valances, political uses, and its glossing over of racism in the United States are not ignored; however, fuller appreciation is given to the ways in which its creators conceived of it as aligned with exhibition-based education suited to participatory democracy. That social instrumentality may have persisted in some way at MoMA or Newark would not be surprising, but without further study the degree to which it remained in practice, even as ongoing imperfect experiments, through specific individuals and institutions cannot yet be known.

Another area bearing further scrutiny is the role of US museum professionals and practices in shaping the development of ICOM and UNESCO's Museums Division (which underwent a series of name changes and reconfigurations after 1949).[21] Likewise, global influences on US museum practice resulting from American participation in these international circuits is poorly understood. When this aspect of US museums history is told, it will need to analyze the organizational development of these international museum networks, as well as the ideas and directives they supported. The role of national ideologies in such bodies cannot be adequately studied apart from the structures that shaped participation in them if we are to write the history of US museums' work in a nation and world newly, if all too briefly, dedicated to peace.

Although this book is temporally bound to the concerns, practices, and cultural work of US museums during the late 1930s and World War II, it connects to other lines of inquiry. One is the matter of museums' wartime work during other conflicts. While museums' part in memorializing past wars—and war's part in giving rise to memorializing museums—receives deserved attention, there is still much to be understood about the varied ways in which museums and wars have intersected across time. As the range of international papers presented at the Museums and Galleries

History Group Biennial Conference in 2018 on the theme "Museums, Collections and Conflict, 1500–2010" demonstrated, research into this topic expands historical perspectives on such issues as women's contributions to the profession, community initiated museums, imperialism, settler colonialism, forms of cultural resistance under fascism and military occupation, and emergency adaptations to practice.[22] The second line of inquiry concerns the material rhetorics of museal display and the techne used to marshal, either loosely or more determinatively, the vibrancies of matter for sensory, affective, and narrative effects that are directed toward social ends. "Techne," as used here, is meant in the sense of cultural and technical apparatuses and practices used to structure or direct the production of narrative, sensory, and embodied encounter.[23]

Social Instrumentality for a New Century: Storytelling, Senses, and Affect

What was still a novel and controversial idea to museums in the 1930s and '40s—that exhibitions take explicitly narrative forms appealing to the mental, emotional, and physical—has now become normative practice. By the 2000s, scholarly interest had coalesced around the sensory, the affective, the narrative, and the ways in which the three are imbricated within museums. One author, calling for renewed attention to connecting museum publics to the materiality of collections, argued, "creative, materialist thinking about the embodied and emotional engagements with objects can provide more powerful alternatives or additions to textual interpretation in enabling visitors to understand and empathize with the stories objects may represent.[24] Others argued that the arrival of the sensory turn in museum practice and studies might constitute a new institutional paradigm, that of the "sensory gymnasium."[25]

Indeed, writing chiefly of digitally mediated multisensory experiences, the American Alliance of Museums anticipated in its *TrendsWatch 2014* report, "The availability of these techniques, along with consumer preferences for multisensory experiences, might reset the baseline expectation for museums, from providers of primarily visual experiences, occasionally embellished with scent, sound or taste, to experts in synesthesia."[26] Certainly, museums have long used low-cost strategies to engage visitors' senses, such as setting out jars of aromatic spices for sniffing in the kitchen of a house museum; and important work is being done to detail museums' historical uses of and relationships with the sensory.[27] There are connections, too, with earlier conceptualizations of museumgoers as "experience consumers" and with developments in educational strategies for engaging varied learning styles and sensory abilities.[28] In this latter regard, museum engagements with the human sensorium square with their efforts to become more democratic civic spaces by expanding access and inclusivity.[29]

The sensory is, of course, inextricable from affect, which has received attention within museum education as a means of productively disrupting what counts as knowledge *and* as normative within museal presentations.[30] Viv Golding, writing of activist museums and the sociopolitical potential of human-object encounters, describes museal affect as potentially productive of deep relationship. Affect offers more than engagement, she argues, if its transformative co-recognitions of self in other and other in self become the bedrock for sustained "wit(h)ness."[31] This "participative witnessing," as Golding terms it, places an "ethical demand" on museums and museumgoers alike.[32] It structures the generativity of the witness dynamic instantiated through exhibition craft or programming toward *being with* and *acting in concert with* those whose testimonial witness forms the substance of the presentation so that empathy might become productive of civic action on contemporary issues.

This matter of ethics is the essential question that must be asked of all efforts seeking to produce affect and direct its potentialities toward heightened, focused, or otherwise modified states of feeling, being, and acting.[33] Also, as the material rhetoric of modern social instrumentality turns to digital technologies whose somatic cues ever more precisely "convince" the perceiver's limbic system that they do indeed inhabit a different person, time, or place, the need for practitioners to develop an understanding of the neuroscience behind the mediated experiences we create has become imperative. Works pointing the way for future scholarship include that of Elena Gonzales and Jenny Kidd. Gonzales integrates consideration of the mind sciences into her assessments of and recommendations for "purposeful" exhibitions designed to advance the aims of social justice.[34] The result is a social instrumentality whose awareness of museal power and museumgoer agency is rooted in both a humanistic and scientific understanding of the human person.

Kidd brings similar interdisciplinarity to bear in her examination of ethical issues raised by the growing suite of digital media technologies, practices, and value systems that are being integrated into museum's public-facing work.[35] For example, in her analysis of Web-browser-based museum games, each designed to provoke strong emotional identification with the interactive narrative's historical protagonist (i.e., the player character), she illustrates why more nuanced understandings are needed of "the fine line between 'affective design'" for educative purposes and "less considered form[s] of 'emotioneering.'"[36] While the issues raised are not dissimilar from those posed by historic reenactment, role playing, and similar analog strategies for heightening museumgoers' sense of immersive "otherness" with respect to time, place, and subjecthood, Kidd convincingly argues for an examination of whether the field's codes of ethics adequately account for digitally mediated psychophysiological interventions.

The agent tasked with directing sensory and affect strategies, analog and digital alike, toward meaning, impact, and action is story. "An immersive heritage encounter," argues Kidd, "can be understood as a bounded experience at the nexus of a story, the body, and the senses."[37] As for distinctions between narrative and story with regard to national imaginaries, narrative is the mosaic, and stories are the discrete but connected tesserae of which the narrative is composed.[38] In other words, if narrative is the big-picture framework structuring information, story can be understood as focused on a more particular, personal, and, therefore, intentionally relatable instance. This, I think, is why story recurs as a meaning-making paradigm for the field. As an ancient human practice it betokens deeper connection of museumgoers to the past, to others, to object knowledge, to the museum, and ultimately to themselves. In 2013, for example, the American Association of Museums took "The Power of Story" as its annual meeting theme, noting, "At the heart of every museum is a story. It is often a compelling story, authentic and moving. Recognizing that story, telling it convincingly and well, are skills that can be key to a museum's success."[39] A year later *Inside Philanthropy* pointed to the popularity of such programs as *The Moth, StoryCorps,* and *This American Life* to suggest that storytelling might be the "next big thing" in museum work as funders and institutions alike sought to engage wider audiences.[40]

Story has a history of being the next big thing for museums, as Carlos E. Cummings's proclamation "Today's Museums Should Tell a Story" reminds us.[41] What is meant by "story" and the means by which museums tell "stories" now have different contours, of course.[42] In 2019, I attended a conference titled "The Future of Museum Storytelling," which again highlighted stories as both possessing and exerting "power."[43] Several speakers considered this power in relation to inclusivity, activism, shared authority, and participatory agency. Program topics dealing with technologies and strategies being adapted from the corporate sector included multimedia, transmedia, and data-driven approaches to storytelling, the latter being the use of audience, media, and other analytics to inform plot, character, and other creative decisions. Research fronts included the Peabody Essex Museum's Neuroscience Initiative, which, in the museum's words, fosters applied and new research on "the nature of perception, information processing and attention systems—in order to create new interpretative and design strategies that foster indelible, transformational museum experiences."[44] The artist-activist Karen Palmer, who turns artificial intelligence technologies and immersive storytelling to liberatory ends, presented her "emotionally responsive" film environments, in which viewer-participants' emotional reactions (as extrapolated from their expressions by a customized facial recognition program) determine how the narrative unfolds.[45] Palmer's ambition with this "film that watches you back" and similar projects, which have open source components, is to both to democratize and deconstruct the biases baked into artificial intelligence, machine learning, facial recognition, and other algorithmic systems.[46]

Story power, much like propaganda when that term retained its broader meanings, receives much popular attention. It is, by turns, the essence of our humanity and a tool of our inhumanity.[47] It is deemed advantageous for promoting personal or community healing and empowerment, for building iconic brands and securing customer loyalties, and for winning friends and influencing people.[48] The latter category extends from individual spheres of power attainment to the geopolitical arena of international affairs, where narrative remains a favored tool of soft-power politics.[49] In fact, Joseph S. Nye Jr., who is credited with coining the term "soft power," notes that in international affairs, as elsewhere, success in garnering public favor very often boils down to "whose story wins."[50] Or, as other scholars have put it, "Strategic narrative *is* soft power in the 21st century."[51] In relation to museums, soft power understood in its diplomatic dimensions has been described as "the ability to influence behavior using persuasion, attraction or agenda setting," which, if exercised with transparency, inclusive pluralism, and local focus, holds the potential to enrich a city's culture, economics, reputation, and connectedness.[52] The term "soft" can, however, obscure the ways in which story and other rhetorical modes rely on representational force to invite or enlist attraction. As one scholar aptly summarizes, "soft power should not be understood [only] in juxtaposition to hard power but [also] as a continuation of it by different means."[53]

The truth of this is heard in intensified calls for museums to dismantle the deep inequities of their own internal power structures—inequities that sustain the patriarchal whiteness of museum governance, staffing, and cultural power.[54] The idea that museums should be active instruments for civic education and change, that museums are part of the political order, has risen to new visibility within the field's white mainstream due in considerable part to antiracist, social justice movements, such as Museums Are Not Neutral and #museumsrespondtoferguson, that use social media and other open-access platforms to amplify their messages.[55] To grasp and understand this moment—for what is new and what is resurgent, for what has been learned in the longer struggle—continued rediscovery and amplification of the histories of those who have pushed museums to, in Scott's words, "more inclusion, civic discourse and public engagement," is needed as well.

Looking at the longer sweep of museum history, it is also critical to question why the wartime work of US museums in any period has infrequently been a topic of concern in museological literature. Scholars interested in exhibitions' ideological content and relationships to state power, particularly through cultural diplomacy abroad, have given attention to select examples from this period but generally not within the broader context of developments within the field. A few reasons seem likely. To the degree that times of war are cast as periods of disruption in which museums break temporarily from their "proper" work, the easier it is to presume lack of consequence to the longer arc of practice. In a similar vein, for histories focused on the field's progress, moments of rupture or incubation that do not mark a clear transformation are of lesser value. Certainly, the tendency to view museums' wartime work chiefly through the lens of propaganda feeds the impulse to view the period as aberrant rather than instructive. So, too, the habit of considering museum work between 1941 and 1945 as a chronological island suspended apart from developments before and after.

Broadening the ways in which museum history and wartimes are considered both separately and in relation to one another will, as noted, invite reconsideration of existing classifications, particularly if, as some historians propose, we accept that by most measures the United States has been on active military footing since the start of World War II.[56] Museal treatments of 9/11 instituted during the various operations in Iraq and Afghanistan (2001–14), for example, constitute more than the memorialization of tragedy; they are also a form of war work awaiting analysis as such.[57] Analysis along these lines would trace the field's initial responses to the attacks, which included museums offering themselves as sites for solace and (fewer) for action on citizens' rights and combatting anti-Muslim hate.[58] It would consider, too, such later exhibitions as *Inconvenient Evidence: Iraqi Prison Photographs from Abu Ghraib* (September 11–November 28, 2004), which offered a disturbing spin on what the "boys" send home.[59] This and other efforts highlighting the human costs of armed aggression both on and off the battlefield edged closer to being antiwar statements despite many host institutions professing their own neutrality. This points to another reason why examination of museums' war work, whether long past or more contemporary, whether obvious in its incarnations or more subtle, is needed. In a collective US culture accustomed to suppressing the nation's near-permanent state of war, of taking as common sense the systems and structures that sustain it, certainly, museums—and not only those memorializing wars—must be counted among the sites where such sense making occurs.[60]

NOTES

PREFACE

1. Jane Lusaka, "Community Gathering: A Report from the Field," *Museum News*, November/December 2001, 37.
2. Larry M. Small, secretary of the Smithsonian Institution in an open letter to the public, November 3, 2001, http://www.si.edu (no longer accessible).
3. Philippe de Montebello, director of the Metropolitan Museum of Art, quoted in Edward H. Able Jr., "To Fix the Soul," *Museum News*, November/December 2001, 87.

INTRODUCTION: THE AMERICAN MUSEUM AS SOCIAL INSTRUMENT

1. Central Press, "Museums Recruited in Defense Drive Now Under Fire of Art Leaders," *Evening Independent* (Massillon, OH), June 19, 1941, 15. Until now Russell Lynes's memoir has served as the sole source for this frequently quoted line; he attributed it to a June 20, 1941, wire story that ran "in many newspapers." See Russell Lynes, *Good Old Modern: An Intimate Portrait of the Museum of Modern Art* (New York: Atheneum, 1973), 233.
2. Here I take George Hein's definition of the progressive museum as one committed to the belief that an informed citizenry was essential to a viable democracy and, thus, its education and other efforts were directed to social and political agendas. See George E. Hein, *Progressive Museum Practice: John Dewey and Democracy* (Walnut Creek, CA: Left Coast Press, 2012).
3. "Nevada Museum Installs Emergency Hospital," *Museum News* 10, no. 8 (October 15, 1942): 2; and "Some Wartime Activities," *Museum News* 21, no. 4 (June 15, 1943): 12. Note: During the period covered in this book, the American Association of Museums published its member newsletter, *The Museum News*, semimonthly except for July and August. Prior to the May 1, 1945, issue, volume numbers were denoted by Roman numerals (converted here for conformance to style guide).
4. "Wartime Activities in Two N.Y.C. Museum Reports," *Museum News* 21, no. 17 (March 1, 1944): 1 and 8; and "Telecast on War Armor," *Museum News* 23, no. 4 (June 1, 1945): 1.
5. Pamela M. Henson, "The Smithsonian Goes to War: The Increase and Diffusion of Scientific Knowledge in the Pacific," in *Science and the Pacific War: Science and Survival*

in the Pacific, 1939–1945, ed. Roy M. MacLeod (Lancaster, UK: Kluwer Academic Publishers, 2000), 27–50.

6. Samuel Redman, "The Smithsonian at War: Museums in US Society during World War II," *Journal of the History of Collections* (January 2019): 1–14.

7. Mary L. Dudziak, *War Time: An Idea, Its History, Its Consequences* (Oxford: Oxford University Press, 2012), 36. Among the recent histories of World War II that reframe its span is Andrew N. Buchanan, *World War II in Global Perspective, 1931–1953: A Short History* (Newark, NJ: Wiley Blackwell, 2019).

8. One exception is Nancy J. Parezo, "'Our Native Allies': The Denver Art Museum's WWII Outreach Exhibits," *Museum History Journal* 1, no. 1 (2008): 9–50. Chapters in books on broader topics include Jasmine Alinder, *Moving Images: Photography and the Japanese American Incarceration* (Urbana: University of Illinois Press, 2009); Inez Roach, *A History of the Science Museum of Minnesota, 1907–1975* (Saint Paul: Science Museum of Minnesota, 1981); and Marjorie Schwarzer, *Riches, Rivals, and Radicals: 100 Years of Museums in America* (Washington, DC: American Association of Museums, 2006).

9. Gaynor Kavanagh, *Museums and the First World War: A Social History* (London: Leicester University Press, 1994); and Catherine Pearson, *Museums in the Second World War: Curators, Culture and Change* (New York: Routledge, 2017).

10. Jennifer Wellington, *Exhibiting War: The Great War, Museums, and Memory in Britain, Canada, and Australia* (Cambridge: Cambridge University Press, 2017).

11. "A Report on the Museums and Art Galleries of the British Isles (Other Than the National Museums) to the Carnegie United Kingdom Trustees" (1938), quoted in Pearson, *Museums in the Second World War*, 26.

12. Ibid., 32–39.

13. Ibid., 54.

14. Paul Marshall Rea, *The Museum and the Community, with a Chapter on the Library and the Community: A Study of Social Laws and Consequences* (Lancaster, PA: Science Press, 1932), 25.

15. Thomas R. Adam, *The Civic Value of Museums*, Studies in the Social Significance of Adult Education in the United States, 4 (New York: American Association of Adult Education, 1937), 33, 102–3.

16. Laurence Vail Coleman, *The Museum in America: A Critical Study*, 3 vols. (Washington, DC: American Museum Association, 1939).

17. Clarissa Ceglio, "Imperfectly Progressive: The Social Mission of U.S. Museums in the 1930s," in *Radical Roots: Public History and a Tradition of Social Justice Activism*, ed. Denise Meringolo (Amherst, MA: Amherst College Press, 2021), 363–93.

18. Hannah Mitchell, "The Part of a Museum Visitors Don't See," *New-York Tribune*, May 15, 1921, SM7; and Hannah Freece, "'A New Era for Museums': Professionalism and Ideology in the American Association of Museums, 1906–1935," thesis, Wesleyan University, 2009, https://doi.org/10.14418/wes01.1.1631.

19. Coleman, *Museum in America*, 1:3.

20. Theodore Lewis Low, *The Museum as Social Instrument* (New York: Metropolitan Museum of Art, 1942).

21. Sally Anne Duncan and Andrew McClellan, *The Art of Curating: Paul J. Sachs and the Museum Course at Harvard* (Los Angeles, CA: Getty Research Institute, 2018), 198–99; and Hein, *Progressive Museum Practice*, 138–39.

22. Low, *Museum as a Social Instrument*, 7.

23. Ibid., 12.

24. See Jeffrey Trask, *Things American: Art Museums and Civic Culture in the Progressive Era* (Philadelphia: University of Pennsylvania Press, 2012); and Carol Duncan, *A Matter of Class: John Cotton Dana, Progressive Reform, and the Newark Museum* (Pittsburgh, PA: Periscope, 2009).
25. Quoted in Edgar Kaufman Jr., "The Department of Industrial Design," *Bulletin of the Museum of Modern Art* 14, no. 1 (Autumn 1946): 2. MoMA's first efforts in this direction included its *Machine Art* exhibition (1934), the *Useful Objects* series (inaugurated in 1938), and the formation of a Department of Industrial Design in 1940. On the Metropolitan Museum of Art, see Richard F. Bach, *Museums and the Industrial World* (New York: Metropolitan Museum of Art, 1926).
26. Richard F. Bach, "Neighborhood Circulating Exhibitions," *Museum News* 14, no. 12 (December 15, 1936): 7–8.
27. Erica Doss, *Benton, Pollock, and the Politics of Modernism: From Regionalism to Abstract Expressionism* (Chicago, IL: University of Chicago Press, 1991), 135.
28. "WPA Provides Museums with 2,774 Workers," *Museum News* 15, no. 18 (March 15, 1938): 4; and Ellen S. Woodward [assistant administrator, Works Progress Administration], "WPA Museum Projects," *Museum News* 15, no. 13 (January 1, 1938): 7–8.
29. Thomas R. Adam, *The Museum and Popular Culture*, Studies in the Social Significance of Adult Education in the United States, 14 (New York: American Association of Adult Education, 1939), vi.
30. Ibid., 7.
31. Ibid., 15.
32. Ibid. Low also quotes this line in *Museum as a Social Instrument*, 28.
33. Ibid., 135.
34. Janowitz Morris, "Sociological Theory and Social Control," *American Journal of Sociology* 81, no. 1 (1975): 82–108.
35. Christiaan Beyers, "The Cultural Politics of 'Community' and Citizenship in the District Six Museum, Cape Town," *Anthropologica* 50, no. 2 (January 1, 2008): 359–73.
36. Benedict Anderson, *Imagined Communities: Reflections on the Origin and Spread of Nationalism* (London: Verso, 1991), 178; Carol Duncan and Alan Wallach, "The Museum of Modern Art as Late Capitalist Ritual: An Iconographic Analysis," *Marxist Perspectives* 4 (1978): 28–51; Amy Lonetree, *Decolonizing Museums: Representing Native America in National and Tribal Museums* (Chapel Hill: University of North Carolina Press, 2012); James Clifford, *Routes: Travel and Translation in the Late Twentieth Century* (Cambridge, MA: Harvard University Press, 1997), 188–219; and Robert R. James and Richard Sandell, eds., *Museum Activism* (London: Routledge, 2019).
37. Homi K. Bhabha, "Introduction: Narrating the Nation," in *Nation and Narration*, ed. Homi K Bhabha (New York: Routledge, 1990), 2.
38. Patrick Colm Hogan, *Understanding Nationalism: On Narrative, Cognitive Science, and Identity* (Columbus: Ohio State University Press, 2009), 25.
39. Tony Bennett, "The Exhibitionary Complex," *New Formations*, no. 4 (Spring 1988): 76. For Bennett's continued refinements of the concept, see "Exhibition, Difference, and the Logic of Culture," in *Museum Frictions: Public Cultures/Global Transformations*, ed. Ivan Karp et al. (Durham, NC: Duke University Press, 2006), 46–69.
40. Tony Bennett, "Thinking (with) Museums: From Exhibitionary Complex to Governmental Assemblage," in *Museum Theory*, ed. Andrea Witcomb and Kylie Message (West Sussex, UK: Wiley-Blackwell, 2020), 3–20.

41. Susan Smulyan, *Popular Ideologies: Mass Culture at Mid-Century* (Philadelphia: University of Pennsylvania Press, 2007).
42. M. Elizabeth Weiser, *Museum Rhetoric: Building Civic Identity in National Spaces* (University Park: Penn State University Press, 2017); and Greg Dickinson, Carole Blair, and Brian Ott, eds., *Places of Public Memory: The Rhetoric of Museums and Memorials* (Tuscaloosa: University of Alabama Press, 2010).
43. Christopher Tilley, "Materializing Identities: An Introduction," *Journal of Material Culture* 16, no. 4 (December 1, 2011): 350. To consider how exhibited things—the showcased objects as well as the showcasing itself—exert a form of agency that shapes human-thing encounters, my work looks to such foundational texts as Alfred Gell, *Art and Agency: An Anthropological Theory* (Oxford: Clarendon Press, 1998); Don Ihde, *Technology and the Lifeworld from Garden to Earth* (Bloomington: Indiana University Press, 1990); and Bruno Latour, *Reassembling the Social: An Introduction to Actor-Network-Theory* (Oxford: Oxford University Press, 2005).
44. Jane Bennett, *Vibrant Matter: A Political Ecology of Things* (Durham, NC: Duke University Press, 2010), 34.
45. Ibid., 34–36. The author invokes the Chinese concept of *shi* to describe this type of ensemble agency.
46. See, for example, Nicole Boivin, *Material Cultures, Material Minds: The Impact of Things on Human Thought, Society, and Evolution* (New York: Cambridge University Press, 2008); Carl Knappett, *Thinking through Material Culture: An Interdisciplinary Perspective* (Philadelphia: University of Pennsylvania Press, 2005); and Christopher Y. Tilley, *A Phenomenology of Landscape: Places, Paths, and Monuments* (Oxford: Berg, 1994), 12–15.
47. Sara Ahmed, *The Cultural Politics of Emotion* (New York: Routledge, 2004), 12; and M. L. Lyon and J. M. Barbalet, "Society's Body: Emotion and the 'Somatization' of Social Theory," in *Embodiment and Experience: The Existential Ground of Culture and Self*, ed. Thomas J. Csordas (New York: Cambridge University Press, 1994), 48–66.
48. See, for example, Laurajane Smith, Margaret Wetherell, and Gary Campbell, eds., *Emotion, Affective Practices, and the Past in the Present* (London: Routledge, 2018); Emma Waterton and Jason Dittmer, "The Museum as Assemblage: Bringing Forth Affect at the Australian War Memorial," *Museum Management and Curatorship* 29, no. 2 (March 15, 2014): 122–39; Andrea Witcomb, "Understanding the Role of Affect in Producing a Critical Pedagogy for History Museums," *Museum Management and Curatorship* 28, no. 3 (2013): 255–71; Andrea Witcomb, "Remembering the Dead by Affecting the Living: The Case of the Miniature Model of Treblinka," in *Museum Materialities: Objects, Engagements, Interpretations*, ed. Sandra H Dudley (London: Routledge, 2010), 39–52; Patrizia Di Bello and Gabriel Koureas, eds., *Art, History and the Senses: 1830 to the Present* (Burlington, VT: Ashgate, 2010); David Howes, ed., *Empire of the Senses: The Sensual Culture Reader* (Oxford: Berg, 2005); and Jonathan Crary, *Techniques of the Observer: On Vision and Modernity in the Nineteenth Century* (Cambridge, MA: MIT Press, 1990).
49. For example, Alison Griffiths, *Shivers down Your Spine: Cinema, Museums, and the Immersive View* (New York: Columbia University Press, 2008); and Constance Classen and David Howes, "The Museum as Sensescape: Western Sensibilities and Indigenous Artifacts," in *Sensible Objects Colonialism, Museums, and Material Culture*, ed. Elizabeth Edwards, Chris Gosden, and Ruth B. Phillips (Oxford: Berg, 2006), 199–222.

50. In this work, I am mindful of the fact that the five senses are a culturally, geographically, and historically contingent Euro-Western rubric. Also, just as the nation-state has been configured as a body with senses, so too have citizenship and hierarchies of belonging within that political corpus been predicated on prescribed uses and relationships among the senses. Lastly, there is no universal human body. Bodies perform and are inscribed with sex, gender, ethnic, and other identities, making them "as much a cultural phenomenon" as they are biological in nature. See Thomas J. Csordas, "The Body as Representation and Being in the World," in Csordas, *Embodiment and Experience*, 4.
51. Clarissa Ceglio, "Conceptualizing Community at the Charleston Museum," in *Radical Roots: Public History and a Tradition of Social Justice Activism*, ed. Denise Meringolo (Amherst, MA: Amherst College Press, 2021), 374–76.

CHAPTER ONE: TOWARD A MATERIAL RHETORIC OF SOCIAL INSTRUMENTALITY

1. Gilbert Seldes, "Your World of Tomorrow," 1939 World's Fair booklet (New York: Rogers-Kellogg-Stillson, 1939).
2. Harold D. Lasswell and Dorothy Blumenstock, *World Revolutionary Propaganda: A Chicago Study* (New York: Knopf, 1939), v and 3.
3. "Milwaukee, Baltimore, and Denver WPA Projects Varied in Product," *Museum News* 16, no. 17 (March 1, 1941): 1, 9.
4. "San Francisco Program to Include Day of Visits," *Museum News* 17, no. 1 (May 1, 1939): 1.
5. Carlos Emmons Cummings, *East Is East and West Is West: Some Observations on the World's Fairs of 1939 by One Whose Main Interest Is in Museums* (East Aurora, NY: Buffalo Museum of Science, 1940); and *Exhibition Techniques: A Summary of Exhibition Practice Based on Surveys Conducted at the New York and San Francisco World's Fairs of 1939* (New York: Museum of Science and Industry, 1940).
6. Quoted in Steven Conn, *Do Museums Still Need Objects?* (Philadelphia: University of Pennsylvania Press, 2010), 4. Correspondence of William Wilson, director of the Philadelphia Commercial Museum, to Edward Everett Ayer, benefactor of Chicago's Field Museum.
7. Steven Conn, *Museums and American Intellectual Life, 1876–1926* (Chicago: University of Chicago Press, 1998), 4–9.
8. Conn, *Do Museums Still Need Objects?*, 218–23.
9. Ibid., 22–26.
10. Manon Niquette and William J. Buxton, "'Sugar-Coating the Education Pill': Rockefeller Support for the Communicative Turn in Science Museums," in *Patronizing the Public: American Philanthropy's Transformation of Culture, Communication, and the Humanities*, ed. William Buxton (Lanham, MD: Lexington Books, 2009), 153–93.
11. Ibid., 156.
12. Cummings, *East Is East*, 97.
13. Niquette and Buxton, "Sugar-Coating the Education Pill," 154.
14. Cummings, *East Is East*, 114.
15. The primary focus of Niquette and Buxton's article is the implication of this communicative turn in the dissemination of eugenics, evolutionism, and other racialist ideologies through museums.

16. Rooted in ethnological approaches, *Kulturgeschichte* had influenced German museum installations in the late 1800s and, by the early 1900s, had made its way to a few arts institutions in the United States. See Kathleen Curran, *The Invention of the American Art Museum: From Craft to Kulturgeschichte, 1870–1930* (Los Angeles, CA: Getty Research Institute, 2016), 1 and 13–15; and Charles R. Richards, *Industrial Art and the Museum* (New York: Macmillan Company, 1927).
17. Laurence Vail Coleman, *The Museum in America: A Critical Study,* 3 vols. (Washington, DC: American Association of Museums, 1939), 1:116; and Louise Anderson Allen, *A Bluestocking in Charleston: The Life and Career of Laura Bragg* (University of South Carolina Press, 2001), 163–67. Allen credits Coleman as being among those who recommended Bragg for the position (3) and cites her reputation as progressive reformer in museum education as one reason she was sought out (165).
18. Arthur C. Parker, "The History Museum—An Opportunity," *New York History* 15, No. 3 (July 1934): 328.
19. Clarissa Ceglio, "Imperfectly Progressive: The Social Mission of U.S. Museums in the 1930s," in *Radical Roots: Public History and a Tradition of Social Justice Activism*, ed. Denise Meringolo (Amherst, MA: Amherst College Press, 2021), 368–70.
20. On Parker's training, work, and life, see Chip Colwell, *Inheriting the Past: The Making of Arthur C. Parker and Indigenous Archaeology* (Tucson: University of Arizona Press, 2009); and Joy Porter, *To Be Indian: The Life of Iroquois-Seneca Arthur Caswell Parker* (Norman: University of Oklahoma Press, 2001).
21. Arthur C. Parker, *A Manual for History Museums,* New York State Historical Association Series 3 (New York: Columbia University Press, 1935), 67.
22. Edward P. Alexander, *Museums in Motion: An Introduction to the History and Functions of Museums,* 1st ed. (Nashville, TN: American Association for State and Local History, 1979). This volume has twice undergone updates and remains a basic primer for those studying the field.
23. Edward P. Alexander, "Functional History in the Small Museum," *Museum News* 14, no. 8 (October 13, 1936): 7–8. Paper read at the annual meeting of the American Association of Museums, May 11–13, 1936.
24. Ibid., 7.
25. Ibid., 8.
26. Ezra Shales, *Made in Newark Cultivating Industrial Arts and Civic Identity in the Progressive Era* (New Brunswick, NJ: Rivergate Books, Rutgers University Press, 2010), 245–51.
27. Alexander, "Functional History in the Small Museum," 7.
28. Parker, "History Museum," 328.
29. Lillian Perricone, "The WPA Museum Extension Project in Context: Historical Precedents in Visual Education," in *WPA Museum Extension Project, 1935–1943: Government Created Aids for Children from the Collections of the Bienes Museum of the Modern Book,* by James A. Findlay and Lillian Perricone (Fort Lauderdale, FL: Broward County Libraries Division, 2009), 8, 14–15.
30. Findlay and Perricone, *WPA Museum Extension Project,* 6.
31. Charles F. Hoban, director of visual education, Pennsylvania Department of Public Instruction and director, Pennsylvania State Library and Museum, quoted in Perricone, "WPA Museum Extension Project," 18. Second quote from Charles F. Hoban, "Enlisting Visual-Sensory Aids," *Journal of Education* 115, no. 17 (1932): 517.

32. See Perricone, "WPA Museum Extension Project," for a more detailed accounting of visual education's roots, relationships to progressive education and museums, and its developments into the 1930s.
33. Hoban, "Enlisting Visual-Sensory Aids," 517.
34. British museums also partook in the adult education movement, which prompted experiments with audio technology and other aids to learning. See Alison Griffiths, *Shivers down Your Spine: Cinema, Museums, and the Immersive View* (New York: Columbia University Press, 2008), 247.
35. Thomas R. Adam, *The Museum and Popular Culture*, Studies in the Social Significance of Adult Education in the United States, 14 (New York: American Association of Adult Education, 1939), 35.
36. Thomas R. Adam, *The Civic Value of Museums*, Studies in the Social Significance of Adult Education in the United States, 4 (New York: American Association of Adult Education, 1937), 10.
37. Roland Marchand, *Creating the Corporate Soul: The Rise of Public Relations and Corporate Imagery in American Big Business* (Berkeley: University of California Press, 1998), 235.
38. Adam, *Civic Value of Museums*, 11.
39. Mary Anne Staniszewski, *The Power of Display: A History of Exhibition Installations at the Museum of Modern Art* (Cambridge, MA: MIT Press, 1998), 13–25. I follow Staniszewski's definition of "the international avant-gardes"; see 310.
40. Ibid., 27.
41. Fred Turner, *The Democratic Surround: Multimedia and American Liberalism from World War II to the Psychedelic Sixties* (Chicago, IL: University of Chicago Press, 2013), 5. Turner analyses several MoMA exhibitions, including *Road to Victory* (1942) and *The Family of Man* (1955), both of which came after *Wartime Housing* (1942) and not only lacked many of the multisensory technologies (e.g., sound, moving images) and techniques that *Wartime Housing* employed but suffered, too, for favoring emotional ends over educational ones.
42. John Cotton Dana, *The Gloom of the Museum* (Woodstock, VT: Elm Tree Press, 1917); Tony Bennett, *The Birth of the Museum: History, Theory, Politics* (London: Routledge, 1995); Duncan, *A Matter of Class: John Cotton Dana, Progressive Reform, and the Newark Museum* (Pittsburgh, PA: Periscope Pub, 2009), 142–43; and Victoria Cain, "'Attraction, Attention, and Desire': Consumer Culture as Pedagogical Paradigm in Museums in the United States, 1900–1930," *Paedagogica Historica: International Journal of the History of Education* 48, no. 5 (2012): 1–25.
43. Philip N. Youtz, "Museums among Public Services," *Museum News* 11, no. 6 (September 15, 1933): 6–8.
44. After his time at the People's Institute of New York (1926–30), Youtz next headed the cited Philadelphia experiment in applying the Carnegie Library branch model to museums (1931–33). As for the Brooklyn Museum, he resigned his directorship there in 1938, becoming a consultant to the Department of the Pacific Area of the Golden Gate International Exposition.
45. Youtz, "Museums among Public Services," 8.
46. Philip N. Youtz, "The Sixty-Ninth Street Branch of the Pennsylvania Museum of Art," *Museum News* 10, no. 12 (December 15, 1932): 5–8.
47. Edward Stevens Robinson, *The Behavior of the Museum Visitor* (Washington, DC: American Association of Museums, 1928). See also "Carnegie Gives Ass'n $20,000 for Museum

Studies Psychological Work Planned at Art and Science Museums," *Museum News* 8, no. 2 (May 15, 1930): 1; Edward S. Robinson, "Psychological Problems of the Science Museum," *Museum News* 8, no. 5 (September 1, 1930): 9–11; and "Carnegie Fellowship for Study of Industrial Museum Problems," *Museum News* 10, no. 15 (February 1, 1933): 2. Sites of study included the Art Institute of Chicago, the Pennsylvania Museum of Art, the Buffalo Museum of Science, and the New York Museum of Science and Industry.

48. Clarence S. Stein [architect], "Museum Lighting," *Museum News* 8, no. 7 (October 1, 1930): 8.
49. Davis H. John, "Use of Mirrors in Museum Installations," *Museum News* 10, no. 20 (April 15, 1933): 8.
50. See, for example, Carol Duncan, "Museums and Department Stores: Close Encounters," in *High-Pop: Making Culture into Popular Entertainment*, ed. Jim Collins (Malden, MA: Blackwell Publishers, 2002), 129–54; and Theresa Scandiffio, "'Better'n Any Circus That Ever Come to Town': Cinema, Visual Culture and Educational Programming at Chicago's Field Museum of Natural History, 1921–1935" (PhD diss., University of Chicago, 2008), 12.
51. "Baltimore Museum of Art Campaigns for Members," *Museum News* 16, no. 20 (April 15, 1933): 1, 3.
52. Duncan, *Matter of Class*, 149.
53. Youtz, "Museums among Public Services," 6.
54. Edsel B. Ford [President, Arts Commission of the City of Detroit], "The New Public Museum from the Standpoint of a Trustee," *Museum News* 18, no. 5 (September 1, 1940): 9. Paper read at annual meeting of the American Association of Museums in Detroit, May 22, 1940.
55. Theodore Lewis Low, *The Museum as a Social Instrument* (New York: Metropolitan Museum of Art for the American Association of Museums, 1942), 33 and 39.
56. See, for example, Robert W. Rydell, *All the World's a Fair: Visions of Empire at American International Expositions, 1876–1916* (Chicago, IL: University of Chicago Press, 1984); and Robert W. Rydell, John E. Findling, and Kimberly D. Pelle, *Fair America: World's Fairs in the United States* (Washington, DC: Smithsonian Institution Press, 2000).
57. On the New York World's fair, see Helen A. Harrison and Joseph P. Cusker, eds., *Dawn of a New Day: The New York World's Fair, 1939/40* (New York: The Queens Museum and New York University Press, 1980); Peter J. Kuznick, "Losing the World of Tomorrow: The Battle over the Presentation of Science at the New York World's Fair," *American Quarterly* 46, no. 3 (1994): 341–73; David E. Nye, *American Technological Sublime* (Cambridge, MA: MIT Press, 1994); and Sevan G. Terzian, "The 1939–1940 New York World's Fair and the Transformation of the American Science Extracurriculum," *Science Education* 93, no. 5 (September 1, 2009): 892–914. The latter details similar struggles between Progressive ethics and corporate interests as educator groups sought to use the fair as a means to promote science as the everyman's path to rational, democratic citizenship while corporations increasingly foregrounded the specialist manpower needed for military mobilization. On the Golden Gate International Exposition, see Andrew Shanken, *Into the Void Pacific: Building the 1939 San Francisco World's Fair* (Berkeley: University of California Press, 2015); and Lisa Rubens, "The 1939 San Francisco World's Fair: The New Deal, the New Frontier and the Pacific Basin," (PhD diss., University of California, Berkeley, 2004).
58. Robert W. Rydell, *World of Fairs: The Century-of-Progress Expositions* (Chicago, IL: University of Chicago Press, 1993).
59. Marchand, *Creating the Corporate Soul*, 249–311.

60. Quoted from corporate memos in ibid., 292.
61. Neil Harris, "Museums, Merchandising, and Popular Taste: The Struggle for Influence," in *Material Culture and the Study of American Life*, ed. Ian M. G. Quimby (New York: W. W. Norton, Winterthur Book, 1978), 67–70.
62. *Exhibition Techniques*, 4.
63. Chauncey J. Hamlin, introduction to Cummings, *East Is East*, viii. The pool of researchers included participants in a Rockefeller-funded internship program designed to promote professionalization through hands-on experience at the Buffalo Museum of Science, regarded as one of the nation's leading museums. The intern-researchers were directors, educators, public relations staff, and others from the City Museum of Greater Shanghai, the Southwestern Museum (Los Angeles), the Free Public Museums (Liverpool, England), the New England Museum of Natural History, the Anthropology Laboratory (Santa Fe), and the Rochester Museum of Arts and Science.
64. Ibid., xviii.
65. *Exhibition Techniques*, 11.
66. Cummings, *East Is East*, 51.
67. Ibid., 25.
68. Ibid., 16.
69. Ibid.
70. See, for example, the doubters quoted in Cummings, *East Is East*, 97–98; and Coleman's objections in *Museum in America*, 2:25–59.
71. Coleman, *Museum in America*, 1:99; emphasis in source.
72. While supplying museums (and even founding them) with stock after an exposition closed was a longstanding practice, the NYMSI endeavored to position itself as a knowledge resource to industry.
73. Adam, *Museum and Popular Culture*, 131.
74. Coleman, *Museum in America*, 2:265.
75. Cummings, *East Is East*, 117.
76. Ibid., 106.
77. Ibid.
78. Ibid, 40. As Niquette and Buxton, who also quote this passage, note, Cummings allowed that such effects did not always reflect a knowing application of theory by corporate exhibitors. Harris, too, uses this quote but gives Cummings little credit for understanding what this and other insights meant for museums (69).
79. Ibid., 326. Here Cummings contemplated specifically the role that music and sound in museums could play in creating an amenable receptivity in museumgoers, noting that sensory cues conducive to creating the right "frame of mind may actually be of much greater importance in putting the story across than any amount of detail applied to the [visual] treatment of object themselves."
80. Coleman, *Museum in America*, 2:323.
81. Coleman, *Museum in America*, 1:99.
82. Ibid., 100.
83. Parker, "History Museum," 330; and *Manual for History Museums*, 15.
84. Parker, *Manual for History Museums*, 199.
85. Ibid., 55; emphasis in source.
86. This exhibition is sometimes called *America Can't Have Housing*, after the accompanying volume, Carol Aronovici, ed., *America Can't Have Housing* (New York: The Committee on the Housing Exhibition by the Museum of Modern Art, 1934).

87. Julie K. Brown, "The Chicago Municipal Museum: An Experiment in Urban Display, 1904–1907," *Museum History Journal* 3, no. 2 (July 2010): 231–56; and Ross Wilson, "The Museum of Safety: Responsibility, Awareness and Modernity in New York, 1908–1923," *Journal of American Studies* 51, no. 3 (August 2017): 915–38.
88. See Deborah Martin Kao and Michelle Lamunière, eds., *Instituting Reform: The Social Museum of Harvard University, 1903–1931* (Cambridge, MA / New Haven, CT: Harvard Art Museums / Yale University Press, 2012); Julie K. Brown, *Health and Medicine on Display International Expositions in the United States, 1876–1904* (Cambridge, MA: MIT Press, 2009); and Julie K. Brown, *Making Culture Visible: The Public Display of Photography at Fairs, Expositions, and Exhibitions in the United States, 1847–1900* (Amsterdam: Harwood Academic, 2001).
89. Geraldine Santoro, "'To Stamp Out the Plague Consumption': 1908–1909," *Curator: The Museum Journal* 36, no. 1 (1993): 13–28.
90. Nader Vossoughian, "The Language of the World Museum: Otto Neurath, Paul Otlet, Le Corbusier," *Transnational Associations* 1–2 (2003): 82–93; and Nader Vossoughian, "Mapping the Modern City: Otto Neurath, the International Congress of Modern Architecture (CIAM), and the Politics of Information Design," *Design Issues* 22, no. 3 (2006): 48–65.
91. Picture-symbols, as defined by Neurath and Vreeland, constituted a specific type of image that, like a letter of the alphabet, functioned as part of an "internally organized and orderly language system." Francis McLennan Vreeland, "The Teaching Uses of a Sociology Museum," *American Sociological Review* 3, no. 1 (1938): 36.
92. Ibid.
93. Coleman, *Museum in America*, 2:258–59.
94. Brett Gary, *The Nervous Liberals: Propaganda Anxieties from World War I to the Cold War* (New York: Columbia University Press, 1999), 380.
95. Alexander, "Functional History in the Small Museum," 11.
96. Youtz, "Sixty-Ninth Street Branch," 8.
97. Cummings, *East Is East*, 336–37.
98. O. E. Jennings, "The Place of the Natural History Museum in Adult Education," *Museum News* 16, no. 2 (May 15, 1938): 6–7; emphasis in source.
99. B. F. Ruskin "The Technique of Gallery Decoration," *Museum News* 18, no. 19 (April 1940): 6.
100. For a history of these developments in Europe and the United States, see Griffiths, *Shivers down Your Spine*.
101. See Karen A. Rader and Victoria E. M. Cain, *Life on Display: Revolutionizing US Museums of Science and Natural History in the Twentieth Century* (Chicago, IL: University of Chicago Press, 2014); Karen Wonders, *Habitat Dioramas: Illusions of Wilderness in Museums of Natural History* (Stockholm: Almqvist & Wiksell, 1993); and Donna Haraway's "Teddy Bear Patriarchy: Taxidermy for the Garden of Eden, New York City, 1908–1936," *Social Text*, no. 11 (Winter 1984–85): 20–64.
102. On house museums as "other world" immersions, see Patricia West, *Domesticating History: The Political Origins of America's House Museums* (Washington, DC: Smithsonian Institution Press, 1999).
103. Waldemar Kaempffert, *From Cave-Man to Engineer: The Museum of Science and Industry Founded by Julius Rosenwald an Institution to Reveal the Ascent of Man* (Chicago, IL: Museum of Science and Industry, 1933), 11–12.

104. Ibid., 12.
105. Ibid., 13.
106. Coleman, *Museum in America*, 1:98.
107. Chicago Museum of Science and Industry website, https://www.msichicago.org/explore/whats-here/exhibits/coal-mine/.
108. Cummings, *East Is East*, 325.
109. Ibid., 113.
110. Coleman, *Museum in America*, 2:323.
111. Ceglio, "Imperfectly Progressive," 378–79.
112. Clayton D. Laurie, *The Propaganda Warriors: America's Crusade against Nazi Germany* (Lawrence: University Press of Kansas, 1996), 29.
113. Gary, *Nervous Liberals*, 2–3.
114. As scholars of both events note, attendance alone is not an accurate gauge of public investment in the ideologies espoused by these exhibitions. Jeffrey T. Schnapp, "Epic Demonstrations: Fascist Modernity and the 1932 Exhibition of the Fascist Revolution," in *Fascism, Aesthetics, and Culture*, ed. Richard Joseph Golsan (Hanover, NH: University Press of New England, 1992), 1–37.
115. Arnaldo Cortesi, "Mussolini Marks Fascists' Holiday: Dedicates a Railroad and Other Works on Eve of Anniversary of March on Rome," *New York Times*, October 28, 1932, 5.
116. Sergio Cortesini, "Invisible Canvases: Italian Painters and Fascist Myths across the American Scene," *American Art* 25, no. 1 (2011): 52–73. It also showed in Hamilton, Ontario, Canada.
117. Arthur Millier, "Mussolini's Sponsorship of Art Shows Striking Results: Several Masterpieces among Collection Sent to Coast by Italian Government, Now at Los Angeles Museum Advance Seen in Italian Art," *Los Angeles Times*, February 24, 1935, A1.
118. Bruce Altshuler, *The Avant-Garde in Exhibition: New Art in the 20th Century* (New York: Abrams, 1994), 136–46.
119. Cummings, *East Is East*, 74.
120. See, for example, Marco Duranti, "Utopia, Nostalgia and World War at the 1939–40 New York World's Fair," *Journal of Contemporary History* 41, no. 4 (October 1, 2006): 663–83; Nicholas J. Cull, "Overture to an Alliance: British Propaganda at the New York World's Fair, 1939–40," *Journal of British Studies* 36, no. 3 (1997): 325–54; and Anthony Swift, "The Soviet World of Tomorrow at the New York World's Fair, 1939," *Russian Review* 57, no. 3 (1998): 364–80.
121. Jack James and Earle Vonard Weller, *Treasure Island, "the Magic City," 1939–1940: The Story of the Golden Gate International Exposition* (San Francisco: Pisani, 1941), 240 and 254; and Mathew Walker, "To America's Two Fairs," *Living Age* 358, no. 4485 (June 1940): 385.
122. See, for example, "Paris and London Offices Remain Open," *Museum News* 17, no. 8 (October 15, 1939): 1; and "The Museums Association Issues War Circulars," *Museum News* 17, no. 10 (November 15, 1939): 2.

CHAPTER TWO: MATERIALIZING THE GOOD NEIGHBORHOOD

1. Franklin D. Roosevelt, "Annual Message to the Congress," January 3, 1940, ed. Gerhard Peters and John T. Woolley, *The American Presidency Project*, https://www.presidency.ucsb.edu/node/210437.

2. Ibid. For a summation of the Good Neighbor Policy, see Mark T. Gilderhus, *The Second Century: US-Latin American Relations Since 1889* (Wilmington, DE: Scholarly Resources, 2000), 71–111.
3. Associated Press, "Argentine Art Exhibit Opens at Richmond: R. Walton Moore and Envoy Emphasize Close Cultural Ties," *Washington Post*, January 17, 1940, 3.
4. "Mexican Songs and Dances to Feature Culture Exhibit," *Los Angeles Times*, January 2, 1940, A5; and "Museum Attendance Breaks Records," *Los Angeles Times*, January 24, 1940, 11. The other exhibits on view featured the Impressionists and the "Camera Pictorialists."
5. Andy Campbell, "Floor, Ceiling, Wall, Garden, Market: The Curatorial Scene of *Twenty Centuries of Mexican Art*," in *Modern in the Making: MoMA and the Modern Experiment, 1929–1949*, ed. Austin Porter and Sandra Zalman (London: Bloomsbury Visual Arts, 2020): 65–80.
6. Art museums predominated in terms of cultural power, but according to Coleman's count, domination by the numbers belonged to history museums, an aggregate that included house museums, public institutions, and historical society collections; see Laurence Vail Coleman, *The Museum in America: A Critical Study*, 3 vols. (Washington, DC: American Association of Museums, 1939), 1:61.
7. Teddy Hartmann [consul general of Bolivia, New York] to Beatrice Winser [secretary and director of the Newark Museum], September 29, 1941, Exhibit Files, box 42, folder: "Latin-America Exhibit 1941." Archives of the Newark Museum (hereafter ANM).
8. S. E. Durán-Ballén [consul general of Ecuador, New York] to Beatrice Winser, September 29, 1941, Exhibit Files, box 42, folder: "Latin-America Exhibit 1941." ANM.
9. "Speech of Nelson A. Rockefeller, Coordinator of Inter-American Affairs, at Macy's Latin American Fair, New York City," January 16, 1942, in *Addresses of Nelson A. Rockefeller, 1940–1944*, CIAA Bound Volumes, subseries 1: CIAA, 1940–1944, series O: Washington, DC, RG 4 NAR Personal, Rockefeller Family Archives, Rockefeller Archive Center (hereafter RAC).
10. "Radio address by Nelson A. Rockefeller at the Opening of the Toledo Chilean Art Exhibition," March 25, 1942, in *Addresses by Nelson A. Rockefeller, 1940–1944*, CIAA Bound Volumes, subseries 1: CIAA, 1940–1944, series O: Washington, DC, RG 4 NAR Personal, Rockefeller Family Archives, RAC.
11. On earlier Pan-American politics and imaginaries, see Alonso Aguilar Monteverde, *Pan-Americanism from Monroe to the Present: A View from the Other Side*, rev. English ed. (New York: MR Press, 1968); and Robert Alexander Gonzalez, *Designing Pan-America: U.S. Architectural Visions for the Western Hemisphere* (Austin: University of Texas Press, 2011).
12. Emily S. Rosenberg, *Spreading the American Dream: American Economic and Cultural Expansion, 1890–1945* (New York: Hill and Wang, 1982), 125.
13. Frank A. Ninkovich, *The Diplomacy of Ideas: U.S. Foreign Policy and Cultural Relations, 1938–1950* (New York: Cambridge University Press, 1981), 35.
14. On the DCR's shifts in budget and tactics, see Clark A. Miller, "'An Effective Instrument of Peace': Scientific Cooperation as an Instrument of U.S. Foreign Policy, 1938–1950," *Osiris* 21, no. 1 (January 1, 2006): 133–60.
15. Charles A. Thomson, "The Cultural-Relations Program of the Department of State," *Journal of Educational Sociology* 16, no. 3 (1942): 135–38.

16. The OCIAA remained under Rockefeller's leadership until December 1944. In 1945, it became the Office of Inter-American Affairs. By the time of its disbanding in April 1946, its functions had been assumed by other agencies or terminated.
17. Gisela Cramer and Ursula Prutsch, "Nelson A. Rockefeller's Office of Inter-American Affairs (1940–1946) and Record Group 229," *Hispanic American Historical Review* 86, no. 4 (2006): 785–806.
18. Rosenberg, *Spreading the American Dream*, 207.
19. Catha Paquette, "Soft Power: The Art of Diplomacy in US-Mexican Relations, 1940–1946," in *¡Américas Unidas!: Nelson A. Rockefeller's Office of Inter-American Affairs (1940–46)*, ed. Gisela Cramer and Ursula Prutsch (Madrid: Iberoamericana, 2012), 143–80; and Holly Barnet-Sanchez, "The Necessity of Pre-Columbian Art in the United States: Appropriations and Transformations of Heritage, 1933–1945," in *Collecting the Pre-Columbian Past*, ed. Elizabeth Hill Boone (Washington, DC: Dumbarton Oaks Research Library and Collection, 1993), 177–207.
20. Paquette, "Soft Power," 176.
21. Irwin F. Gellman, *Good Neighbor Diplomacy: United States Policies in Latin America, 1933–1945* (Baltimore, MD: Johns Hopkins University Press, 1979), 43.
22. Ninkovich, *Diplomacy of Ideas*, 37.
23. Reinhold Wagnleitner, "Propagating the American Dream: Cultural Policies as Means of Integration," *American Studies International* 24, no. 1 (1986): 60–84.
24. "Philosophy and Objectives of the Office of Inter-American Affairs," undated, 16; folder 61, box 8, subseries 1: Coordinator of Inter-American Affairs (CIAA), 1940–1944, series O: Washington, DC, RG 4 NAR Personal, Rockefeller Family Archives, RAC. *N.b.*: Folder title indicates contents' date as 1942–43.
25. Ibid., 10–11.
26. Ibid., 16–17.
27. Darlene J. Sadlier, *Americans All: Good Neighbor Cultural Diplomacy in World War II* (Austin: University of Texas Press, 2012), 16–21.
28. Breanne Robertson, "Textbook Diplomacy: The New World Neighbors Series and Inter-American Education during World War II," *Hemisphere: Visual Cultures of the Americas* 4 (2011): 67–93.
29. Helen Delpar, *The Enormous Vogue of Things Mexican: Cultural Relations between the United States and Mexico, 1920–1935* (Tuscaloosa: University of Alabama Press, 1992); and Ilaria Scaglia, "The Diplomacy of Display: Art and International Cooperation in the 1920s and 1930s" (PhD diss., State University of New York at Buffalo, 2011).
30. "Pan-American Cooperation Is Projected. Wissler Committee to Develop Work," *Museum News* 3, no. 4 (June 15, 1925): 1.
31. Ibid.
32. "Meeting Hears Report of AAM Work for Year: Association Gains Stability and Outlines Work for Future," *Museum News* 6, no. 3 (June 1, 1928): 1–2, 4.
33. "Coleman to Visit Museums in Latin America," *Museum News* 6, no. 4 (June 15, 1928): 2.
34. "Directory of South American Museums Offered to Members," *Museum News* 7, no. 3 (June 1, 1929): 1.
35. "Personals," *Museum News* 8, no. 8 (October 15, 1930): 3.
36. James Brown Scott, "Intellectual Cooperation," *American Journal of International Law* 24 (January 1, 1930): 762–65.

37. Herbert Hoover, "Proclamation 1912—Pan American Day," May 28, 1930, ed., Gerhard Peters and John T. Woolley, *The American Presidency Project*, https://www.presidency.ucsb.edu/node/210223.
38. "The Study of International Relations in the United States: Survey for 1934," *Museum News* 12, no. 14 (January 15, 1935): 5; and Edith Ellen Ware, *The Study of International Relations in the United States: Survey for 1934* (New York: Columbia University Press, 1934): 72–74.
39. "Beatrice Winser, Newark Librarian," *New York Times*, September 16, 1947, 23.
40. Obituary, "Miss Beatrice Winser," *Courier-News* (Bridgewater, NJ), September 15, 1947, 18.
41. "Library and Museum Directed by Woman Widen Their Service in Decade of Stress," *New York Times*, December 24, 1939, 22; and Ezra Shales, *Made in Newark Cultivating Industrial Arts and Civic Identity in the Progressive Era* (New Brunswick, NJ: Rivergate Books, Rutgers University Press, 2010), 87, 208–9.
42. Julia Sabine, "Winser, Beatrice (1869–1947)," in *Dictionary of American Library Biography*, ed. Bohdan S. Wynar (Littleton, CO: Libraries Unlimited, 1978): 567–68.
43. Beatrice Winser to Sumner Welles, January 3, 1940, (unless otherwise noted, all cited Winser–Welles correspondence is archived in box 44, folder: "Latin America Exhibit, 1941 Correspondence S–Z." ANM.
44. Richard L. Lael, *Arrogant Diplomacy: U.S. Policy toward Colombia, 1903–1922* (Wilmington, DE: Scholarly Resources, 1987): 120–24.
45. Emily S. Rosenberg, "World War I and 'Continental Solidarity,'" *Americas* 31, no. 3 (1975): 313–34.
46. "Colombia, South American Republic," undated, promotional handbill, box 8, folder: "Colombian Exhibit." ANM. The exhibit ran from May 11 through June 30, was closed except by appointment July through August, and reopened on a larger scale September through November 30, 1918.
47. Leo S. Rowe to Chairman, Board of Trustees, July 22, 1918, box 8, folder: "Colombian Exhibit." ANM.
48. Woodrow Wilson to Richard C. Jenkinson [vice-president of Newark Library board of trustees, Newark Museum trustee, and owner of the Newark-based metal goods manufactory, R. C. Jenkinson and Company], telegram, May 20, 1918, box 8, folder: "Colombian Exhibit." ANM.
49. "Wilson Endorses Colombia Exhibit," *Evening Post* (New York, NY), May 25, 1918, final edition. Likewise, "Colombia Exhibit Here Is Indorsed by Wilson," clipping from unspecified Newark newspaper, May 25, 1918, Exhibit Files, box 9, folder: "Colombia, Clippings, 1918." ANM.
50. Richard C. Jenkinson to Beatrice Winser, May 21, 1918, Exhibit Files, box 10, folder: "Colombia, President 1918." ANM. To do something "up brown" is to do something just right or with great effect.
51. Cordell Hull to Beatrice Winser, November 11, 1939, Exhibit Files, box 44, folder: "Latin America Exhibit, 1941 Correspondence S–Z." ANM. See also "State Dept. Conferences on Cultural Relations in the Americas," *Museum News* 17, no. 8 (October 15, 1939): 1.
52. Sumner Welles to Beatrice Winser, January 13, 1940.
53. Ronn F. Pineo, *Ecuador and the United States: Useful Strangers* (Athens: University of Georgia Press, 2007), 125–26. In July 1941, these tensions erupted into a

three-week-long armed conflict; its grievances continued during the planning and exhibition of *Three Southern Neighbors*.
54. George M. Lauderbaugh, "Bolivarian Nations: Securing the Northern Frontier," in *Latin America during World War II*, ed. Thomas M. Leonard and John F. Bratzel (Lanham, MD: Rowman & Littlefield, 2007), 113.
55. Fredrick B. Pike, *The United States and the Andean Republics: Peru, Bolivia, and Ecuador* (Cambridge, MA: Harvard University Press, 1977): 236–68; and Kenneth Duane Lehman, *Bolivia and the United States: A Limited Partnership* (Athens: University of Georgia Press, 1999): 72–90.
56. Beatrice Winser to Sumner Welles, January 16, 1940.
57. Sadlier, *Americans All*, 169.
58. Beatrice Winser to Sumner Welles, October 14, 1940; and Sumner Welles to Beatrice Winser, November 18, 1940.
59. Sumner Welles to Beatrice Winser, January 7, 1941.
60. Beatrice Winser to Nelson Rockefeller, 21 January 1941, box 43, folder: "Correspondence, O–R." ANM.
61. Robert G. Caldwell [chairman, Cultural Relations Program, Office for Coordination of Commercial and Cultural Relations between the American Republics] to Beatrice Winser, January 27, 1941, box 43, folder: "Correspondence, O–R." ANM.
62. Mrs. Dick, "Costs: Latin-American Exhibit (Apr. 14, 1941–Jan. 27, 1942)," June 2, 1942, Exhibit Files, box 44, folder: "Latin American Exhibit 1941, Costs." ANM.
63. T. R. Kennedy Jr., "World's Largest 'Classroom': More Than 1,000 Delegates from Twenty-Two American Nations to Map Broader Use of Radio for Pan-American Unity," *New York Times*, February 23, 1941, 17. The First International Conference of the School of the Air of the Americas was a joint enterprise of the National Education Association, the Columbia Broadcasting System, and the Pan-American Union.
64. "Museum Plan Aids Amity in Americas," *New York Times*, March 1, 1941.
65. Press release, "John Hay Whitney Announces Museum of Modern Art Will Serve as Weapon of National Defense," February 28, 1941. The Museum of Modern Art, New York. [https://www.moma.org/momaorg/shared/pdfs/docs/press_archives/676/releases/MOMA_1941_0015_1941-02-28_41228-14.pdf].
66. "Mexican Murals at the American Museum," *Museum News* 18, no. 19 (April 1, 1941): 7.
67. Barnet-Sanchez, "Necessity of Pre-Columbian Art," 196–98. MoMA handled national circulation of all three sections.
68. Grace L. McCann Morley, "Grace L. McCann Morley: Art, Artists, Museums, and the San Francisco Museum of Art," interview by Suzanne B. Riess, 1960, in Berkeley, CA, transcript, 151–60. Regional Cultural History Project, the Bancroft Library, University of California, Berkeley. Available online http://digitalassets.lib.berkeley.edu/roho/ucb/text/morley_grace_l_mccann.pdf.
69. Ibid.
70. The word "Modern" was added to the museum's name in 1975. Berit Potter, "Grace McCann Morley and the Dialectical Exchange of Modern Art in the Americas, 1935–1958" (PhD diss., New York University, 2015), 30.
71. Ibid., 61–63.
72. Brooklyn Museum press release, "Opening of Exhibition 'America South of U.S.,'" November 10, 1941, Records of the Department of Public Information. Press releases, 1939–1941. 10–12/1941, 201. Brooklyn Museum Archives.

73. "Latin American Galleries at the Brooklyn Museum," *Museum News* 20, no. 16 (February 15, 1943): 1–2; and Nancy B. Rosoff, "As Revealed by Art: Herbert Spinden and the Brooklyn Museum," *Museum Anthropology* 28, no. 1 (March 1, 2005): 47–56.
74. "Defense and Hemisphere Solidarity Sessions Focus Interest at Columbus," *Museum News* 19, no. 3 (June 1, 1941): 1–2.
75. Ibid., 1.
76. Grace L. McCann Morley, "Inter-American Cooperation in Art," *Museum News* 19, no. 9 (November 1, 1941): 11.
77. Charles H. Sawyer, "A Visitor's Impressions of Exchange Exhibitions with the Central American Republics," *Museum News* 19, no. 10 (November 15, 1941): 9.
78. Ibid., 10.
79. Ibid.
80. Philip Adams, "A Plan of Inter-American Cooperation," *Museum News* 19, no. 8 (October 8, 1941): 9–11.
81. Ibid., 10.
82. On the differences between the *Carte de Tendre* as conceived by Madeleine de Scudéry and subsequent masculinizations of it, see Gloria Feman Orenstein, "Journey through Mlle. De Scudery's *Carte de Tendre*: A 17th-Century Salon Woman's Dream/Country of Tenderness," *Femspec* 3, no. 2 (2002): 53–66; and Anthony Vidler, "Terres Inconnues: Cartographies of a Landscape to Be Invented," *October* 115 (2006): 13–30.
83. Adams, "Plan of Inter-American Cooperation," 11.
84. Margaret Jarden to Beatrice Winser, "Re: Latin-American Exhibit (Peru, Bolivia, Ecuador)," December 9, 1940, Exhibit Files, box 45, folder: "Latin-America Exhibit 1941 Notes." ANM.
85. Exhibition plan and script for *Three Southern Neighbors: Ecuador, Peru, Bolivia; Part II: Viewing the Present,* n.d., Exhibit Files, box 43, folder: "Latin American Exhibit 1941." ANM.
86. "Three Southern Neighbors: Ecuador, Peru, Bolivia Exhibition; Part II—Viewing the Present," *Museum* 4, no. 11 (October 1941): 41. ANM.
87. Beatrice Winser to Sumner Welles, "Museum Exhibit," December 18, 1940, Exhibit Files, box 44, folder: "Latin-America Exhibit, 1941, Correspondence O–R." ANM.
88. Ibid.
89. Ibid.
90. Michael J. Francis, "The United States at Rio, 1942: The Strains of Pan-Americanism," *Journal of Latin American Studies* 6, no. 1 (May 1, 1974): 77.
91. Macy's display advertisement, "It Opens Tomorrow! Macy's Latin American Fair; Greatest Exposition of Its Kind Ever Staged by a Department Store," *New York Times,* January 16, 1942, 7.
92. Agnes Adams, "Macy Latin American Fair a Bond of Good Will: Craftsmanship of Neighbors to the South to Be Presented Saturday," *New York Post,* January 14, 1942, H41.
93. "Macy's to Conduct Latin American Fair as Aid to Trade with Southern Republics," *Wall Street Journal,* October 15, 1941, 3; and "Latin America Fair Ends," *New York Times,* February 8, 1942, 51.
94. Augustine Sedgewick, "'The Spice of the Department Store': The 'Consumers' Republic,' Imported Knock-Offs from Latin America, and the Invention of International Development, 1936–1941," *International Labor and Working Class History* 81 (January 1, 2012): 49–68.

95. Jeffrey Trask, *Things American: Art Museums and Civic Culture in the Progressive Era* (Philadelphia: University of Pennsylvania Press, 2012), 209–11.
96. "Design Is Started in Volume Range," *New York Times*, July 13, 1941; and Press Release, "Executives of Museum of Modern Art and Bloomingdale's, Inc. Explain Purpose of Design Competition and Introduce Mexican and South American Winners," June 14, 1941, 4–5. MoMA, NY. [https://www.moma.org/momaorg/shared/pdfs/docs/press_archives/710/releases/MOMA_1941_0047_1941-06-14_41614-46.pdf].
97. Press Release, "Work of Prize-Winning American Designers Goes on Exhibition at Museum of Modern Art and in Department Stores throughout the Country," September 22, 1941, 5. MoMA, NY. [https://www.moma.org/momaorg/shared/pdfs/docs/press_archives/734/releases/MOMA_1941_0071_1941-09-22_41922-70.pdf].
98. Press Release, Number 41924, September 22, 1941. MoMA, NY. [https://www.moma.org/momaorg/shared/pdfs/docs/press_archives/737/releases/MOMA_1941_0074_1941-09-24_41924-73.pdf].
99. David Mark Carletta, "Frances R. Grant's Pan-American Activities, 1929–1949" (PhD diss., Michigan State University, 2009), 316–21.
100. Macy's, "Macy's Latin American Fair" brochure, 1942, 6. folder 6, box 1, series 2, Record Unit 7386: Carl W. Mitman Papers, 1937–1946, 1949, Smithsonian Institution Archives.
101. Quoted in Sadlier, *Americans All*, 182.
102. David Crouch and Luke Desforges, "The Sensuous in the Tourist Encounter; Introduction: The Power of the Body in Tourist Studies," *Tourist Studies* 3, no. 1 (April 1, 2003): 5–22.
103. John Urry, *Consuming Places* (London: Routledge, 1995); John Urry and Jonas Larsen, *The Tourist Gaze 3.0* (London: Sage, 2011); and Michael K. Goodman, David Goodman, and Michael R. Redclift, eds., *Consuming Space: Placing Consumption in Perspective* (Farnham, UK: Ashgate, 2010).
104. "It Opens Tomorrow!"
105. Daryle Williams, *Culture Wars in Brazil: The First Vargas Regime, 1930–1945* (Durham, NC: Duke University Press, 2001), 52–89; and Lisa Crossman, "Macy's Latin American Fair: A Temple Built on the Anxieties of Inter/Americanism," *Material Culture Review* 79 (Spring 2014): 60–77.
106. *Exhibition Techniques: A Summary of Exhibition Practice Based on Surveys Conducted at the New York and San Francisco World's Fairs of 1939* (New York: Museum of Science and Industry, 1940), 115–16.
107. Exhibition plan and script.
108. Urry and Larsen, *Tourist Gaze 3.0*, 167.
109. Veronica Della Dora, "Putting the World into a Box: A Geography of Nineteenth-Century 'Travelling Landscapes,'" *Geografiska Annaler* 89, no. 4 (January 1, 2007): 287–306.
110. "Latin Americans Honored at Fair," *New York Times*, January 17, 1942, 30.
111. "Macy Fair Contest," *New York Times*, January 18, 1942, XX7.
112. See correspondence between Rafael Valdez [commissioner of the Ecuadorean Pavilion] and Winser in Exhibit Files, box 42, folder: "Correspondence C–G"; and also Margaret Jarden, "Report on Visit to the Consul General of Ecuador by Sabine and Jarden on 1/20/41," January 22, 1941, Exhibit Files, box 45, folder: "Latin-America Exhibit 1941 Notes." ANM.

113. Beatrice Winser to Kathryn B. Greywacz, January 28, 1941, Exhibit Files, box 42, folder: "Correspondence C–G." ANM.
114. Kathryn B. Greywacz to Beatrice Winser, February 1, 1941, Exhibit Files, box 42, folder: "Correspondence C–G." ANM. The State Museum's *Latin American Arts and Crafts* ran from March 2 through April 20, 1941.
115. C. J. Fraissinet [president, Button Machinery Company] to Beatrice Winser, March 21, 1941, Exhibit Files, box 42, folder: "Latin American Exhibition 1941." ANM. Once the United States entered the war, demand for buttons for military uniforms temporarily boosted Ecuador's tagua nut industry.
116. See, for example, Jason M. Colby, *The Business of Empire: United Fruit, Race, and U.S. Expansion in Central America* (New York: Cornell University Press, 2011).
117. Lawrence A. Clayton, *Grace: W. R. Grace & Co.: The Formative Years, 1850–1930* (Ottawa, IL: Jameson Books, 1985); and C. A. Secada, "Arms, Guano, and Shipping: The W. R. Grace Interests in Peru, 1865–1885," *Business History Review* 59, no. 4 (1985): 597–621.
118. Fredrick B. Pike, *The United States and Latin America: Myths and Stereotypes of Civilization and Nature* (Austin: University of Texas Press, 1992), 288.
119. "Lists America's Discovery as a Catastrophe," *New York Herald Tribune*, April 15, 1939, 3.
120. Carl Greenleaf Beede, "Antiques: Arts of Latin-American Colonial Era," *Christian Science Monitor*, December 10, 1941, 3.
121. Quoted in Beede, "Antiques," 3.
122. Campbell, "Floor, Ceiling," 73–77.
123. "Macy's Latin American Fair" brochure, 20.
124. "Latin-American Fair Aids Peasant Women, Sale Here Gives Outlet to 20 Southern Nations," *New York Times*, January 19, 1942, 14.
125. Exhibition plan and script, 43.
126. Ibid.
127. "Suggested Approach for Exhibition on Ecuador-Peru-Bolivia," Exhibit Files, box 45, folder: "Latin-America Exhibit 1941, Notes." ANM.
128. *Museum* 4, no. 11 (October 1941): 42.
129. Exhibition plan and script, 46.
130. Richard Foster Howard [director, Dallas Museum of Fine Arts] to Beatrice Winser, March 15, 1941, Exhibit Files, box 42, folder: "Latin America Exhibition 1941." ANM.
131. Margaret Jarden, "Report on Visit to Peruvian Consul General by Sabine & Jarden 1/22/41," January 23, 1941, Exhibit Files, box 45, folder: "Latin-America Exhibit 1941 Notes." ANM.
132. Office of Public Opinion Research (1940), cited in Frederick B. Pike, *FDR's Good Neighbor Policy: Sixty Years of Generally Gentle Chaos* (Austin: University of Texas Press, 1995), 287.
133. Margaret Jarden, "Report on Visit to Bolivian Consul General–Sabine & Jarden 1/21/41," January 22, 1941, Exhibit Files, box 45, folder: "Latin-America Exhibit 1941 Notes." ANM. The meeting was not with Hartman.
134. Jarden, "Report on Visit Visit to the Consul General of Ecuador by Sabine and Jarden on 1/20/41."
135. Untitled memorandum, August 15, 1941, Exhibit Files, box 43, folder: "Correspondence O–R." ANM.
136. Georgina Smith [of *Pan-American* magazine] to Irvine White [Newark Museum public relations], October 10, 1941, Exhibit Files, box 43, folder: "Correspondence M–N,"

AMN. Smith passes along the comments of a Mr. O'Neill who viewed the exhibition with her. Smith, who wrote about *Three Southern Neighbors: Ecuador, Peru, Bolivia*; *Part I* for the magazine, did not give coverage to *Part II*. See Georgina Smith, "Masterpieces of Unknowns Exhibited," *Pan-American* 2, no. 3 (June 1941): 23–30.

137. "Una exhibición ecuatoriana de gran valor educacio nal y mucho interés propagandistico, en EE. UU," *El Comercio*, November 9, 1941, Exhibit Files, box 45, folder: "Latin-America Exhibit 1941 Publicity & Programs." ANM.

138. "Department of United States Activities and Special Services," undated, 4–5, folder 36, box 5, subseries: Division of Inter-American Activities in the U.S., 1942–44, series O: Washington, DC, RG 4 NAR Personal, Rockefeller Family Archives, RAC.

139. "Status of Projects as of March 31, 1944," 205, in *Project Reports, 1944*, vol. I, CIAA Bound Volumes, subseries 1: CIAA, 1940–1944, series O: Washington, DC, RG 4 NAR Personal, Rockefeller Family Archives, RAC.

140. Barnet-Sanchez, "Necessity of Pre-Columbian Art," 174–80.

141. Michael L. Krenn, *Fall-out Shelters for the Human Spirit: American Art and the Cold War* (Chapel Hill: University of North Carolina Press, 2005), 18–26.

142. Alvaro A. Araujo, "On Exchange of Exhibitions between United States and Latin America," *Museum News* 19, no. 16 (February 15, 1942): 7–8.

143. Arthur Preston Whitaker, introduction to *Inter-American Affairs 1943: An Annual Survey: No. 3*, ed. Arthur Preston Whitaker (New York: Columbia University Press, 1944), 5.

144. "Parranda Pan Americana," *Museum News* 22, no. 20 (April 15, 1945): 4.

145. "To Depict Our Life in War: Macy's to Give Exhibition of How We Use Substitutes," *New York Times*, August 30, 1942; and "Art of Camouflage Is Demonstrated Here as Army Men Open Department Store Show," *New York Times*, February 6, 1943.

146. Russell Lynes, *Good Old Modern: An Intimate Portrait of the Museum of Modern Art* (New York: Atheneum, 1973), 237; and "The Minutes of the Sixteenth Annual Meeting of the Board of Trustees and Members of the Corporation of the Museum of Modern Art," *Bulletin of the Museum of Modern Art* 13, no. 3 (September 1946): 5. See also Mary Anne Staniszewski, *The Power of Display: A History of Exhibition Installations at the Museum of Modern Art* (Cambridge, MA: MIT Press, 1998), 224–25.

147. Victoria Cain, "'The Direct Medium of the Vision': Visual Education, Virtual Witnessing and the Prehistoric Past at the American Museum of Natural History, 1890–1923," *Journal of Visual Culture* 9, no. 4 (2010): 284–303.

148. Ana Douglass and Thomas A Vogler, introduction to *Witness and Memory: The Discourse of Trauma*, ed. Ana Douglass and Thomas A Vogler (New York: Routledge, 2003), 1–53.

149. Greg Grandin, *Empire's Workshop: Latin America, the United States, and the Rise of the New Imperialism* (New York, 2006), 33–39.

CHAPTER THREE: WAR COMES TO THE MUSEUM

1. "The Museum in America," *Museum News* 17, no. 19 (April 1, 1940): 7.
2. "Unsurpassed Hospitality, Large Attendance Mark Detroit Meeting," *Museum News* 18, no. 3 (June 1, 1940): 1.
3. "Museums of Honolulu Go through Japanese Air Raids Unharmed," *Museum News* 19, no. 14 (January 15, 1942): 1, 4.
4. "Committee to Study Air Raid Hazards," *Museum News* 19, no. 1 (May 1, 1941): 1. The committee was convened by the government's National Resource Planning Board.

5. See John E. Graf [associate director, U.S. National Museum], "Emergency Protection Measures for Museums," *Museum News* 19, no. 4 (June 15, 1941): 8–9; and Robert G. Rosegrant [registrar, Museum of Fine Arts, Boston], "The Preservation of Museum Collections during War, Parts I and II," *Museum News* 19, no. 4 (June 15, 1941): 9–12. Both articles from papers read at the Annual Meeting at Columbus, OH, May 15–16, 1941.
6. Ralph H. Lewis [field curator, Museum Division, National Park Service], "Museums in Wartime—The British Example," *Museum News* 18, no. 20 (April 15, 1941): 11–12.
7. Ibid., 11.
8. Ibid.
9. "Three San Diego Museums Become Navy Hospitals," *Museum News* 20, no. 20 (April 15, 1943): 1. See also, "Nevada Museum Installs Emergency Hospital," *Museum News* 20, no. 8 (October 15, 1942): 2.
10. Clarissa Ceglio, "Imperfectly Progressive: The Social Mission of U.S. Museums in the 1930s," in *Radical Roots: Public History and a Tradition of Social Justice Activism*, ed. Denise Meringolo (Amherst, MA: Amherst College Press, 2021), 365–67.
11. Lewis, "Museums in Wartime," 11–12.
12. "War-time Service by Museums and Museum Men," *Museum Work* 1, no. 2 (November 1918): 34.
13. "Mineral and Munitions," *Museum Work* 1, no. 3 (December 1918): 69.
14. "The Program for Springfield Meeting," *Museum News Letter* 1, no. 8 (April 1918): 1.
15. "St. Paul Museum Builds Defense Exhibitions," *Museum News* 19, no. 2 (May 15, 1941): 1, 4; and "Eastern Museums Circuit Saint Paul National Security Exhibit," *Museum News* 19, no. 11 (December 1, 1941): 1–2.
16. Brian McMahon, "Can America Be Bombed? The St. Paul Science Museum's Answer," *Ramsey County History* 52, no. 2 (Summer 2017): 22–26.
17. Arthur C. Parker, "Museums in the World Crisis," *Museum News* 21, no. 5 (September 1, 1943): 6–8. Paper read at the Annual Meeting of the American Association of Museums at Williamsburg, VA, May 18–19, 1942.
18. "Art: Globes on Parade," *Time Magazine,* Monday, Dec. 22, 1941, http://content.time.com/time/magazine/article/0,9171,932000,00.html.
19. Louis H. Powell, "New Uses for Globes and Spherical Maps," *Geographical Review* 35, no. 1 (1945): 49–58.
20. Ibid., 49.
21. A. Philpott, "War Cartoons by David Low at Boston Fine Arts Museum," *Daily Boston Globe,* December 13, 1940, 11.
22. *War Comes to the People: A Story Written with the Lens,* MoMA Exh. #119.
23. "Toledo Museum Stresses the Art of Our Allies," *Museum News* 20, no. 6 (September 15, 1942): 6.
24. Office of War Information, "A Pilot Study of American Sentiment toward the British; Surveys Division Special Memorandum No. 47," March 29, 1943, 2, folder 0027, box 002, John Marshall Papers, Series 1: General Files, Record Group IV 2A 37, Rockefeller Related Special Collections Family Archives, Rockefeller Archive Center.
25. Ibid., 1.
26. "Emergency Planning," *Museum News* 19, no. 13 (January 1, 1942): 1 and 4.
27. Ceglio, "Imperfectly Progressive," 365.
28. Ibid., 366.

29. L. Hubbard Shattuck [director, Chicago Historical Society], "Wartime Duties of Historical Museums," *Museum News* 20, no. 7 (October 1, 1942): 6–8. Paper read at the Annual Meeting of the American Association of Museums at Williamsburg, May 18–19, 1942.
30. "NY Museum Attendance," *Museum News* 21, no. 3 (June 1, 1943): 2.
31. This represented a 2 percent increase, and, given the variability inherent in attendance-taking methods of the time, such a modest increase may just as likely signal stability, if not actual growth, in visitation. The other museum enjoying an attendance bump was the New York Museum of Science and Industry.
32. Maren Stange, *Symbols of Ideal Life; Social Documentary Photography in America, 1890–1950* (New York: Cambridge University Press: 1989), 139.
33. "Annual Meeting Announcements," *Museum News* 19, no. 20 (April 1, 1942): 1.
34. "Constructive Ideas Mark a Well Attended Meeting at Williamsburg," *Museum News* 20, no. 3 (June 1, 1942): 1–2.
35. See, for example, "No A.A.M. Meeting in 1943," *Museum News* 20, no. 17 (March 1, 1943): 1. Almost identical wording was used in announcing the cancellation of the 1944 and 1945 meetings.
36. A. E. Parr, "The Wartime Duties of Natural History Museums," *Museum News* 20, no. 5 (September 1, 1942): 8.
37. Shattuck, "Wartime Duties of Historical Museums," 8.
38. Edward L. Bernays, "The Museum's Job in Wartime," *Museum News* 20, no. 20 (April 15, 1943): 11–12. Paper read at the Annual Meeting of the American Association of Museums at Williamsburg, May 18–19, 1942. See also Edward L. Bernays, *Propaganda* (New York: H. Liveright, 1928).
39. Ibid., 11.
40. Ibid., 12.
41. Ibid.
42. Ned J. Burns, "Park Museums and Public Morale," *Museum News* 19, no. 10 (November 15, 1941): 12.
43. Ibid., 11.
44. Ibid.
45. Ibid.
46. Ibid., 12.
47. Shattuck, "Wartime Duties of Historical Museums," 6.
48. Ibid., 8.
49. Ibid. It is unknown whether AAM or regional museum bodies took up the issue.
50. Ibid., 7.
51. "Wartime Duties of Historical Museums: Address Given by L. Hubbard Shattuck, Director of the Chicago Historical Society" (Chicago, IL: Chicago Historical Society, July 1942).
52. Parr, "Wartime Duties of Natural History Museums," 7.
53. Ibid., 8.
54. Ibid., 7.
55. Ibid.
56. Fiske Kimball [director, Philadelphia Art Museum], "Art Museums in War Time," *Museum News* 20, no. 6 (September 15, 1942): 7–8. Paper read at the Annual Meeting of the American Association of Museums at Williamsburg, May 18–19, 1942.

57. Ibid., 7.
58. Lewis, "Museums in Wartime," 12.
59. Fiske Kimball, *Annual report of the Philadelphia Museum of Art, 1943*, quoted in *Museum News* 21, no. 10 (November 15, 1943): 1.
60. Horace H. F. Jayne [vice director, Metropolitan Museum of Art, New York], "The Art Museum in War Time," *Museum News* 20, no. 14 (January 15, 1943): 8. Paper read at the Annual Meeting of the American Association of Museums at Williamsburg, May 18–19, 1942.
61. "Art Museum Directors Hold New York Meeting on War Emergency," *Museum News* 19, no. 13 (January 1, 1942): 1 and 4.
62. Ibid., 4.
63. Ceglio, "Imperfectly Progressive," 388.
64. Theodore L. Low, "Museums Need Vitamin A," *Museum News* 20, no. 17 (March 1, 1943): 1 and 4.
65. Theodore Lewis Low, *The Museum as a Social Instrument* (New York: Metropolitan Museum of Art for the American Association of Museums, 1942), 23.
66. Low, "Museums Need Vitamin A," 1.
67. "Theodore Low, of Walters Gallery, Dies," *Baltimore Sun*, Monday, July 27, 1987, 29.
68. Ibid. The quote is by Edward S. King, former director of the Walters and a friend of Low's.
69. A. Parker, "Museums in the World Crisis," 6.
70. Quoted in ibid., 7.
71. Ibid.
72. Clark Wissler [dean of scientific staff and curator in chief, Department of Anthropology, American Museum of Natural History, and president of the American Association of Museums], "Some Fundamentals in the Philosophy of Science Museums," *Museum News* 20, no. 15 (February 1, 1943): 9–12. Paper read at the Annual Meeting of the American Association of Museums at Williamsburg, May 18–19, 1942.
73. Ibid., 11.
74. *Animals and the War*, photo file drawer 225: "Temporary Exhibitions, 1900–1950," Central Archives, American Museum of Natural History, New York.
75. "Nature at War," *New York Times*, November 22, 1942: Sec. 7, 20–21.
76. Margaret Mead, "Museums in the Emergency," *Natural History* 48, no. 2 (1941): 67. Copyright © Natural History Magazine, Inc., 1941. Reprinted by permission.
77. Fred Turner, *The Democratic Surround: Multimedia and American Liberalism from World War II to the Psychedelic Sixties* (Chicago, IL: University of Chicago Press, 2013), 63–76.
78. Frank L. DuMond, "Presenting the Museum to the Community," *Museum News* 18, no. 13 (January 1, 1941): 10–12.
79. Ibid., 10.
80. Karla V. Parker, "A Museum 'as Accessible as a Dime Store,' as Friendly as a Next-Door Neighbor," *Christian Science Monitor*, December 23, 1941, 15.
81. Whitman, Walt, *Leaves of Grass* (1881–82), Walt Whitman Archive, ed. Ed Folsom and Kenneth M. Price, http://www.whitmanarchive.org.
82. "Racial Freedom Shown at Vassar: Museum Has Graphic Exhibit on Life Here and in Other Countries," *New York Times*, February 1, 1942, D6.
83. Jane Wilkinson, "The Great Idea at the Social Museum," *Vassar Alumni Magazine* (March 1942): 17–18.

84. In 1943 budget and staff cuts all but eliminated Vassar's Social Museum, which closed in the 1950s.
85. Gregory Clark, "Rhetorical Experience and the National Jazz Museum in Harlem," in *Places of Public Memory: The Rhetoric of Museums and Memorials*, ed. Greg Dickinson, Carole Blair, and Brian Ott (Tuscaloosa: University of Alabama Press, 2010): 113–35.

CHAPTER FOUR: WITNESSING WAR FARE

1. National Resources Planning Board leaflet quoted in Bertha L. Heilbron, "Local Historical Museums and the War Program," *Minnesota History* 23, no. 1 (March 1942): 16.
2. Bernice Stevens, "Museum Demonstrates Methods of Household Management," *Christian Science Monitor*, September 2, 1942, 11.
3. "Exhibition of Home Front Homes," *Museum News* 21, no. 2 (May 15, 1943): 2.
4. Stuart C. Henry [director], "Program for Today," *Museum News* 21, no. 6 (September 15, 1943): 7–8.
5. Harvey A. Anderson [chief of the Conservation and Substitution Branch, Conservation Division, War Production Board] to Alice M. Carson [acting director of Industrial Design], November 17, 1942, quoted in "Useful Objects in Wartime: Fifth Annual Exhibition of Useful Objects under $10.00," *Bulletin of the Museum of Modern Art* 10, no. 2 (December 1942): 7.
6. "American-Soviet War Exhibit Here Opened by Wife of Red Ambassador," *New York Times*, 2 June 1943, 5.
7. Andrew James Wulf, *U.S. International Exhibitions during the Cold War: Winning Hearts and Minds through Cultural Diplomacy* (Lanham, MD: Rowman & Littlefield, 2015), 135–42.
8. "Wartime Housing," *Bulletin of the Museum of Modern Art* 9, no. 4 (May 1942): 2.
9. "Roosevelt's Address on the Museum of Modern Art," *Herald Tribune*, May 11, 1939. Monroe Wheeler Papers, I.146. The Museum of Modern Art Archives, New York.
10. Alan Wallach, "The Museum of Modern Art: The Past's Future," *Journal of Design History* 5, no. 3 (1992): 207.
11. Alfred H. Barr, "Research and Publication in Art Museums," *Museum News* 23, no. 13 (January 1, 1946): 6–8. Paper presented at a conference entitled "The Future of the Art Museum as an Educational Institution," Chicago, March 24–25, 1944.
12. "Circulating Exhibitions, 1931–1954," *Bulletin of the Museum of Modern Art* 21, no. 3–4 (Summer 1954): 11–12, 28.
13. John D. Rockefeller Jr. [JDR Jr.] to Victor E. D'Amico, March 10, 1949, folder 1743, box 157, series A: Activities, Record Group (hereafter RG) 4 Nelson A. Rockefeller Personal (hereafter NAR Personal), Rockefeller Family Archives, Rockefeller Archive Center (hereafter RAC); and "Art for Veterans," *Bulletin of the Museum of Modern Art* 13, no. 1 (September 1945): 1–15.
14. John Jay Whitney, preface to *Bulletin of the Museum of Modern Art* 7, no. 6 (September 1941): 2. *Image of Freedom* invited photographers to submit work that "most deeply signifies America" and also affirmed faith in the nation's core principles.
15. "Schedule of Income," n.d., enclosed with Stephen C. Clark to JDR Jr., January 8, 1942, folder 241, box 23, series E: Cultural Interests, RG 2, Office of the Messrs. Rockefeller (hereafter OMR), Rockefeller Family Archives, RAC.

16. "Some Wartime Activities among the Museums," *Museum News* 21, no. 1 (May 1, 1943): 1–2.
17. "Re: Gov't Bureau of Design," Julian Street Jr. to Elliot Noyes, November 20, 1940, p. 2, folder 1307, box 133, subseries: MoMA, series L: Projects, RG 4, NAR Personal, Rockefeller Family Archives, RAC.
18. Alfred H. Barr to John Abbott, August 8, 1940, folder 1203, box 123, series L: Projects, RG 4, NAR Personal, Rockefeller Family Archives, RAC.
19. Frances Hawkins to Abby Aldrich Rockefeller, June 9, 1942, folder 115, box 9, RG 2, OMR, Abby Aldrich Rockefeller Papers, Rockefeller Family Archives, RAC; and "Museum and the War," 15.
20. Fiske Kimball, "Art Museums in War Time," *Museum News* 20, no. 6 (September 15, 1942): 7.
21. Fiske Kimball, *Annual Report of the Philadelphia Museum of Art*, for fiscal year ended May 31, 1943, quoted in *Museum News* 21, no. 10 (November 15, 1943): 1.
22. Frances Hawkins to Nelson A. Rockefeller (hereafter NAR), October 29, 1943, folder 1203, box 123, subseries: MoMA, series L: Projects, RG 4, NAR Personal, RAC.
23. Museum of Modern Art, "Project Memorandum," June 9, 1948, p. 2, folder 1611, box 158, series L: Projects, RG 4, NAR; Museum of Modern Art, "Project Memorandum," December 31, 1942, p. 4, folder 219, box 22, series E: Cultural Interests, RG 2, OMR, RAC; and "The Minutes of the Sixteenth Annual Meeting," *Bulletin of the Museum of Modern Art* 13, no. 3 (February 1946): 8.
24. Herman Kashins to Frances Hawkins, April 2, 1943, folder 1203, box 123, series L: Washington, DC, RG 4, NAR Personal, Rockefeller Family Archives, RAC.
25. Hawkins to NAR, October 29, 1943, 2.
26. "75,000 Tanks, 414,000 Houses," *Time* 39, no. 19 (May 11, 1942): 44.
27. Kristin Szylvian, "The Federal Housing Program during World War II," in *From Tenements to the Taylor Homes: In Search of an Urban Housing Policy in Twentieth-Century America*, ed. John F. Bauman, Roger Biles, and Kristin Szylvian (University Park: Pennsylvania State University Press, 2000), 121.
28. Data on population movement can be found in John E. Jeffries, *Wartime America: The World War II Home Front* (Chicago, IL: Ivan R. Dee, 1996), 69–71; and Michael C. C. Adams, *The Best War Ever: America and World War II* (Baltimore, MD: Johns Hopkins University Press, 1994), 119.
29. Andrew M. Shanken, *194X: Architecture, Planning, and Consumer Culture on the American Home Front* (Minneapolis: University of Minnesota Press, 2009), 10.
30. "Committee Forms for Cooperation in Defense Housing," *Washington Post*, March 24, 1941, 13.
31. Catherine Bauer, *Modern Housing* (New York: Houghton Mifflin, 1934).
32. Szylvian, "Federal Housing Program," 129.
33. *T.V.A. Architecture and Design*, MoMA Exh. #125, April 30–June 7, 1941; Geoffrey Baker, "Exhibition at the Museum of Modern Art Reveals Democracy in a Mood of Creation on a Project of Gigantic Size," *New York Times*, May 4, 1941, X9.
34. Allen Freeman Davis, *Spearheads for Reform: The Social Settlements and the Progressive Movement, 1890–1914* (New Brunswick, NJ: Rutgers University Press, 1994), 70–72.
35. Frederick A. Gutheim, "Federal Participation in Two World's Fairs," *Public Opinion Quarterly* 3, no. 4 (October 1, 1939): 608–22.

36. Rixt Woudstra, "Exhibiting Reform: MoMA and the Display of Public Housing (1932–1939)," *Architectural Histories* 6, no. 1 (September 11, 2018): 1–17; Joan A. Saab, *For the Millions: American Art and Culture between the Wars* (Philadelphia: University of Pennsylvania Press, 2004), 121–27; Mary Anne Staniszewski, *The Power of Display: A History of Exhibition Installations at the Museum of Modern Art* (Cambridge, MA: MIT Press, 1998), 196–99; and Suzanne Spencer, "'Housing on Trial': The Museum of Modern Art and the Campaign for Modern Housing in the United States, 1932–1952" (PhD diss., Emory University, 2004).
37. Press Release, "Museum of Modern Art Opens Exhibition of Therese Bonney's War History Written with the Lens," December 10, 1940, 2. MoMA, NY. [https://www.moma.org/momaorg/shared/pdfs/docs/press_archives/654/releases/MOMA_1940_0085_1940-12-10_401210-76.pdf].
38. "The Lens Writes History," *New York Times*, December 15, 1940, 115.
39. "Museum of Modern Art Opens Exhibition of Therese Bonney's War History Written with the Lens," 1–2.
40. Erin Kathleen O'Toole, "No Democracy in Quality: Ansel Adams, Beaumont and Nancy Newhall, and the Founding of the Department of Photographs at the Museum of Modern Art" (PhD diss., University of Arizona, 2010); and Kristen Gresh, "The Politics of Photography: The Family of Man and the Museum of Modern Art's War Program," in *On Display: Visual Politics, Material Culture, and Education*, ed. Karin Priem and Kerstin te Heesen (Münster, Germany: Waxmann Verlag, 2016), 127–43.
41. On photography as an act and product of witness, see, for example, Gretchen Garner, *Disappearing Witness: Change in Twentieth-Century American Photography* (Baltimore, MD: Johns Hopkins University Press, 2003).
42. "The Lens Writes History," 115.
43. Installation view of exhibition *War Comes to the People: A Story Written with the Lens* (MoMA Exh. #119, December 10, 1940–January 5, 1941). Photographic Archive. The Museum of Modern Art Archives, New York.
44. Frances Guerin and Roger Hallas, introduction to *The Image and the Witness: Trauma, Memory, and Visual Culture*, ed. Frances Guerin and Roger Hallas (New York: Wallflower Press, 2007), 12.
45. Thomas A. Vogler, "Poetic Witness: Writing the Real," in *Witness and Memory: The Discourse of Trauma*, ed. Ana Douglass and Thomas A. Vogler (New York: Routledge, 2003), 190.
46. Quoted in David Phillips, "Actuality and Affect in Documentary Photography," in *Using Visual Evidence*, ed. Robert W. Matson and Richard Howells (Maidenhead, UK: Open University Press/McGraw-Hill, 2009), 65.
47. O'Toole, "No Democracy in Quality," 187.
48. Alfred Barr to Philip L. Goodwin, Esq., June 30, 1941. Registrar Exhibition Files (REG), Exh. #178. MoMA Archives, NY.
49. John E. Abbott to I. Edwin Goldwasser, October 31, 1941. REG, Exh. #178. MoMA Archives, NY.
50. National Committee on the Housing Emergency memo, "Housing for Victory," March 24, 1942. REG, Exh. #178. MoMA Archives, NY.
51. Winslow Ames to Philip Goodwin, December 26, 1941. REG, Exh. #178. MoMA Archives, NY.

52. Janet Henrich to Mary [no last name], October 3, 1941. REG, Exh. #178. MoMA Archives, NY. The recipient was likely architect Mary Goldwater.
53. Janet Henrich to Mary [no last name], October 6, 1941. REG, Exh. #178. MoMA Archives, NY.
54. "War Emergency Housing," undated memorandum. REG, Exh. #178. MoMA Archives, NY.
55. The idea of an exhibition staged as a "drama" and partitioned into "scenes" may have been inspired by the proposed treatment for a never-realized MoMA effort "For Us the Living," also called "Exhibition X," which had been sketched out in mid-1940 in response to Abby Rockefeller's desire to combat isolationist sentiments in the United States. See Robert R. Janes, *Museums in a Troubled World: Renewal, Irrelevance or Collapse?* (London: Routledge, 2009), 60–61, and Fred Turner, *The Democratic Surround: Multimedia and American Liberalism from World War II to the Psychedelic Sixties* (Chicago, IL: University of Chicago Press, 2013), 99–102.
56. "Photographs: Wartime Housing Exhibition," undated exhibition script. REG, Exh. #178. MoMA Archives, NY.
57. Ibid.
58. "Report of Discussion of Wartime Housing Exhibition by the Architecture Committee of the Museum of Modern Art," February 17, 1942. REG, Exh. #178. MoMA Archives, NY.
59. Don E. Hatch, "Notes on Meeting at Coffee House; Modern Museum of Art Show on Housing," January 19, 1942. REG, Exh. #178. MoMA Archives, NY.
60. "Wartime Housing Show: Final Script #1," undated. REG, Exh. #178. MoMA Archives, NY.
61. Catherine Bauer to Eliot Noyes, March 11, 1942. REG, Exh. #178. MoMA Archives, NY.
62. . Eliot Noyes to Catherine Bauer, March 16, 1942. REG, Exh. #178. MoMA Archives, NY.
63. *Two Years of War in England: Photographs by William Vandivert*, MoMA Exh. #177, April 15–June 10, 1942; and *Art Sale for the Armed Services*, MoMA Exh. #179, May–June 16, 1942.
64. *Anti-Hoarding Pictures by New York School Children* (MoMA Exh. #180, May 13 to June 8, 1942); and Press Release, "N.Y. School Children Invited by Museum of Modern Art and City Women's Club to Participate in Anti-Hoarding Picture Project," March 27, 1942. MoMA, NY. [https://www.moma.org/momaorg/shared/pdfs/docs/press_archives/783/releases/MOMA_1942_0025_1942-03-27_42327-23.pdf].
65. *Mexican Costumes by Carlos Mérida* (MoMA Exh. #181, May 13 to May 24, 1942); and Press Release, "Museum of Modern Art Announces Summer Exhibition Schedule," May 8, 1942. MoMA, NY. [http://www.moma.org/pdfs/docs/press_archives/794/releases/MOMA_1942_0036_1942-05-08_42508-31.pdf?2010].
66. Undated exhibition script with 11 scenes, 2. REG, Exh. #178. MoMA Archives, NY.
67. Ibid.
68. "Wartime Housing Show: Final Script #1."
69. "75,000 Tanks."
70. Carl Mydans's work later featured in MoMA's Cold War effort, *Korea: The Impact of War in Photographs* (February 13–April 22, 1951).

71. On the use of photomontage in earlier exhibitions, see Jorge Ribalta, ed., *Public Photographic Spaces: Exhibitions of Propaganda, from Pressa to The Family of Man, 1928–55* (Barcelona: Museu d'Art Contemporani de Barcelona, 2008).
72. "Wartime Housing Show: Final Script #1," 1.
73. Ibid.
74. "Script Wartime Housing Exhibition, Scene III," April 6, 1942. REG, Exh. #178. MoMA Archives, NY. *Nb*: Small deviations exist between the final script and the audio production, preserved in cassette format for research access.
75. Clayton Funk, "The 'Art in America' Radio Programs, 1934–1935," *Studies in Art Education* 40, no. 1 (October 1, 1998): 42–43.
76. Susan Douglas, *Listening In: Radio and the American Imagination* (New York: Times Books, 1999), 29–30.
77. Sheila Watson, "Myth, Memory and the Senses in the Churchill Museum," in *Museum Materialities: Objects, Engagements, Interpretations*, ed. Sandra H Dudley (London: Routledge, 2010), 212–14.
78. Roland Marchand, *Creating the Corporate Soul: The Rise of Public Relations and Corporate Imagery in American Big Business* (Berkeley: University of California Press, 1998), 326–36.
79. Ibid., 322.
80. Erskine Caldwell and Margaret Bourke-White, *You Have Seen Their Faces* (New York: The Viking Press, 1937); James Agee and Walker Evans, *Let Us Now Praise Famous Men* (New York: Houghton Mifflin, 1941); and Archibald MacLeish, *Land of the Free* (New York: Harcourt, Brace and Co., 1938).
81. Christopher Gerould authored the scripts, and stage and screen actor Myron McCormick served as commentator.
82. "75,000 Tanks."
83. Ibid.
84. "In Fields as They Worked," *Time* 34, no. 16 (October 16, 1939): 47.
85. Darlene J. Sadlier, *Americans All: Good Neighbor Cultural Diplomacy in World War II* (Austin: University of Texas Press, 2012), 90; and James Spiller, "This Is War! Network Radio and World War II Propaganda in America," *Journal of Radio Studies* 11, no. 1 (May 2004): 67.
86. "75,000 Tanks."
87. Ibid.
88. "Script-Wartime Housing Exhibition (Scene 7), undated, 2. REG, Exh. #178. MoMA Archives, NY.
89. "75,000 Tanks."
90. "Wartime Housing Show: Final Script #1," 5.
91. Margaret Crawford, "Daily Life on the Home Front: Women, Blacks, and the Struggle for Public Housing," in *World War II and the American Dream*, ed. Donald Albrecht (Washington, DC / Cambridge, MA: National Building Museum / MIT Press, 1995), 90–143.
92. Nicholas Natanson, *The Black Image in the New Deal: The Politics of FSA Photography* (Knoxville: University of Tennessee Press, 1992), 42–46.
93. Mrs. Samuel I. Rosenman to Frances Hawkins, March 3, 1942. REG, Exh. #178. MoMA Archives, NY.

94. Edward Alden Jewell, "A Mélange of New York Activities," *New York Times*, April 26, 1942, X5.
95. John J. Horowitz quoted in Mrs. Samuel I. Rosenman to Charles [sic] Noyes, April 29, 1942. Department of Circulating Exhibitions Records (hereafter CE), II.1.118.4.2. Museum of Modern Art Archives, NY.
96. Eliot Noyes to Mrs. Samuel I. Rosenman, May 1, 1942. CE, II.1.118.4.2. MoMA Archives.
97. *Wartime Housing* appeared at a diverse range of venues, as was often the case with circulating exhibitions organized by MoMA: Washington County Museum Hagerstown, MD; Utah War Services Center, Salt Lake City, UT; Denver Art Museum, CO; San Francisco Museum of Art, CA; Portland Art Museum, OR; Baltimore Museum of Art, MD; Houston Community Planning Association and University of Texas, Austin, Houston TX; and University of North Carolina, Chapel Hill, NC.
98. "Exhibitions Are Opening Today," *Morning Herald*, August 24, 1942. CE III.29.5; mf 16:0321. MoMA Archives, NY.
99. "Museum Plans for New Shows," *Daily Mail*, August 17, 1942. CE III.29.5; mf 16:0321. MoMA Archives, NY.
100. "Wartime Housing Exhibit to Give Contrast," *American*, March 9, 1943, CE III.29.5; mf 16:0324. MoMA Archives, NY.
101. "Wartime Housing: Comments about the Exhibition," undated. CE III.29.5; mf 16:0334. MoMA Archives, NY.
102. Press Release, "Museum of Modern Art Opens Exhibition of Wartime Housing," April 20, 1942, 1. MoMA, NY. [https://www.moma.org/momaorg/shared/pdfs/docs/press_archives/790/releases/MOMA_1942_0032_1942-04-20_42420-28.pdf].
103. Walter Nash, *Rhetoric: The Wit of Persuasion* (Oxford, UK: Blackwell, 1989), 37.
104. Carol Duncan and Alan Wallach, "The Museum of Modern Art as Late Capitalist Ritual: An Iconographic Analysis," *Marxist Perspectives* 4 (1978): 28–51; and Carol Duncan, "Art Museums and the Ritual of Citizenship," in *Exhibiting Cultures: The Poetics and Politics of Museum Display*, ed. Ivan Karp and Steven D. Lavine (Washington, DC: Smithsonian Institution Press, 1991), 88–103.
105. Carole Blair, "Contemporary U.S. Memorial Sites as Exemplars of Rhetoric's Materiality," in *Rhetorical Bodies*, ed. Jack Selzer and Sharon Crowley (Madison: University of Wisconsin Press), 16–57.
106. Kenneth S. Zagacki and Victoria J. Gallagher, "Rhetoric and Materiality in the Museum Park at the North Carolina Museum of Art," *Quarterly Journal of Speech* 95, no. 2 (2009): 171–91.
107. Staniszewski, *Power of Display*, 209–24; Turner, *Democratic Surround*, 95–109; and Christopher Phillips, "Steichen's Road to Victory," *Exposure* 18, no. 2 (1981): 38–48.
108. "Road to Victory: A Procession of Photographs of the Nation at War," *Bulletin of the Museum of Modern Art* 9, no. 5–6 (June 1942): 19.
109. Edward Alden Jewell, "Portrait of the Spirit of a Nation," *New York Times*, May 24, 1942, sec. 8, p. 5.
110. "The Museum and the War," *Bulletin of the Museum of Modern Art* 10, no. 1 (October–November 1942): 6.
111. Staniszewski, *Power of Display*, 212 and 215.
112. Archibald MacLeish quoted in John Morton Blum, *V Was for Victory: Politics and American Culture During World War II* (New York: Harcourt Brace Jovanovich, 1976), 29.

113. Jeffries, *Wartime America*, 190.
114. Frances Hawkins to NAR, June 25, 1942, folder 1131, box 136, subseries: MoMA, series L: Projects, RG 4, NAR Personal, Rockefeller Family Archives, RAC.
115. George H. Roeder, *The Censored War: American Visual Experience during World War Two* (New Haven, CT: Yale University Press, 1993), 430.

CHAPTER FIVE: GATEWAYS TO GLOBAL CITIZENSHIP IN A POSTWAR WORLD

1. Theodore Lewis Low, *The Museum as a Social Instrument* (New York: Metropolitan Museum of Art for the American Association of Museums, 1942), 16.
2. Frank A. Ninkovich, *The Diplomacy of Ideas: U.S. Foreign Policy and Cultural Relations, 1938–1950* (New York: Cambridge University Press, 1981), 64–73.
3. Andrew Justin Falk, *Upstaging the Cold War: American Dissent and Cultural Diplomacy, 1940–1960* (Amherst: University of Massachusetts Press, 2010), 39–62.
4. Laura A. Belmonte, *Selling the American Way: U.S. Propaganda and the Cold War* (Philadelphia: University of Pennsylvania Press, 2010), 45–62.
5. Fred Turner, *The Democratic Surround: Multimedia and American Liberalism from World War II to the Psychedelic Sixties* (Chicago, IL: University of Chicago Press, 2013), 110.
6. Charles E. Slatkin [coordinator, New York City Schools–Museums program], "Aims and Methods in Museum Education," *College Art Journal* 7, no. 1 (Autumn 1947): 28.
7. George H. Roeder, *The Censored War: American Visual Experience during World War Two* (New Haven, CT: Yale University Press, 1993), 83.
8. Paul S. Wingert, "Oceana," *American Anthropologist*, no. 45 (1943): 286.
9. *American Museum of Natural History. Seventy-Sixth Annual Report for the Year 1944* (New York: American Museum of Natural History, 1944), 1. See also Samuel Redman, "The Smithsonian at War: Museums in US Society during World War II," *Journal of the History of Collections* (January 2019): 9.
10. "Some Wartime Activities of the Museums," *Museum News* 9, no. 18 (March 15, 1942): 2; and "The Living Map," *Living Museum* 3, no. 11 (March 1942): 91.
11. H. B. Hart, "'War Theatres' Exhibit to Keep Pace with Current Front Page News: Museum Displays Material from Battle Areas for Information of Fighters and their Families," *Field Museum News* (April–May 1943): 1.
12. "Museums, Libraries Join in Exhibits at Buffalo," *Museum News* 20, no. 18 (March 15, 1943): 1.
13. New York Zoological Society, *Annual Report of the New York Zoological Society* (New York: New York Zoological Society, 1943), 3 and 23; and "The Zoo in Wartime," *New York Times*, January 15, 1944, 2.
14. Nancy J. Parezo, "'Our Native Allies': The Denver Art Museum's WWII Outreach Exhibits," *Museum History Journal* 1, no. 1 (2008): 9.
15. Ibid., 33–37.
16. Tracy Teslow, *Constructing Race: The Science of Bodies and Cultures in American Anthropology* (Cambridge: Cambridge University Press, 2014), 228–83; and "Races Exhibit Available," *Museum News* 21, no. 16 (February 15, 1944): 7–8.
17. Teslow, *Constructing Race*, 278.
18. "Pan-American Women's Association Urges Better Race Relations: See Need for United Front on Home Front," *New York Amsterdam News*, May 15, 1943, 12.

19. David Mark Carletta, "Frances R. Grant's Pan American Activities, 1929–1949" (PhD diss., Michigan State University, 2009), 353–56.
20. "Museum to Depict Nature on the Job: New Natural History Exhibits to Present Forces at Work Instead of Stuffed Objects to Show Culture Trends. Races Are Not 'Superior' or 'Inferior,' but Only 'Different,' Scientists Emphasize," *New York Times*, May 4, 1943, 20.
21. American Museum of Natural History, "Seventy-Fourth Annual Report for the Year 1942" (New York: American Museum of Natural History, May 1, 1943), 2–3.
22. "Business and Professional Women to Have International Forum: Well Known Group to Have Modern Art Museum Forum," *New York Amsterdam News*, May 1, 1943, 9.
23. Ibid.
24. "Press Comments upon *Airways to Peace*," *Bulletin of the Museum of Modern Art* 11, no. 1 (August 1943): 24.
25. Monroe Wheeler, "A Note on the Exhibition," *Bulletin of the Museum of Modern Art* 11, no. 1 (August 1943): 24.
26. Mary Anne Staniszewski, *The Power of Display: A History of Exhibition Installations at the Museum of Modern Art* (Cambridge, MA: MIT Press, 1998), 227–35; and Turner, *Democratic Surround*, 109–13.
27. "Press Release, "Airways to Peace Exhibition with Text by Wendell L. Willkie Opens at Museum of Modern Art," June 30, 1943, 4. MoMA, NY. [https://www.moma.org/momaorg/shared/pdfs/docs/press_archives/886/releases/MOMA_1943_0038_1943-06-30_43630-36.pdf]; and "Airways to Peace," *Bulletin of the Museum of Modern Art* 11, no. 1 (August 1943): 20. The photograph of the children on the monkey bars was by Eliot Elisofon from a series for *LIFE* magazine.
28. Richard F. Bach, et al., "Museums in Occupational Therapy and Rehabilitation," *Museum News* 21, no. 15 (February 1, 1944): 7, 8.
29. "Wartime Work," *Museum News* 22, no. 14 (January 15, 1945): 2.
30. "Therapeutics at Detroit," *Museum News* 23, no. 4 (June 15, 1945): 8.
31. For recent work on this topic, see Suzanne Hudson, "'Toward a Happier and More Successful Life,' or When Veterans Made Art in the Modern Museum, 1944–1948," in *Modern in the Making: MoMA and the Modern Experiment 1929–1949*, ed., Austin Porter and Sandra Zalman (London: Bloomsbury Visual Arts, 2020), 181–93.
32. Alfred H. Barr, "Research and Publication in Art Museums," *Museum News* 23, no. 13 (January 1, 1946): 6. From a paper presented at "The Future of the Art Museum as an Educational Institution" conference, Chicago, IL, March 24–25, 1944.
33. W. Douglas Burden, "A New Vision of Learning," *Museum News* 21, no. 12 (December 15, 1943): 9–12.
34. Ibid., 9.
35. Ibid., 12.
36. Ibid.
37. "Recorded Gallery Tours Succeed at St. Paul," *Museum News* 19, no. 16 (February 15, 1942): 1.
38. Daniel Catton Rich, "Special Exhibitions," *Museum News* 23, no. 7 (October 1, 1945): 6.
39. "*Life*'s War Art Show at National Gallery," *Museum News* 21, no. 4 (June 15, 1943): 2; and *The Abbott Collection: Paintings of Naval Aviation*, undated catalog, 2 and 18.

40. Melissa Renn, "Fine Arts under Fire: *Life* Magazine and the Display of Architectural Destruction," in *Architecture and Armed Conflict: The Politics of Destruction*, ed., JoAnne Mancini and Keith Bresnahan (New York: Routledge, 2015), 82.
41. "Life Magazine Offers Traveling Shows," *Museum News* 23, no. 18 (March 15, 1946): 2; and Renn, "Fine Arts under Fire," 82–83.
42. Albright Art Gallery, *Gallery Notes* 10, no. 1 (May 1943): 10.
43. "Newark Program on Newark in War," *Museum News* 23, no. 1 (May 1, 1945): 1.
44. "Company Museum Opens in Empire State Building," *Museum News* 21, no. 9 (November 1, 1943): 1.
45. Obituary, "Miss Beatrice Winser," *Courier-News* (Bridgewater, NJ), September 15, 1947, 18; and "Miss B. Winser Quits Newark Library Post," *Montclair Times* (Montclair, NJ), July 30, 1942, 18.
46. Rich, "Special Exhibitions," 6.
47. Ibid., 7.
48. Ibid., 8.
49. "Chicago Art of the United Nations," *Bulletin of the Art Institute of Chicago* 38, no. 6 (November 1944): 89–95; and "Chicago Institute Opens United Nations Art," *Museum News* 22, no. 12 (December 15, 1944): 1, 8.
50. "Exhibitions," *Museum News* 22, no. 14 (January 15, 1945): 12.
51. *Art of the United Nations* (Chicago, IL: Art Institute of Chicago, 1944), 7–8.
52. Ibid., 8.
53. György Kepes, *Language of Vision* (Chicago, IL: P. Theobald, 1944), 13.
54. Michael Golec, "A Natural History of a Disembodied Eye: The Structure of György Kepes's 'Language of Vision,'" *Design Issues* 18, no. 2 (2002): 5.
55. Julia Moszkowicz, "Gestalt and Graphic Design: An Exploration of the Humanistic and Therapeutic Effects of Visual Organization," *Design Issues* 27, no. 4 (2011): 66.
56. *Art of the United Nations*, 25 and 36.
57. Eugene R. Gaddis, *Magician of the Modern: Chick Austin and the Transformation of the Arts in America* (New York: Alfred A. Knopf, 2000), 347–71.
58. Minutes of Annual Trustees' Meeting, January 17, 1942, Trustees RG1, Minutes S.1, box 2: "January 1923–January 1943," 186, Wadsworth Atheneum Archives (hereafter WAA), Hartford, CT. See also Gaddis, *Magician of the Modern*, 348–51.
59. Berger, the institution's first professionally trained staff member, had come to the Atheneum in 1918, after twenty years at the Museum of Fine Arts, Boston. Gaddis, *Magician of the Modern*, 75–76. See also Elizabeth J. Normen, "From Atheneum to Art Museum: 'Mrs. Berger's Great Contribution,'" *Hog River Journal* 5, no. 1 (Winter 2006/2007): 38–43.
60. "Mrs. Willing, Author, Dies at Age 65," *Hartford (CT) Courant*, September 1, 1962, 4; and Minutes of Special Trustees' Meeting, December 28, 1944, Trustees RG1, Minutes S.1, box 3: "April 1943–February 1948," WAA.
61. Marjorie Fay, "Mrs. Pratt's Ambition: Open Atheneum to All," *Daily Herald*, February 10, 1946. From Wadsworth Atheneum Scrapbook, Printed Material RG8, Scrapbooks, box 31: "November 1944–May 1946," WAA.
62. "What Have You to Lend?," *Wadsworth Atheneum Members' Bulletin*, March 1945, Auerbach Art Library of the Wadsworth Atheneum Museum of Art.
63. "Atheneum Plans Souvenir Exhibit," *Hartford (CT) Times*, February 22, 1945, 25.

64. Gladys Lynwall Pratt, "Report on Membership Efforts and Results," 1945, 1, Trustees RG1, Records, Reports, Correspondence, S.4 1955–1949, folder 1945, box 4, WAA.
65. Marian Murray, "Museum at Avery Colorful with Servicemen's Curios," *Hartford (CT) Times*, April 7, 1945, 3.
66. Brochure for membership drive, "Your Share in the Postwar World," WAA.
67. John E. Jeffries, *Wartime America: The World War II Home Front* (Chicago, IL: Ivan R. Dee, 1996), 190.
68. John Bodnar, *Remaking America: Public Memory, Commemoration, and Patriotism in the Twentieth Century* (Princeton, NJ: Princeton University Press, 1992), 14.
69. The position went to Charles C. Cunningham, a former assistant curator at the Museum of Fine Arts, Boston, who had served in the navy during World War II. He held the director's position at the Atheneum from 1946 to 1966.
70. "Mrs. Willing Author Dies at Age 65."
71. Winston Churchill, "Sinews of Peace," March 6, 1946, http://www.nationalchurchill museum.org/sinews-of-peace-iron-curtain-speech.html.
72. Anders Greenspan, *Creating Colonial Williamsburg: The Restoration of Virginia's Eighteenth-Century Capital. Chapel Hill* (Chapel Hill: University of North Carolina Press, 2009), 63–72.
73. "AAM Washington Meeting Record for Interest and Attendance," *Museum News* 24, no. 3 (June 1, 1946): 1–2.
74. "AAM Washington Meeting Will Consider Timely Museum Problems," *Museum News* 23, no. 19 (April 1, 1946): 1.
75. Samuel J. Redman, "Museum Tours and the Origins of Museum Studies: Edward W. Gifford, William R. Bascom, and the Remaking of an Anthropology Museum," *Museum Management and Curatorship* 30, no. 5, October 20, 2015, 444–61.
76. Archibald MacLeish, "Museums and World Peace," *Museum News* 24, no. 2 (June 1, 1946): 6; emphasis in source.
77. Ibid., 7.
78. Ibid.
79. Ibid., 8.
80. At the end of the war, the State Department's Division of Cultural Relations briefly took on this new name as it assumed vestiges of the Office of the Coordinator of Inter-American Affairs and Office of War Information; a series of name changes followed.
81. The word "modern" was not added to the San Francisco Museum of Art's name until 1975.
82. Oral history interview with Grace Morley, February 6 and March 24, 1982, http://www.aaa.si.edu/collections/interviews/oral-history-interview-grace-morley-12774, Archives of American Art, Smithsonian Institution.
83. Grace L. McCann Morley, "Grace L. McCann Morley: Art, Artists, Museums, and the San Francisco Museum of Art," interview by Suzanne B. Riess, 1960, in Berkeley, CA, transcript, 151–60. Regional Cultural History Project, the Bancroft Library, University of California, Berkeley. Available online http://digitalassets.lib.berkeley.edu/roho/ucb/text/morley_grace_l_mccann.pdf.
84. Oral history interview with Grace Morley.
85. Sid Ahmed Baghli, Patrick Boylan, and Yani Herreman, *History of ICOM: 1946–1996* (Paris: International Council of Museums, 1998), 9 and 71.

86. "National Commission Has Museum Representation," *Museum News* 26, no. 6 (September 15, 1946): 1.
87. "International Council of Museums Organized," *Museum News* 24, no. 9 (November 1, 1946): 1; and "International Council Has Meeting in Paris," *Museum News* 24, no.12 (December 15, 1946): 1.
88. Raymonde Frin, "Museum: 'for the Benefit of the Museums of the World,'" *Museum International* 50, no. 1 (January 1998): 6.
89. Oral history interview with Grace Morley.
90. Samuel Zipp, *The Idealist: Wendell Willkie's Wartime Quest to Build One World* (Cambridge, MA: Harvard University Press, 2020), 303–35.
91. Office of War Information, quoted in Jonathan Spaulding, *Ansel Adams and the American Landscape: A Biography* (Berkeley: University of California Press, 1995), 209. In addition to Spaulding's treatment of the controversy over *Manzanar: Photographs by Ansel Adams of Loyal Japanese-American Relocation Center* (207–34), see Jasmine Alinder, *Moving Images: Photography and the Japanese American Incarceration* (Urbana: University of Illinois Press, 2009), 103–16, Erin Kathleen O'Toole, "No Democracy in Quality: Ansel Adams, Beaumont and Nancy Newhall, and the Founding of the Department of Photographs at the Museum of Modern Art," (PhD diss., University of Arizona, 2010), 267–87; and Thy Phu, "The Spaces of Human Confinement: Manzanar Photography and Landscape Ideology," *Journal of Asian American Studies* 11, no. 3 (2008): 337–71.
92. Jospeh Klimberger, "The Races of Mankind Exhibition at the Detroit Public Library," *Library Journal* 69 (November 1944): 919–21.
93. Ibid., 920.
94. Quoted in Greg Barnhisel, *Cold War Modernists: Art, Literature, and American Cultural Diplomacy* (New York: Columbia University Press, 2015), 27.
95. Leon Whipple, "Culture Repositories: Museums Are Suggested for the Guidance of Posterity," *New York Times*, January 19, 1947, 101. Hamlin quoted this line in the article cited below.
96. Chauncey J. Hamlin, "Arsenals of Knowledge," Buffalo Society of Natural Sciences, Buffalo Museum of Science, *Hobbies* 27, no. 3 (February 1947): 65.
97. Chauncey J. Hamlin, "Museums and the Post-War World," Buffalo Society of Natural Sciences, Buffalo Museum of Science, *Hobbies* 27, no. 1 (October 1946): 1.
98. "Opening Night at The Brooklyn Museum," September 16, 1947, Records of the Department of Public Information, Press releases, 1947–1952, 07–09/1947, 118–20. Brooklyn Museum Archives.
99. Ibid., 119.
100. "What Inspired the Exhibition," September 16, 1947, Records of the Department of Public Information, Press releases, 1947–1952, 07–09/1947, 101. Brooklyn Museum Archives. Several newspaper articles quoted or rephrased Nagel's remarks.
101. "U.N. Exhibit at Boro Museum Appeals to Peace Aspirations of Little Man," *Brooklyn Daily Eagle*, September 28, 1947, 19, Brooklyn Newsstand database, Brooklyn Public Library.
102. "Soviet Opens Exhibit in Rockefeller Center; Gromyko and New Ambassador View Display," *New York Times*, March 5, 1948, 6; and Casimir Viltis, Vytautas Liaudis, Gediminas Kova, et al., "Statement," folder 196, box 20, series E: Cultural Interests, RG 2, Rockefeller Family Archives, Rockefeller Archive Center (hereafter RAC).

103. Robert P. Shaw to Francis L. Corcoran, January 26, 1948, folder 196, box 20, series E: Cultural Interests, RG 2, Rockefeller Family Archives, RAC.
104. Barton P. Turnbull to John D. Rockefeller Jr., April 2, 1948, folder 196, box 20, series E: Cultural Interests, RG 2, Rockefeller Family Archives, RAC. This letter quotes the decision reached by the Rockefeller Center board on January 28, 1947, and subsequently communicated to Shaw.
105. "Russian Exhibit at Museum of Science and Industry," Inter-Office Correspondence from Caroline Hood to Francis L. Corcoran, March 5, 1948, folder 196, box 20, series E: Cultural Interests, RG 2, Rockefeller Family Archives, RAC.
106. Laurence Vail Coleman, *The Museum in America: A Critical Study*, 3 vols. (Washington, DC: American Association of Museums, 1939), 2:259; and Jaume Sastre-Juan, "'Science in Action': The Politics of Hands-on Display at the New York Museum of Science and Industry," *History of Science* (June 8, 2018): 16–19.
107. Coleman, *Museum in America*, 2:257.
108. Ibid., 2:265.

CONCLUSION: MUSEUM STORIES, OLD AND NEW

1. Grace L. McCann Morley, "Museums and UNESCO," *Museum* 2, no. 1 (1949): 13.
2. George Hein, "'The Museum as a Social Instrument': A Democratic Conception of Museum Education," in *Museum Gallery Interpretation and Material Culture*, ed. Juliette Fritsch (New York: Routledge, 2011), 22.
3. Clarissa Ceglio, "Imperfectly Progressive: The Social Mission of U.S. Museums in the 1930s," in *Radical Roots: Public History and a Tradition of Social Justice Activism*, ed. Denise Meringolo (Amherst, MA: Amherst College Press, 2021), 363–93.
4. Jennifer Scott, case statement for "Museums and Civic Discourse: Past, Present, and Emerging Futures," a 2016 National Council of Public History Working Group, February 2016, https://ncph.org/phc/ncph-working-groups/museums-civic-discourse-2016-working-group/scott-case-statement/.
5. Denise D. Meringolo, "Social Justice and Public History: The Networks, Goals, and Practices that Shaped Our Noble Dream" in Meringolo, *Radical Roots*, 4.
6. Melissa Jayne Fawcett, *Medicine Trail: The Life and Lessons of Gladys Tantaquidgeon* (Tucson: University of Arizona Press, 2000), 89–94; and Majel Boxer, "'2,229': John Joseph Mathews, the Osage Tribal Museum, and the Emergence of an Indigenous Museum Model," *Wicazo Sa Review* 31, no. 2 (2016): 69–93.
7. Bill V. Mullen, *Popular Fronts: Chicago and African-American Cultural Politics, 1935–46* (Urbana: University of Illinois Press, 1999), 81–105; and John E. Fleming and Margaret T. Burroughs, "Dr. Margaret T. Burroughs: Artist, Teacher, Administrator, Writer, Political Activist, and Museum Founder," *Public Historian* 21, no. 1 (1999): 31–55.
8. Andrea A. Burns, *From Storefront to Monument: Tracing the Public History of the Black Museum Movement* (Amherst: University of Massachusetts Press, 2013), 1–20.
9. Mabel O. Wilson, *Negro Building: Black Americans in the World of Fairs and Museums* (Berkeley: University of California Press, 2012), 233–41; and Ian Rocksborough-Smith, *Black Public History in Chicago: Civil Rights Activism from World War II into the Cold War* (Urbana: University of Illinois Press, 2018), 48–74.
10. Federal Bureau of Investigation, "FBI file for Frank Marshall Davis," main file no. 100-328955-4, Chicago file no. 100–15799, February 18, 1945, 44, Internet Archive, https://archive.org/details/FrankMarshallDavisFBIFile.

11. Maureen Honey, *Creating Rosie the Riveter: Class, Gender, and Propaganda during World War II* (Amherst: University of Massachusetts Press, 1984), 85; and George H. Roeder, *The Censored War: American Visual Experience during World War Two* (New Haven, CT: Yale University Press, 1993), 44.
12. Michael C. C. Adams, *The Best War Ever: America and World War II* (Baltimore, MD: Johns Hopkins University Press, 1994).
13. Roeder, *Censored War*, 3.
14. Ibid., 63.
15. James H. S. Bossard, "Family Backgrounds of Wartime Adolescents," *Annals of the American Academy of Political and Social Science*, 246 (November 1944): 33–42, excerpted in *America at War: The Home Front, 1941–1945*, ed. Richard Polenberg (Englewood Cliffs, NJ: Prentice-Hall, 1968), 126.
16. Tom Brokaw, *The Greatest Generation* (New York: Random House, 1998).
17. Andrew Edmund Kersten, *Labor's Home Front: The American Federation of Labor during World War II* (New York: New York University Press, 2006); and Kevin Allen Leonard, *The Battle for Los Angeles: Racial Ideology and World War II* (Albuquerque: University of New Mexico Press, 2006).
18. A sample of such works includes Robert H. Haddow, *Pavilions of Plenty: Exhibiting American Culture Abroad in the 1950s* (Washington, DC: Smithsonian Institution Press, 1997); Walter L. Hixson, *Parting the Curtain: Propaganda, Culture, and the Cold War, 1945–1961* (New York: St. Martin's Press, 1997); Jack Masey and Conway Lloyd Morgan, *Cold War Confrontations: US Exhibitions and Their Role in the Cultural Cold War* (Zürich: Lars Müller, 2008); and Yale Richmond, *Cultural Exchange and the Cold War: Raising the Iron Curtain* (University Park: Pennsylvania State University Press, 2003).
19. In addition to Wilson, Burns, and Rocksborough-Smith, see the work of Fath Davis Ruffins, including "Building Homes for Black History: Museum Founders, Founding Directors, and Pioneers, 1915–95," *Public Historian* 40, no. 3 (2018): 13–43, and "Mythos, Memory, and History: African American Preservation Efforts, 1820–1990," in *Museums and Communities: The Politics of Public Culture*, ed. Ivan Karp, Christine Mullen Kreamer, and Steven Lavine (Washington, DC: Smithsonian Institution Press, 1992), 506–611.
20. Fred Turner, "The Family of Man and the Politics of Attention in Cold War America," *Public Culture* 24, no. 1 (2012): 55–84; and Eric J. Sandeen, *Picturing an Exhibition: The Family of Man and 1950s America* (Albuquerque: University of New Mexico Press, 1995).
21. English-language works on the founding and early work of ICOM and UNESCO's Museums Division are largely limited to histories written by the organizations themselves. In addition to Sid Ahmed Baghli, Patrick Boylan, and Yani Herreman, *History of ICOM: 1946–1996* (Paris: International Council of Museums, 1998), see Roger-Pol Droit, *Humanity in the Making: Overview of the Intellectual History of UNESCO, 1945–2005* (Paris: UNESCO, 2005).
22. Select contributions from the conference, in which the author participated, can be found in *Museums, Modernity and Conflict: Museums and Collections in and of War since the Nineteenth Century*, ed. Kate Hill (London: Routledge, 2021).
23. Greg Dickinson, Carole Blair, and Brian Ott, introduction to *Places of Public Memory: The Rhetoric of Museums and Memorials*, ed. Greg Dickinson, Carole Blair, and Brian Ott (Tuscaloosa: University of Alabama Press, 2010), 3.
24. Sandra H, Dudley, ed. *Museum Materialities: Objects, Engagements, Interpretations* (London: Routledge, 2010), 4.

25. David Howes, "The Secret of Aesthetics Lies in the Conjugation of the Senses: Reimaging the Museum as a Sensory Gymnasium," in *The Multisensory Museum: Cross-Disciplinary Perspectives on Touch, Sound, Smell, Memory, and Space*, ed. Nina Sobol Levent, Alvaro Pascual-Leone, and Simon Lacey (Lanham, MD: Rowman & Littlefield, 2014), 285–300.
26. Center for the Future of Museums, "Synesthesia: Multisensory Experiences for a Multisensory World," *TrendsWatch 2014* (Washington, DC: American Alliance of Museums, 2014), 21.
27. Constance Classen, "Museum Manners: The Sensory Life of the Early Museum," *Journal of Social History* 40, no. 4 (2007): 895–914; and Helen Rees Leahy, *Museum Bodies: The Politics and Practices of Visiting and Viewing* (Burlington, VT: Ashgate, 2012).
28. See Barbara Kirshenblatt-Gimblett, *Destination Culture: Tourism, Museums, and Heritage* (Berkeley: University of California Press, 1998); and B. Joseph Pine and James H Gilmore, *The Experience Economy: Work Is Theatre and Every Business a Stage* (Boston, MA: Harvard Business School Press, 1999).
29. Jennie Morgan, "The Multisensory Museum," *Glasnik Etnografskog Instituta* 60, no. 1 (2012): 69.
30. See, for example, Viv Golding, "Museums, Poetics and Affect," *Feminist Review*, no. 104 (2013): 80–99; Lynne Dierking, "Museums, Affect, and Cognition: The View from Another Window," in *Beyond Cartesian Dualism: Encountering Affect in the Teaching and Learning of Science*, ed. Stephen Alsop (Dordrecht, Netherlands: Springer, 2005), 111–22; and Lisa Roberts, "Affective Learning, Affective Experience: What Does It Have to Do with Museum Education?" *Visitor Studies: Theory, Research and Practice* 4, no. 1 (1992): 162–68.
31. Viv Golding, "Feminism and the Politics of Friendship in the Activist Museum," in *Museum Activism*, ed. Robert R. James and Richard Sandell (London: Routledge, 2019), 135.
32. Ibid.
33. Work in this area includes Paul Williams, "Memorial Museums and the Objectification of Suffering," in *Routledge Companion to Museum Ethics: Redefining Ethics for the Twenty-First Century Museum*, ed. Janet Marstine (New York: Routledge, 2011), 220–35; and, in the same volume, Bjarne Sode Funch, "Ethics of Confrontational Drama in Museums," 414–26.
34. Elena Gonzales, *Exhibitions for Social Justice* (New York: Routledge, 2019), 7.
35. Jenny Kidd, *Museums in the New Mediascape: Transmedia, Participation, Ethics* (Farnham, UK: Ashgate, 2014).
36. Jenny Kidd, "Gaming for Affect: Museum Online Games and the Embrace of Empathy," *Journal of Curatorial Studies* 4, no. 3 (2015): 425. Kidd attributes the terms "affective design" and "emotioneering" to the following works, respectively: Daniel M. Johnson and Janet Wiles "Effective Affective User Interface Design in Games," *Ergonomics* 46, no. 13–14 (October 2003): 1332–45; and David Freeman, "Creating Emotion in Games: The Craft and Art of Emotioneering," *Computers in Entertainment* 2, no. 3 (2004): 1–11.
37. Jenny Kidd, "'Immersive' Heritage Encounters," *Museum Review* 3, no. 1 (2018), https://themuseumreviewjournal.wordpress.com/2018/04/16/tmr_vol3no1_kidd/amp/.

38. My distinction between "narrative" and "story" is taken from Jeffry R. Halverson, H. L. Goodall Jr., and Steven R. Corman, *Master Narratives of Islamist Extremism* (London: Palgrave Macmillan, 2011), 1–26.
39. "2013 AAM Annual Meeting: The Power of Story." This online call for proposals initially posted in 2012 on the American Alliance of Museums website is no longer accessible.
40. Mike Scutari, "Why Storytelling May Be the Next Big Thing in Museum Funding," *Inside Philanthropy*, May 2, 2014, http://www.insidephilanthropy.com/home/2014/5/2/why-storytelling-may-be-the-next-big-thing-in-museum-funding.html.
41. Carlos Emmons Cummings, *East Is East and West Is West: Some Observations on the World's Fairs of 1939 by One Whose Main Interest Is in Museums* (East Aurora, NY: Buffalo Museum of Science, 1940), 97.
42. On narrative and storytelling as tools of constructivist museums, see Lisa C. Roberts, *From Knowledge to Narrative: Educators and the Changing Museum* (Washington, DC: Smithsonian Institution Press, 1999); and Leslie Bedford, "Storytelling: The Real Work of Museums," *Curator: The Museum Journal* 44, no. 1 (January 1, 2001): 27–34.
43. Museum Next, "Future of Museum Storytelling," November 7–8, 2019, New York City.
44. "PEM to Assess How Neuroscience Can Enhance the Museum Experience," Peabody Essex Museum, March 13, 2017, https://www.pem.org/press-news/pem-to-assess-how-neuroscience-can-enhance-the-museum-experience.
45. Karen Palmer, "Resume," Storyteller from the Future website, http://karenpalmer.uk/resume/.
46. Karen Palmer, "The Film That Watches You Back," TED Residency video, 6:56, November 2017, https://www.ted.com/talks/karen_palmer_the_film_that_watches_you_back.
47. Jonathan Gottschall, *The Storytelling Animal: How Stories Make Us Human* (Boston, MA: Mariner Books, 2013); and Christian Salmon, *Storytelling: Bewitching the Modern Mind* (London: Verso Books, 2010).
48. Michael Jackson, *Politics of Storytelling: Violence, Transgression, and Intersubjectivity* (Copenhagen: Museum Tusculanum Press, 2002); Jonah Sachs, *Winning the Story Wars: Why Those Who Tell and Live the Best Stories Will Rule the Future* (Boston, MA: Harvard Business Review Press, 2012); and Annette Simmons, *Whoever Tells the Best Story Wins: How to Use Your Own Stories to Communicate with Power and Impact* (New York: AMACOM, 2007).
49. Joseph S. Nye Jr., "Soft Power," *Foreign Policy*, no. 80 (October 1, 1990): 153–71; and Joseph S. Nye Jr., *The Future of Power* (New York: Public Affairs, 2011).
50. Quoted in Laura Roselle, Alister Miskimmon, and Ben O'Loughlin, "Strategic Narrative: A New Means to Understand Soft Power," *Media, War & Conflict* 7, no. 1 (April 1, 2014): 71.
51. Ibid.; emphasis in source.
52. In Gail Lord and Ngaire Blankenberg, eds., *Cities, Museums, and Soft Power* (Washington, DC: AAM Press, 2015), see Gail Lord and Ngaire Blankenberg, "Introduction: Why Cities, Museums and Soft Power," 9; Ngaire Blankenberg, "When Soft Powers Collide," 100; Javier Jimenez, "The Economics of Museums and Cities," 29–47; and Frederica Olivares, "Museums in Public Diplomacy," 51.
53. Janice Bially Mattern, "Why 'Soft Power' Isn't So Soft: Representational Force and the Sociolinguistic Construction of Attraction in World Politics," *Millennium—Journal of International Studies* 33, no. 3 (June 1, 2005): 583–612.

54. Mike Murawski, "Interrupting White Dominant Culture in Museums," Art Museum Teaching (blog), May 31, 2019, https://artmuseumteaching.com/2019/05/31/interrupting-white-dominant-culture/.
55. La Tanya S. Autry and Mike Murawski, "Museums Are Not Neutral: We Are Stronger Together," *Panorama: Journal of the Association of Historians of American Art* 5, no. 2 (Fall 2019): https://doi.org/10.24926/24716839.2277; Adrianne Russell, "Museums & #BlackLivesMatter," *CODE | WORDS: Technology and Theory in the Museum, an Experiment in Online Publishing and Discourse,* September 20, 2015, https://medium.com/code-words-technology-and-theory-in-the-museum/museums-blacklivesmatter-ba-28c7111bec; Kami Fletcher, "#MuseumsRespondtoFerguson: An Interview with Aleia Brown and Adrianne Russell," *AAIHS* (blog), September 29, 2016, https://www.aaihs.org/museumsrespondtoferguson-an-interview-with-aleia-brown-and-adrianne-russell/; and Jennifer Wingate, "#museumsrespond: Social Justice and the Engaged Museum," in *Museums and Public Art?* ed. Cher Krause Knight and Harriet F. Senie (Newcastle upon Tyne, UK: Cambridge Scholars Publishing, 2018): 238–56.
56. On the militarization of US culture and its role in obscuring the nation's near-perpetual state of war and military engagements abroad, see Michael S. Sherry, *In the Shadow of War: The United States since the 1930s* (New Haven, CT: Yale University Press, 1995); and A. J. Bacevich, *The New American Militarism: How Americans Are Seduced by War* (New York: Oxford University Press, 2005).
57. The dates ascribed by the US government to the Iraq War (Operation Iraqi Freedom and Operation New Dawn) are March 20, 2003–December 15, 2011. Those recorded for Operation Enduring Freedom in Afghanistan are October 7, 2001–December 28, 2014. See Barbara Salazar, Torreon, "U.S. Periods of War and Dates of Recent Conflicts," Congressional Research Service, RS21405 (June 5, 2020): 6–10, https://crsreports.congress.gov.
58. Institutions whose missions already aligned to antiracist work, such as the Japanese American National Museum in Los Angeles, most directly addressed these issues. See "Where Do We Go from Here: Five Directors on the Aftermath," *Museum News,* January/February 2002, 43.
59. Co-organized by the Andy Warhol Museum (Pittsburgh, PA) and the International Center for Photography (New York), *Inconvenient Evidence* showed simultaneously at both venues but with different contextualization. On these exhibitions, see Malini Johar Schueller, "Techno-Dominance and Torturegate: The Making of U.S. Imperialism," in *Exceptional State: Contemporary U.S. Culture and the New Imperialism,* ed. Ashley Dawson and Malini Johar Schueller (New York: Routledge, 2007), 162–88; and Douglas Kellner, *Media Spectacle and the Crisis of Democracy: Terrorism, War, and Election Battles* (New York: Routledge, 2005), 77–105.
60. David Vine, *The United States of War: A Global History of America's Endless Conflicts, from Columbus to the Islamic State* (Oakland: University of California Press, 2020): 192.

INDEX

Page numbers in *italics* reference figures.

AAM. *See* American Alliance of Museums; American Association of Museums
Abbott, John E., 44, 97, 98, 107
Abbott Laboratories, 139, 141; *Art in War: The Abbott Collection of Paintings of Naval Aviation* (1943), *139*, 141
"action" exhibits, 19
Adam, Thomas Ritchie: on neutrality, 23–24, 29; on visual-sensory approaches, 22–23
Adams, Ansel, 150–51
Adams, Philip R., 52, 53–54, 66
adult education movement: Adam and, 22–24; background, 5–6, 8, 17; MacLeish on, 148; museums and, ix, 5, 17, 23, 70, 86–87, 114; Neurath and, 32; postwar reflections on, 159; in postwar world, 129, 136–38; radio programming, 114; visual-sensory approaches, 22–24; Youtz and, 25
affective encounters, 54–57, *55*
Agee, James: *Let Us Now Praise Famous Men* (& Evans), 116
AIC. *See* Art Institute of Chicago
Airways to Peace: An Exhibition of Geography for the Future (MoMA, 1943), 135–36, *136*
Albany Institute of History and Art, 76
Albright Art Gallery (Buffalo), 132–33; *Airacobra* (1943), *139*
Alexander, Edward P., 21–22, 32
American Alliance of Museums (AAM), 166–67; annual meeting (2013, "The Power of Story"), 168. *See also* American Association of Museums

American Association of Adult Education, 22–23
American Association of Museums (AAM): on Allied nations' museum reports, 38; annual meeting (1918), 74; annual meeting (1936), 21; annual meeting (1939, "The Interpretation through Exhibits"), 16–18; annual meeting (1940, "The New Public Museum"), 27, 70–71; annual meeting (1941, "Defense and Hemisphere Solidarity"), 52, 79, 147; annual meeting (1942, "Wartime Duties of Museums"), 79–81, 147; annual meeting (1946), 147–49; annual meeting (1947), 147–48; Coleman as director of, 5, 16, 46; exhibitionary networking of, 45–46; funding and organization of, 46; Hamlin as president of, 148, 149; hemispheric unity efforts by, 45–47, 67, 79, 147; publications background, 173n3; study of visitor behavior, 26; wartime policy recommendations, 72–74, 78, 80, 85; Wissler as president of, 87
American Association of Museums (AAM), publications: *Directory of Museums in South America*, 46; *The Museum in America: A Critical Study*, 5–6, 70
American Friends Service Committee, 107
American Museum of Natural History (AMNH): attendance and membership rates, 79, 132; Covarrubias and, 132; DCR panel members from, 44; exhibitionary network and, 88, 139; hemispheric unity efforts by, 50–52; loans of artifacts by, 60;

American Museum of Natural History (AMNH) *(continued)*: military support and, 133; mind-body appeal techniques used by, 35; Pratt's tenure at, 144, 145; on race issues, 133–34; Union Settlement and Greenwich House exhibition, 102; wartime duties of, 83–84, 87–88; during WWI, 74

American Museum of Natural History (AMNH), exhibitions: *Animals and the War* (1943), 88; *International Tuberculosis Exhibition* (1908–1909), 32; *Latin American Art* (1941), 50; *Minerals and Munitions* (1918), 74

American Safety Museum, 31

American Smelting and Refining Company, 61

American-Soviet war exhibition. See *Two Allies—One War—One Peace*

Ames, Winslow, 107

AMNH. *See* American Museum of Natural History

anti-hoarding competition, 110

architecture and architectural exhibits, 101–2, 121. See also *Wartime Housing*

Army Air Forces Training Command, 139–40

Art in America (radio program), 114

Art Institute of Chicago (AIC): *Art of the United Nations* (1944–1945), 14–15, 141–43; exhibitionary network and, 141

art museums: cultural power of, 184n6; debates on mission of, 84–86; meaning making with objects in, 17, 41, 141, 143–44; mind-body appeal techniques used by, 34–35, 138, 142; postwar world and, 137–38. *See also specific art museums*

Ask Mr. Foster, 60

Association of Art Museum Directors, 85–86

Austin, A. Everett, Jr., 144

avant-gardes, 24–25

Axis exhibitions, 37–38

Baltimore Museum of Art, 123

Barr, Alfred H., Jr., 44, 96, 98, 107, 137–38

Bauer, Catherine, 101, 102, 109–10

The Behavior of the Museum Visitor (Robinson), 26

Bell Aircraft Corporation, 139

Benedict, Ruth, 133–34

Berger, Florence Paull, 144, 146

Berkshire Museum, 20, 94

Bernays, Edward L.: "The Museum's Job in Wartime" (address), 80–81

Bernice P. Bishop Museum (Honolulu), 71

biases. *See* racism

Black Americans, wartime housing for, 120–21

Black museum movement, 164

Blandford, John, Jr., 117

Bloomingdale's (department store), 56

Board of Education (New York City), 153, *154*

Bolivia, 41–42, 49, 51. See also *Three Southern Neighbors: Ecuador, Peru, Bolivia*

Bonney, Thérèse, 103, 104–5, *106*

Bourke-White, Margaret: *You Have Seen Their Faces* (& Caldwell), 116

Bragg, Laura, 20, 131

British Council, 77

British Ministry of Information, 77

British war cartoons exhibition, 76

Brooklyn Botanic Garden, 79

Brooklyn Museum: attendance during WWII, 79; DCR panel members from, 44; hemispheric unity efforts by, 44, 51, 57, 61–62; home-front exhibitions, 94; postwar world and, 152–54, 157; on race issues, 66; retail partnerships, 26; Youtz as director of, 25

Brooklyn Museum, exhibitions: *America South of U.S.* (1941–1942), 51, 62; *Clothing One World* (1947), 15, 152–53, 157; *The Consumer Front: Essential Wartime Economics* (1942), 94; *Inventions for Victory* (1942–1943), 94; *Know Your United Nations* (1947), 152–55, *153–54*, 157, 163; *Latin American Art* (1941), 50

Bryan, Julien, 116

Buffalo Historical Society, 133

Buffalo Museum of Science, 19, 28, 133, 149, 181n63

Buffalo Public Library, 133

Buffalo Society of Natural Sciences, 148

Buffalo Zoological Gardens, 133

Buhl Planetarium (Pittsburgh), 76

Burns, Ned, 81–82

Burroughs, Margaret Taylor Goss, 162

Button Machinery Company, 60–61

Caldwell, Erskine: *You Have Seen Their Faces* (& Bourke-White), 116

California Academy of Sciences, 139

Canada, 52, 77, 147

Index

Can America Be Bombed? (Science Museum of the St. Paul Institute, 1941), 74–75, 135
Carnegie Corporation, 4, 5, 25, 26, 51, 144
Carnegie Endowment for International Peace, 46
Carnegie Institution of Washington, 46
Carnegie Museum (Pittsburgh), 34
Carolina Art Association (Charleston), 94
Carte de Tendre, 53–54
Centennial International Exhibition (1876), 21
Century of Progress International Exposition (Chicago, 1933–1934), 28
Chicago Historical Society, 74, 82
Chicago Museum of Science and Industry (CMSI): Coal Mine exhibition (1933), 35; corporate funding for, 29; home-front exhibition, 94; *The Homemaker and the War* (1942), 94; Kaempffert as director of, 35
Chicago State Rationing Administrator, 83
Churchill, Winston, 146–47
Cincinnati Art Museum, 51
circulating shows. *See* traveling exhibits
citizenship. *See* home-front citizenship; postwar global citizenship
civic imaginaries. *See* imagined communities
civil rights activism, 162
class dynamics: background, 12, 161; British support and, 77; exhibitionary tourism and, 65; naturalized race and, 133–34; in *Wartime Housing* (1942), 115–16, 120
classification of museums, 83. *See also specific types of museums*
Cleveland Museum of Art, 76
Clothing One World (Brooklyn Museum, 1947), 15, 152–53, 157
CMSI. *See* Chicago Museum of Science and Industry
Cold War nationalism, 69, 130, 146–47
Coleman, Laurence Vail: as American Safety Museum director, 31; on corporate partnerships, 156–57; on culture history, 19–20; on educational approaches, 16, 30–31; exhibitionary network and, 46; on meaning making with objects, 30–31; on mind-body appeal techniques, 35, 36; on museumgoers as learners, 92; *The Museum in America: A Critical Study*, 5–6, 16; on social instrumentality, 5–6, 95; on

storyline technique, 29–30; US National Council appointment of, 46
Colombia, 47–50
colonial imperialism: meaning making with objects and, 18; postwar world and, 130, 150; romanticizing of, 59, 61–62, 126; trade relations through, 61; vestiges of, 10, 14–15, 53–54
Colonial Williamsburg (Virginia), 35, 79, 147
Columbus Gallery of Art, 66
commercial window displays, 28, 33
Committee on Conservation of Cultural Resources, 72
community-engaged exhibitions, 89
community groups, racial equity work of, 134–35
community planning, for housing, 117–21, 118–19
Conference of Inter-American Relations in the Field of Books and Libraries (1939), 48–49
Conference on Inter-American Relations in the Field of Art (1939), 52
Connolly, Louise, 6
Convention on International Civil Aviation, 141
corporate-museum collaborations, 27–29, 139, 156–57
Covarrubias, Miguel, 50, 132
Cranbrook Institute of Science (Michigan), 70, 87; *The Races of Mankind* (1944), 133–34, 151, 157
cultural internationalism, 134–35, 142–43, 150–51
culture history approach, 19–21, 84
Cummings, Carlos E.: *East Is East and West Is West*, 28; on retail sector influences, 28, 30, 181n78; on storyline technique, 19, 33, 169, 181n79; WWII reference by, 38

Dallas Museum of Fine Arts, 64–65
Dana, John Cotton: *The Gloom of the Museum*, 25; influence of, 6, 19–20, 25; as Newark Museum director, 47, 48
DCR (Division of Cultural Relations). *See under* US Department of State
DeForest, Robert W., 6
"democratic surround," 24–25, 89
demonstration exhibits, 21
demountable housing, 117
Denver Art Museum, 123, 133; *Peoples of Our Fighting Fronts*, 133

department stores: hemispheric unity efforts by, 42, 56–57, 59, 60, 62; wartime exhibits by, 67–68; window displays, 28, 33. *See also* retail sector influences; *specific department stores*
DePauw University's social museum, 32
Depression. *See* Great Depression
Detroit (Michigan), racial issues in, 134–35
Detroit Institute of Arts: "A Tour for War Nerves: A Guide to an Hour in the Galleries," 137
Deutsche Lufthansa affiliates, 49
Dewey, John, 22
diorama techniques, 21–22, 35, 59
display craft. *See* exhibition (display) craft; window displays
Division of Cultural Relations (DCR). *See under* US Department of State
Doob, Leonard W.: *Propaganda: Its Psychology and Technique*, 45
Du Bois, W. E. B., 150
DuMond, Frank L., 89
Durán-Ballén, S. E., 40, 42
DuSable Museum of African American History, 162

East Is East and West Is West: Some Observations on the World's Fairs of 1939 by One Whose Main Interest Is in Museums (Cummings), 28
Ecuador, 42, 49, 63, 66. See also *Three Southern Neighbors: Ecuador, Peru, Bolivia*
education. *See* adult education movement; public education
E. I. du Pont de Nemours and Company, 59–60
El Comercio (newspaper), 66
emotional aspects of exhibits, 21–22, 34–35
Empire State Building, 157
Entartete Kunst (Degenerate Art, 1937), 37–38
Evans, Walker: *Let Us Now Praise Famous Men* (& Agee), 116
exhibition (display) craft: adult education through, 23–24; avant-gardes' influence on, 24–25; background, 9–12, 17–18; cultural mobilization and, 91–92; defined, 9, 160; expositions, 27–31; funding for, 19; future directions, 164; graphic communication, 30–32, 36, 141–42; modernization of, 24–25; photographic techniques for, 59–60, 103–7, 126; postwar reflections on, 159–60; postwar world and, 131, 137–38; repurposed exposition materials and, 60; retail sector influences, 25–34 (*see also* retail sector influences); storytelling framework, 19–23 (*see also* storytelling); during wartime, 83, 88–90; at world's fairs, 27–28, 30–32 (*see also* expositions)
exhibitionary network: background, 40–41; corporate collaborations, 27–29, 139–40, 156–57; exhibitionary complex comparison, 10–11; foreign information ministries and, 76, 77; foundations of, 41–50; future directions, 164–65; government partnerships and funding, 13, 42, 68, 74–75, 76–77, 96–98; loans through, 22, 60, 138–39, 149; repurposing of materials through, 59–60, 104, 108–9, 112. *See also* government-museum partnerships
exhibitionary tourism, 54–66; colonial imperialism romanticized through, 59, 61–62; consumption and, 57, 59, 62–64, 64; racism and, 59, 61–66; as tourism substitute, 58–59; trade relations and, 60–61; world-making power of, 59–60
Exhibition Techniques: A Summary of Exhibition Practice Based on Surveys Conducted at the New York and San Francisco World's Fairs of 1939 (1940), 28–29, 59
expositions: corporate and retail ties to, 27–28; graphic communication and, 30–32; study of exhibits at, 19, 27–28, 30, 35–36; WWII references at, 38. *See also* Golden Gate International Exposition; New York World's Fair
"eye witness," 102–3, 104–5, 127–28, 145–46, 163–64

fascist Italy: propaganda by, 37, 62; psychological front against, 81; South American ties of, 43, 49
Federal Works Agency, 121
Field Museum (Chicago): 9/11 response by, x; postwar world and, 132; retail partnerships, 26; *War Theatres* series, 132
Fine Arts Gallery of San Diego, 72
Fisk University (Nashville), 134
Fogg Museum (Harvard University), 51
Force, Juliana R., 44
Ford, Edsel, 27, 70
France, 82–83
Franklin, Benjamin, 116

Frin, Raymonde, 149–50
FSA. *See* US Farm Security Administration

gender issues, 62, 76
Germany. *See* Nazi Germany
Gibbes Memorial Art Gallery (South Carolina): *Home Front Homes*, 94
Gimbel's (department store): *Ancient Arts and Crafts of South America* (1942), 56, 57
global citizenship. *See* postwar global citizenship
The Gloom of the Museum (Dana), 25
Golden Gate International Exposition (San Francisco, 1939): AAM meeting and, 16–17; corporate and retail ties to, 27–28; Covarrubias and, 132; Latin American art collection for, 51; Morley's experience with, 148; Pacific House, 17, 50; Redwood Empire Building, 36; study of exhibitions at, 19, 27–28, 30, 35–36; WWII references at, 38
Good Neighbor policy: background, 40–41; credo of, 44–45; government agencies and, 42–45 (*see also* Office of the Coordinator of Inter-American Affairs); trade relations and, 40, 43–45, 47–48, 60–61. *See also* hemispheric unity efforts
Good Neighbor Tour (book series), 58
Goodwin, Philip L., 107
government-museum partnerships: as exhibitionary network, 13, 96–98; OCIAA (*see* Office of the Coordinator of Inter-American Affairs); postwar world and, 129–30, 133, 139–41; WPA and, 7, 16, 76–77 (*see also* Works Progress Administration)
Grand Rapids Public Museum (Michigan), 89
graphic communication, 30–32, 36, 141–42
Great Britain: Museums Association, 4, 38, 70–73; wartime policies of, 4–5, 72–74
Great Depression, 6, 17, 27, 78, 86–87, 159
Great War. *See* World War I
Greenwich House (New York City), 102
Große Deutsche Kunstausstellung (The Great German Art Exhibition), 37–38
Grosvenor Library (Buffalo), 133
Guayaquil (Ecuador), 54, 59

habitat (nature) groups, 19, 34–35
Hamlin, Chauncey Jerome, 148–49, 151–52
Hammer Galleries (New York City), 57
Harrison, Wallace K., 56–57

Hartmann, Teddy, 41–42
Harvard Social Museum, 31
Hatch, Donald E., 109
Hatt, Robert T., 70
Hayden Planetarium (New York City), 133
hemispheric unity efforts: background, 3, 9, 13, 40–41, 66–67, 69; "Credo for the Individual U.S. Citizen," 44–45 (*see also* Good Neighbor policy); exhibitionary tourism as, 54–66 (*see also* exhibitionary tourism); foundations of, 41–50; heyday of, 50–54, 56; imagined communities and, 38, 57–59, 61, 71, 163; legacy of, 163; at MoMA, 44, 50, 56–57, 60, 62, 65, 110; by retail sector, 42, 56–60, 62; waning of, 66–68
Henrich, Janet, 108, 110
history museums, 34–35, 82–83, 184n6. *See also specific history museums*
home-front citizenship, 93–128; background, 1–2, 3, 9, 14, 93–95; imagined communities and, 97, 125–27, 163; legacy of, 163–64; MoMA's programming and services overview, 95–99, 110; MoMA's *War Comes to the People* (1940–1941), 103–7, 106; MoMA's *Wartime Housing* (1942), 99–128 (*see also Wartime Housing*); postwar world and, 129; racial issues, 120–22
Honolulu Academy of Arts, 71
house museums, 19, 184n6
housing, 99–102, 107–10, 117–20. *See also Wartime Housing*
Housing Act (1937), 101
Houston Public Library, 123
Howard, Richard Foster, 64–65
human sameness. *See* One World spirit
human-thing encounters. *See* material rhetoric of objects

ICOM. *See* International Council of Museums
Illinois State Museum: *The Living Map*, 132
imagined communities: background, 9–10; colonial imperialism and, 10, 14–15, 53–54; hemispheric unity efforts and, 38, 57–59, 61, 71, 163; Home Front imaginary, 97, 125–27, 163; "One World" imaginary, 130–31, 135–36, 137, 141–42, 147–48; storytelling and, 10, 168
imperialism. *See* colonial imperialism
Inconvenient Evidence: Iraqi Prison Photographs from Abu Ghraib (2004), 171
Indigenous museums, 162

industrial arts movement, 6–7
industrial museums, 19, 28–29, 156. *See also* specific industrial museums
in-migrants, 100, 120
institutional disruption, 143–46
Inter-American Conference for the Maintenance of Peace (1936), 43
Inter-American Institute of Intellectual Cooperation, 46
International Council of Museums (ICOM), 14, 130, 148–49, 151–52, 164, 165
internationalism, 130–31, 134–35, 142–43, 147–48, 150–51. *See also* hemispheric unity efforts; One World spirit
International Museums Office, League of Nations, 149
International Style architecture, 101
"Interpretation through Exhibits," 17. *See also* material rhetoric of objects
"interpretive showmanship," 27
"iron curtain," 146–47. *See also* Cold War nationalism
Italy. *See* fascist Italy

Jane Addams Hull-House Museum (Chicago), 159
Japan, 76, 136
Japanese-Americans, 122, 136
Jarden, Margaret, 54, 60, 65
Jayne, Horace H. F., 85
Jenkinson, Richard C., 48
Jewell, Edward Alden, 122

Kaempffert, Waldemar, 35
Kepes, György: *Language of Vision*, 142–43
Kimball, Fiske, 85, 98
knowing through objects. *See* material rhetoric of objects
Know Your United Nations (Brooklyn Museum, 1947), 152–55, 153–54, 157, 163
Kulturgeschichte (culture history), 19–21, 178n16
Kunst- und Wunderkammern, 33

Land of the Free (MacLeish), 116
Language of Vision (Kepes), 142–43
La Revista Du Pont (magazine), 59–60
Latin America. *See* Good Neighbor policy; hemispheric unity efforts
Lend-Lease Act (1941), 71, 112
Let Us Now Praise Famous Men (Agee & Evans), 116

Lewis, Ralph H., 72, 73–74, 78, 85
Library of Congress: MacLeish at, 104; *To Whom the Wars Are Done* (1940), 103
Life magazine, 104, 108, 112; photographic exhibitions department of, 139; *War Art* (1943), 139, 141
living history museums, 21, 147. *See also* Colonial Williamsburg
Los Angeles Museum: Italian art exhibit (1935–1936), 37; *Mexican Cultural Arts* (1940), 40
Low, Theodore Lewis: *The Museum as Social Instrument*, 6, 86, 129; on postwar world, 129; on retail influences, 27; on social instrumentality, 1, 6, 8, 86, 131; "social instrument" term used by, 160; on wartime mission of museums, 86
Lyman Allyn Museum (New London, CT), 107

Mabry, Thomas Dabney, Jr., 139
MacLeish, Archibald: on Americans' postwar outlook, 126–27; on *Land of the Free*, 116; "Museums and World Peace" (address), 147–48; *This Is War!* (radio program), 116; on *War Comes to the People*, 104–5
Macy's (department store): Latin American Fair (1942), 42, 56–57, 59, 60, 62; *Organic Design in Home Furnishings* (1941), 56; wartime exhibits by, 68
Manifest Destiny, 126
A Manual for History Museums (Parker), 20–21, 31
Manzanar Center, 122
maps, popular appeal of, 132
Marchand, Roland, 23, 115
mass media and marketing: approaches employed by, 2–3, 20, 23 (*see also* storytelling); on British support, 77; cultural mobilization and, 91–92; hemispheric unity efforts, 44–45, 48; museums as type of, 19; postwar reflections on, 159; public relations craze and, 23; temporary shows and, 26–27
mass production of housing, 117
material culture, 11, 24, 82, 176n43. *See also* object knowledge
material rhetoric of objects, 16–39; background, 2–3, 11–12, 13, 16–18, 38–39; cultural mobilization and, 91–92; "dynamic interrelation," 24; family heirlooms, 89; mind-body appeal of, 34–36; neutrality dilemma, 29–30; object knowledge,

18–25 (see also object knowledge); and photographic exhibitions, 102–5, 123–24; postwar reflections on, 160; postwar world and, 131, 141–46; propaganda and, 36–38 (see also propaganda); retail sector and, 25–34 (see also retail sector influences); witness-objects, 102–3, 104–5, 127–28, 145–46, 163–64
Mead, Margaret, 88–89
meaning making through exhibits. See material rhetoric of objects
metanarratives of organization, 33–34
Metropolitan Museum of Art: American Wing (period rooms), 35; Arms and Armor Department, 1; attendance during WWII, 79; DCR panel members from, 44; home-front activities of, 1; mission of, 7, 85–86; 9/11 response by, xi; postwar world and, 139; retail partnerships, 26, 56
Mexico, 40, 41, 50, 62, 110
migrant welfare, 100
Mika, Andzia, 116
Mika, Kazimiera, 116
military personnel: reacclimation programs for, 137; training at museums, 133, 147
mind-body appeal techniques: affective encounters and, 54–57, 55; background, 11–12; for exhibitionary tourism, 63; future directions, 166–68; for meaning making with objects, 34–36; for wartime exhibits, 82; in *Wartime Housing* (1942), 112–15, *113–14*, 117, 125
mine exhibits, 33, 35
Minneapolis Institute of Art, 76
Minnesota Art Project, 75
Modern Movement, 101
Mohegan Tribe, 162
MoMA. *See* Museum of Modern Art
Morley, Grace L. McCann: background, 51; DCR panel member, 44; on hemispheric unity efforts, 52, 53; on peace efforts, 129; on race issues, 66; as UNESCO's Museum Division head, 129, 148–50
Mostra della Rivoluzione Fascista (Exhibition of the Fascist Revolution) (1932), 37
multisensory techniques. *See* mind-body appeal techniques; visual-sensory approaches
Municipal Museum of Chicago, 31
Murphy, Michele, 152–53
The Museum as Social Instrument (Low), 6, 86, 129

Museum Council of New York City, 79
museumgoers. *See* visitors' behavior and interpretation
Museum magazine, 149–50
Museum of Fine Arts (Boston), 76
Museum of Man (San Diego), 72
Museum of Modern Art (MoMA, New York City): Architecture Committee, 109; Armed Services Program, 96–97, 98; attendance and membership rates, 79, 98–99, 122, 193n31; DCR panel members from, 44; Department of Architecture, 107; Department of Industrial Design, 107; Department of Photographs, 103–4; exhibitionary networks of, 50, 77; funding and fundraising for, 97, 107; hemispheric unity efforts by, 56, 60, 62, 65, 68, 110; home-front activities, 95–128 (see also home-front citizenship); members' bulletin of, 135; members praise of, 93, 98–99; mission of, 7, 96; photographic exhibitions, 97–99, 102–7, 124–26 (see also *Wartime Housing*); postwar world and, 134–39; racism and, 121–22, 134–35; relocation of, 95–96; retail partnerships, 26, 56; as social instrument, 1; traveling exhibits of, 96; wartime exhibits, 68, 76, 77, 79, 89, 90, 91, 99–128 (see also *Wartime Housing*); War Veterans Art Center, 96–97
Museum of Modern Art (MoMA), exhibitions and programs: *Airways to Peace: An Exhibition of Geography for the Future* (1943), 135–36, *136*; *Architecture and Government Housing* (1936), 102; *Art in America* (radio program, 1930s), 114; *Art Sale for the Armed Services* (fundraiser, 1942), 98, 110; *Britain at War* (1941), 77; *The Family of Man* (1955), 164–65; *Houses and Housing* (1939), 102; *Housing Exhibition of the City of New York* (1934), 31, 102; *Image of Freedom* (competition, 1942), 97; *Manzanar: Photographs by Ansel Adams of Loyal Japanese-American Relocation Center* (1944), 150–51; *Organic Design in Home Furnishings* (1941), 56; *Posters for National Defense* (competition, 1941), 97; *Road to Victory: A Procession of Photographs of the Nation at War* (1942), 79, 98–99, 124–28, 141, 157, 163; *T.V.A. Architecture and Design* (1941), 102; *Twenty Centuries of Mexican Art* (1940), 41, 62; *Two Years of War in*

Museum of Modern Art (MoMA), exhibitions and programs (*continued*)
 England: Photographs by William Vandivert (1942), 110; *Useful Objects in Wartime under $10* (1942–1943), 94; *War Comes to the People* (1940–1941), 76, 103, 104–7, *106*; *Wartime Housing* (1942), 99–128 (see also Wartime Housing)
Museum of Society and Economy (Vienna), 32
Museums and Galleries History Group Biennial Conference (2018), 165–66
"Museums and World Peace" (MacLeish), 147–48
Museums Are Not Neutral (social justice movement), 170
Museums Association (Britain), 4, 38, 70–73
Museums Council of New York, 137, 157
Museums in Motion (Alexander), 21
"The Museum's Job in Wartime" (Bernays), 80–81
Museums Journal, 72
#museumsrespondtoferguson, 170
Muslims, 171
Mussolini, Benito, 37, 76

Nagel, Charles, Jr., 153–54
narrative technique. *See* storytelling
National Association of Negro Business and Professional Women's Clubs (NANBPWC), 134–35
National Committee on the Housing Emergency (NCHE), 95, 101–2, 107–8, 115, 117, 122
National Conference for Christians and Jews, 90
National Council of American-Soviet Friendship, 155
National Gallery (London), 77
National Gallery of Art (Washington, DC), 67, 139, 147
National Geographic maps, 132
National Housing Agency, 95, 102
National Housing Authority, 117
nationalists, 10, 130, 150
National Negro Museum and Historical Foundation (NNMHF), 162
National Park Service, 72, 73, 81–82
National Resources Planning Board, 93
Natural History Museum (San Diego), 72, 137
natural history museums: mind-body appeal techniques used by, 34–35; mission of, 83–84; postwar world and, 138–39. *See also specific natural history museums*
nature (habitat) groups, 19, 34–35
Nazi Germany, 37–38, 43, 49, 62, 81, 134
Nazis (American), 16
NCHE. *See* National Committee on the Housing Emergency
Nelson, Caroline, *140*
Netherlands Information Bureau, 77
Neurath, Otto von, 32, 182n91
neutrality dilemma, 3–4, 24, 29–30
Nevada Museum and Art Institute (Carson City), 1
Newark Museum: auction of artifacts from, 57; Durán-Ballén on, 40; education initiatives by, 68; future directions for, 165; hemispheric unity efforts by, 40–42, 47–50, 51–52, 54–56, 57, 59–63, 67, 68; material publications during WWII, xii; postwar world and, 132, 134, 139–41; racism at, 64–66; retail partnerships, 26; visitor participation exhibits at, 21; Wisner as director, 141
Newark Museum, exhibitions: *Colombia: South American Republic* (1918), 47–48, 49–50; *Look to Latin America for Design* (1942), 67; *Our Neighbor Republics* (1943), 67; *Theatres of War* (1942–1944), 132; *Three Southern Neighbors* (see *Three Southern Neighbors: Ecuador, Peru, Bolivia*); *War and Peace: The Industrial Front in the Newark Area* (1945), 139; *Wings Over America* (1943), 140–41, *140*
Newark Public Library, 48
New Deal, 13
New England Inter-Museum Committee, 137
Newhall, Beaumont, 103, 106–7
Newhall, Nancy, 103
New Jersey State Museum, 60
New York City Housing Authority, 31
New-York Historical Society, 60
New York Museum of Science and Industry (NYMSI): corporate and retail ties, 29; OWI and, 94; postwar world and, 155–57; Powell on, 76; study of exhibitions by, 28–29, 35
New York Museum of Science and Industry (NYMSI), exhibitions and publications: *Exhibition Techniques* (study), 28–29; *Thirty Years of the USSR* (1948), 155–57; *Two Allies—One War—One Peace* (1943), 94, 155

New York Public Library, 79
New York Times, 37, 90, 97, 103, 122, 135
New York World's Fair (1939): background, 16; Brazilian Pavilion, 59; corporate and retail ties to, 27–28; diorama techniques used in, 59; Florida Building, 36; Pavilion of the Republic of Ecuador, 60; study of exhibitions at, 19, 27–28, 30, 35–36; as tourism substitute, 59–60; WWII references at, 38
New York Zoological Garden, 79
New York Zoological Society: *Life in the Jungle*, 133
9/11 responses, x–xi, 171
NNMHF. *See* National Negro Museum and Historical Foundation
North Carolina Historical Commission, 87
Noyes, Eliot, 107–10, 122, 123
Nye, Joseph S., Jr., 169
NYMSI. *See* New York Museum of Science and Industry

object ensembles, 19
object knowledge: avant-gardes' influence on, 24–25; background, 11; colonial imperialism and, 18; culture history approach, 19–21; evolution of, 18–20; visual-sensory approaches, 21–24
Office for Coordination of Commercial and Cultural Relations between the American Republics, 43. *See also* Office of the Coordinator of Inter-American Affairs
Office of Facts and Figures, 139
Office of the Coordinator of Inter-American Affairs (OCIAA): Advisory Committee on Art, 49; creation of, 43–44; disbanding of, 185; hemispheric unity efforts by, 43–45, 49–53, 56, 66–68, 148; Rockefeller (N.) as head of, 42, 43, 52, 155, 185n16
One World (Willkie), 130, 135
One World spirit, 131–55; adult education movement, 131–32, 136–37; background, 9, 13–15, 130–31, 146; flaws, 150–51; imagined communities and, 130–31, 135–36, *137*, 141–42, 147–48; leadership and, 146–50; legacy of, 163; living museums, 132–33; meaning making with objects and, 141–46; racism and, 133–36, 150–51; United Nations and, 130, 141, 150–55; viewed as propaganda, 151–52

Osage Tribal Museum, 162
OWI. *See* US Office of War Information

"Pageant of the Pacific" (Covarrubias), 132
Palmer, Karen, 169
Pan-American Conference (sixth), 46
Pan American Day, 46–47, 50, 67, 71
Pan-American diplomacy. *See* Good Neighbor policy; hemispheric unity efforts
Pan-American Exposition (1901), 28
Pan American–Grace Airways (Panagra), 59
Pan-American Holiday (radio program), 58
Pan-American magazine, 66
Pan-American Union, 46, 67, 147–48
Pan-American Women's Association, 134
Parker, Arthur Casewell: on culture history, 20–21; "Have Schools Improved?" exhibit example, 20–21; *A Manual for History Museums*, 20–21, 31; material rhetoric of objects, 31; on social instrumentality, 86–87, 131; on storyline technique, 20–21, 22
Parr, Albert Eide, 83–84
"participative witnessing," 167
Peabody Essex Museum's Neuroscience Initiative, 169
Pearl Harbor attack (1941), 71, 78, 93, 112, 116
Pennsylvania Museum of Art, 69th Street Branch, 25
Pennypack Woods housing project, 121
People's Institute of New York, 25
period rooms, 35
Peru, 49, 51. *See also Three Southern Neighbors: Ecuador, Peru, Bolivia*
Philadelphia Art Museum, 85, 98
Philadelphia Arts and Crafts Guild, 60
Photographing Science, 139
photography and photographic techniques: Abu Ghraib prison photographs, 171; competitions, 97; evolution of, 32; for exhibitionary tourism, 59–60; for humanization of grim statistics, 102; meaning making with objects and, 102–5; photographic narratives, 97–99, 102–7, 124–26, 133–34, 138–39 (see also *Wartime Housing*)
"picture-symbols," 32, 182n91. *See also* graphic communication
political activism, xi, 161–62
Portland Art Museum (Oregon), 123
postwar global citizenship, 129–58; background, 14–15, 129–31; corporate

postwar global citizenship (*continued*)
funding for museums and, 139–40; government-museum partnerships and, 129–30, 133, 139–41; from grasping the world to one world, 131–37, 141–46 (*see also* One World spirit); recognition in common, 146–50; service climate for, 136–37; social instrument paradigm and, 130–31, 137, 156–58; socially engaged exhibitions on, 137–38; storytelling and, 133–34, 138–39; United Nations and, 130, 141, 150–55

Powell, Louis H., 75–76

Pratt, Gladys Lynwall, 144–46

prerecorded (recorded) narratives, 35–36

professionalization of museum workers, 19

Progressive Era, 1, 6–8, 159, 173n2

propaganda: of Axis countries, 37–38, 62; colonial imperialism romanticized as, 59, 61–62; cultural mobilization and, 91–92; defined, 37, 81; as education initiative, 68; Good Neighbor policy comparison, 43, 45; natural history museums and, 84; postwar world and, 151–52, 157; pre-WWII analysis of, 36–38; storytelling comparison, 169–70; during wartime, 81, 87–89

Propaganda: Its Psychology and Technique (Doob), 45

psychological front: AAM's annual meeting (1942) addressing, 79–81; adult education's mission, 86–87; art museums' mission, 84–86; Bernays on, 80–81; cultural mobilization and, 91–92; exhibition craft and, 83, 88–90; history museums' mission, 82–83; natural history museums' mission, 83–84; propaganda and, 81, 87–89; storytelling and, 81–82

public education: indoctrination comparison, 29–31; as museums' mission, 18–19, 22–23; postwar world and, 129, 131, 153, *154*; pre-WWII analysis of, 36. *See also* adult education movement

public housing, 99–102, 107–8, 117–20. See also *Wartime Housing*

Quito (Ecuador), 63, 66

The Races of Mankind (Cranbrook Institute of Science, 1944), 133–34, 151, 157

racism: anti-Black racism, 120–21, 133–34, 151, 161 (*see also* whiteness); background, xii, 12; community planning for housing and, 120–22; at Dallas Museum of Fine Arts, 64–65; exhibitionary tourism and, 59, 61–66; future directions to address, 170–71; Good Neighbor policy on, 45; Japanese internment camps as, 122; at MoMA, 121–22, 134–35; at Newark Museum, 64–66; postwar reflections on, 161; postwar world and, 133–36, 150–51; racial reductionism, 133

"radical museology," 159, 160–61

radio programing, 58, 112–15, 116

realism, 25, 34–35, 63, 134

repurposed exposition materials, 60

retail sector influences: background, 25–26; criticisms of, 29–32; on expositions, 27–29; on hemispheric unity exhibitions, 56–61, 62; on museum display, 26–27, 33; partnerships with museums, 26, 29, 56, 60–61, 94

Rich, Daniel Catton, 141–42

Road to Victory: A Procession of Photographs of the Nation at War (1942), 79, 98–99, 124–28, 141, 157, 163

Roberts, Laurance, 44, 51

Robinson, Edward Stevens, 26

Rochester Museum of Arts and Sciences, 20, 86; *Parranda Pan Americana* (1945), 67

Rockefeller, Abby Aldrich, 96–97, 98

Rockefeller, John D., Jr., 147

Rockefeller, Nelson A.: Doob and, 45; as head of OCIAA, 42, 43, 52, 155, 185n16 (*see also* Office of the Coordinator of Inter-American Affairs); MoMA and, 13, 43–44, 98, 127; Shaw and, 155; on war-related programming, 98, 127

Rockefeller Foundation, 17, 19, 28

Roosevelt, Eleanor, 56

Roosevelt, Franklin D.: on Americans' postwar outlook, 126–27; on geography, 132; Good Neighbor policy of, 40–41 (*see also* Good Neighbor policy); on housing, 100; MoMA dedication by, 95–96; State of the Union Address (1942), 111, 112, 117

Rose, Hannah, 153

Rosenman, Dorothy, 101–2, 115, 121–22

Rosenman, Samuel Irving, 102

Rowe, Leo S., 46, 48

Sabine, Julia, 47, 48, 54, 60, 65

Sachs, Paul J., 6, 51

Sandburg, Carl, 126

San Francisco Museum of Art: hemispheric unity efforts and, 44, 50–51; *Latin American Art* (1941), 50–51; Morley and, 51, 148, 149

San Francisco World's Fair. *See* Golden Gate International Exposition

Sawyer, Charles H., 52–53

school-museum partnerships, 22, 51–52, 67, 110, 123, 153, *154*

Science Museum of the St. Paul Institute: *Can America Be Bombed?* (1941), 74–75, 135; funding and, 74–75; national security concerns addressed by, 74–76; *Strategic Elements of Naval Warfare* (1941), 75; US Navy and, 75

sensory experience. *See* mind-body appeal techniques; visual-sensory approaches

service climate, in postwar world, 137

Seurat, Georges: *A Sunday on La Grande Jatte*, 142, 143

Shattuck, L. Hubbard, 82–83

Shaw, Richard P., 28, 155

Sixth Pan-American Conference, 46

Smithsonian Institution (Washington, DC): home-front activities of, 1–2, 133; 9/11 response by, x–xi; "Survival on Land and Sea" (guide), 1–2. *See also* United States National Museum

social control, 6–8

social documentary photography, 112, 116, 120

social instrument paradigm: background, ix–xi, 1–6, 159–61; boundaries of, 161–62; defined, 160; exhibitionary networks, 9, 10–11; future research directions, 164–66; future trends, 166–71; home-front citizenship and, 89, 90, 95, 99–102, 107–10, 124–28; imagined communities and, 9–10, 11, 57, 58–59, 71; influences of, 15, 162–65; Low on, 86; material rhetoric of, 16–39; meaning making with objects and (*see* material rhetoric of objects); neutrality dilemma and, 3–4, 29–30; postwar world and, 14–15, 130–31, 137, 156–58; reflections on, 159–66; "social instrument" defined, 160; social progressivism and, 6–8; storytelling and, 2–4, 9, 11–12, 168–71; studies on, 4–5; transitions and, 13–15; during wartime, 86–90

social museums, 31–32, 89–90. *See also specific types of museums*

social progressivism, 6–8, 15, 95, 101

social services, 137

soft power, 169–70

Sojourner Truth housing project, 120

South Side Community Art Center (Chicago), 162

Soviet Union, 94, 155–57

Spinden, Herbert Joseph, 51, 61–62

Springfield Museum of Fine Arts (Massachusetts), 1

Standard Oil, 49

State of the Union Address (Roosevelt, 1942), 111, 112, 117

Steichen, Edward, 103

stereotypes, in exhibitionary tourism, 64–65

stores. *See* department stores; retail sector influences; *specific stores*

store window displays, 25–34

storytelling: background, 2–3, 9, 11–12; criticisms of, 29–32; cultural mobilization and, 91–92; evolution of, 19–24; expositions and, 28–29; future directions, 168–71; imagined communities and, 168; metanarratives, 33–34; for mind-body appeal, 35; neutrality dilemma of, 3–4, 24, 29–30; photographic narratives, 97–99, 102–7, 124–26, 133–34, 138–39; postwar world and, 138–39; social instrument paradigm and, 2–4, 9, 11–12; as soft power, 169–70; structuring of, 166; travelogue exhibits and, 54–55, *55*; verbalism and, 22–23, 32; during wartime, 81–82

Street, Julian, Jr., 97–98

Stryker, Roy, 105

symbols. *See* graphic communication; material rhetoric of objects

"talking labels," 35–36

Tantaquidgeon Museum of the Mohegan Tribe, 162

Taylor, Francis Henry, 44

temporary exhibitions, 26–27

Tennessee Valley Authority, 102, 117

Textile Museum (Washington, DC), 60

Textron War Products Museum, 139

thematic frameworks. *See* storytelling

This Is War! (radio program), 116

Three Southern Neighbors: Ecuador, Peru, Bolivia (Newark Museum, 1941–1942): artifacts on loan for, 60–61; background, 3, 13, 47, 50, 51–52; exhibitionary network and, 59–60, 104; hemispheric unity

Three Southern Neighbors: Ecuador, Peru, Bolivia (Newark Museum, 1941–1942) (continued)
    effort exemplified by, 41–42, 50; opening of, 71; race issues, 64–66; as tourism substitute, 59; on trade relations, 60–63; as a travelogue, 54–56, 55; "unity across difference" as goal of, 25, 157; witnessing of others through, 163
Time magazine, 75, 99, 118, 135
Toledo Museum of Art: *Art of Our Allies* (1942–1943), 76–77; *Chilean Contemporary Art*, 42, 76; exhibitionary network and, 42, 76, 77; hemispheric unity efforts by, 42–43; wartime exhibits by, 76–77
tourism, 58. *See also* exhibitionary tourism
traveling exhibits, 50–52, 77, 96, 109, 123, 141
travelogue exhibits, 54–57, 55
Tulane University Museum (New Orleans), 57
Two Allies—One War—One Peace (1943), 94, 155

unilateralists, 130
Union Settlement (New York City), 102
United Fruit Company, 60
United Nations, 130, 141, 150–55; *Know Your United Nations*, 152–55, 153–54, 157
United Nations Educational, Scientific and Cultural Organization (UNESCO), 151–52; Morley and, 129, 148–50; Museums Division, 14, 129, 130, 147–50, 159, 164, 165
United Services Organization centers, 1, 96
United States National Museum: *International Tuberculosis Exhibition* (1908–1909), 32. *See also* Smithsonian Institution
"unity across difference": Brooklyn Museum's *Clothing One World* as example of, 152; MoMA's *Wartime Housing* as example of, 24–25; Newark Museum's *Three Southern Neighbors* as example of, 25; UN's *Know Your United Nations* as example of, 152
US Council of National Defense, 43
US Department of State: appointments by, 46–47, 147, 149; Conference of Inter-American Relations in the Field of Books and Libraries (1939), 48; Conference on Inter-American Relations in the Field of Art (1939), 52; cultural policies of, 68, 129; Division of Cultural Relations (DCR), 43, 44, 49, 52; Newark Museum and, 41, 42, 47, 49

US Farm Security Administration (FSA), 101, 105, 108, 112
US Housing Authority (USHA), 101, 102, 108, 120
US National Park Service, 72, 73, 81–82
US Navy, 72, 75, 108, 139
US Office of Emergency Management, 110
US Office of Facts and Figures, 116
US Office of War Information (OWI), 68, 77, 94, 96, 108, 112, 151, 155, 163; *Two Allies—One War—One Peace* (1943), 94, 155
USSR, 94, 155–57
US War Production Board, 94

Vaillant, George C., 44
Vassar College Social Museum: *The Great Idea* (1942), 89–90
verbalism, 22–23, 32
"vibrant matter," 11, 82
Victorian-era museums, 18
Virginia Museum of Fine Arts, 40
visitor participation exhibits, 21
visitors' behavior and interpretation: of hemispheric unity efforts, 68–69; of MoMA's wartime exhibits, 93, 98–99; "participative witnessing," 167; study on, 19; of UN exhibits, 154–55; unpredictability of, 30; of *Wartime Housing* (1942), 122, 124
visual aids, 22
visual-sensory approaches: to adult education, 22–24; background, 11–12; to exhibits, 21–25; to expositions, 27–28; future directions, 166–68; mind-body appeal, 34–36; "psychology of attention" and, 26; to wartime exhibits, 82
Vreeland, Francis McLennan, 32, 182n91

Wadsworth Atheneum (Hartford, CT): postwar world and, 143–46; *What the Boys Send Home* (1945), 3, 143–45, 157, 163
Walters Art Gallery (Baltimore), 86
War Comes to the People (MoMA, 1940–1941), 76, 103, 104–7, 106
War on Terror responses, x–xi, 171
Wartime Housing (MoMA, 1942): background, 3, 12, 14, 89, 90, 95, 97, 99–103, 107–8; class dynamics, 115–16, 120; as "democratic surround" example, 24–25; development of, 108–10; exhibition scenes, 110–20, 111, 113–14, 118–19; impact of, 122–28, 131, 157, 163; racial issues, 120–22; traveling exhibitions, 123

Washington County Museum (Hagerstown, MD), 123
Welles, Sumner, 41, 48–50
Westinghouse Electric and Manufacturing Company, 94
What the Boys Send Home (Wadsworth Atheneum, 1945), 3, 143–45, 157, 163
Wheeler, Monroe, 126, 135
Whitby, Beulah, 134
whiteness: anti-Black racism and, 120–21, 133–34, 151, 161; hemispheric unity efforts and, 65–66; museum field and, xii, 12, 18–19, 150, 161, 170; resistance against, 133–34, 170
Whitney, John Hay, 1, 4, 50, 52, 115
Whitney Museum of American Art, 44
Williamsburg. *See* Colonial Williamsburg
Willkie, Wendell L.: *One World*, 130, 135
Wilson, Mabel O., 162
Wilson, Woodrow, 48
window displays, 25–34
Winser, Beatrice: correspondence with Howard, 64–65; correspondence with Jarden, 65; correspondence with Welles, 40–41; on duplication of exhibits, 60; hemispheric unity efforts by, 47–50, 53, 64–66; as Newark Museum director, 141; personal qualities of, 47; on social instrumentality, 131
Wissler, Clark, 87–88
"wit(h)ness," 167
witness-objects, 102–3, 104–5, 127–28, 145–46, 163–64. *See also* material rhetoric of objects
Women's City Club (New York City), 110
Works Progress Administration (WPA): dioramas funded by, 35; "extension" exhibits supported by, 7, 22; funding during WWII by, 78, 89; Indigenous museum funding by, 162; Minnesota Art Project, 75; museum-government relationships of, 7, 16; photographic exhibitions supported by, 32; populism of, 159; temporary exhibitions supported by, 26
world-making, through exhibitionary tourism, 59–60
World's Columbian Exposition (Chicago, 1893), 28
world's fairs. *See* expositions; Golden Gate International Exposition; New York World's Fair
World War I (WWI): art of, 77; hemispheric unity efforts during, 48; impact of, 6, 27, 86–87; museum policies during, 74; propaganda use during, 36; wartime housing and, 100
World War II (WWII): allies' kinship exhibits, 38, 76–77, 94; contribution of museum staff during, 78–79; cultural mobilization during, 91–92; declaration of war in Europe (1939), 111; exhibit craft during, 83, 88–90; home-front activities, 1–2, 93–128 (*see also* home-front citizenship); impact on hemispheric unity efforts, 66–69 (*see also* hemispheric unity efforts); museum attendance during, 79, 80, 98–99, 122, 183n144, 193n31; museum funding during, 78, 80, 89; museum policies during, 4–5, 72–74, 78, 81, 90–91; museums' missions during, 84–87, 96; national security exhibits, 74–76; postwar global citizenship, 129–58 (*see also* postwar global citizenship); psychological front, 79–92 (*see also* psychological front); transitional period in the United States, 70–72
The World You Must Know When the Boys Come Home (1943–1944), 133
WPA. *See* Works Progress Administration
W. R. Grace and Company, 59–60, 61

You Have Seen Their Faces (Bourke-White & Caldwell), 116
Young Men's Hebrew Association, 7
Youtz, Philip N., 25–26, 33, 179n44

CLARISSA J. CEGLIO is associate director of research for Greenhouse Studios at the University of Connecticut, where she is also assistant professor of digital humanities in the Digital Media and Design Department of the School of Fine Arts. She works at the intersections of public history, museum studies, and digital media, and collaborates with museums, archives, and others on public-facing research projects that engage diverse audiences in topics of contemporary concern. Ceglio, who came to academia after a career as a communications specialist in the marketing, museum, and publishing fields, holds a doctoral degree in American studies from Brown University. She serves as an advisory board member for *Public History Weekly*, a multilingual, open, peer review journal, and on the board of *Connecticut Explored*, a magazine of state history. Born in Cardigan, Wales, Ceglio lives in Connecticut with her husband, Jack.